THE FOUNDATIONS OF
ACCOUNTING MEASUREMENT

A Mathematical,
Economic, and
Behavioral Inquiry

PRENTICE-HALL INTERNATIONAL SERIES IN MANAGEMENT

PRENTICE-HALL, INC.
PRENTICE-HALL INTERNATIONAL, INC., UNITED KINGDOM AND EIRE
PRENTICE-HALL OF CANADA, LTD., CANADA
J. H. DE BUSSY, LTD., HOLLAND AND FLEMISH-SPEAKING BELGIUM
DUNOD PRESS, FRANCE
MARUZEN COMPANY, LTD., FAR EAST
HERRERO HERMANOS, SUCS., SPAIN AND LATIN AMERICA

PRENTICE-HALL, INC., Englewood Cliffs, N. J.

YUJI IJIRI

Stanford University

THE FOUNDATIONS OF ACCOUNTING MEASUREMENT

A Mathematical, Economic, and Behavioral Inquiry

PRENTICE-HALL INTERNATIONAL, INC., *London*
PRENTICE-HALL OF AUSTRALIA, PTY. LTD., *Sydney*
PRENTICE-HALL OF CANADA, LTD., *Toronto*
PRENTICE-HALL OF INDIA PRIVATE LTD., *New Delhi*
PRENTICE-HALL OF JAPAN, INC., *Tokyo*

Library of Congress Catalog Card Number 67-15629

Current Printing (last digit):

10 9 8 7 6 5 4 3 2 1

Printed in the United States of America

To Takejiro Ijiri and Taminosuke Nishimura,
whose philosophy is imbedded in this book

Preface

In recent years we have seen the appearance of numerous books, articles, and speeches dealing with contemporary challenges to accounting from those who make growing use of electronic computers, operations research techniques, behavioral science theories, etc. in dealing with business and economic problems. In fact, accounting has now come to a critical turning point which is at least as important as the one it came to in the early 1930's.

Accountants must respond to these challenges. But the response should come after a careful study of the foundations upon which accounting has been constructed. The most dangerous trap that accountants could fall into is to be confused and demoralized by the numerous challenges from the neighboring areas of accounting in business and economics and to adjust their theories and practices here and there with a humble apology to these neighbors. Accounting has its own way of thinking about, observing, and organizing business phenomena. What is more important, accounting has its own discipline and own philosophy, which have been developed over many centuries. This does not mean that they should not be changed. It emphasizes that the response to the challenges should be made keeping always in mind the effects of this response upon accounting foundations. Otherwise, accounting will soon become simply a patchy collection of practices.

This book was motivated primarily by this need to probe into the foundations of accounting. In particular, this book inquires into the measurement aspects of accounting and searches for the foundations of accounting measurement. Measurement is the core of accounting, and without an understanding of what is measured and how it is measured, proper comprehension of accounting is totally impossible. Three basic inquiries are made in this book: a mathematical inquiry, which is made in order to grasp the logical structure of accounting measurement; an economic inquiry, to apprehend what is measured in accounting; and a behavioral inquiry, to perceive the ways in which the measurement system is put into practice by accountants and the ways in which the resulting measures are used by decision makers.

The results of this probe into the foundations of accounting measurement are presented here in the simplest and easiest way but without loss of any essentials. Thus, for example, certain concepts and constructs in mathematics and metamathematics were utilized, but the findings are presented here in such a way that readers with no more mathematical background than high school algebra can read the main text, providing they are willing to pursue the logical thinking contained in it. Similar care was taken in the presentation of the results of the economic and behavioral inquiry. The appendices give a more advanced treatment of some of the topics in the main text for interested readers. Furthermore, this book is also intended for those who are not familiar with accounting per se but who nevertheless are interested in its fundamental modes of reasoning in order to understand the logical bases and possible uses or limitations of this important discipline. Hence, the amount of accounting background required for this book is also minimized.

It is perhaps most important for the readers of this book to keep in mind that the purpose is a better understanding of the foundations of accounting as it is and not as someone thinks it ought to be. Before we make a value judgment, we must comprehend the foundations of accounting as they now exist. Thus the objects of this study are the accounting theories and practices that are now socially accepted. In this sense, the type of analysis in this book may be classified as *meta-accounting* or *accounting sociology* when such areas become more fully developed in the future.

Although an inquiry into the foundations of a field is intrinsically interesting to any scientist, it is also of practical value especially from the following three angles. First, it enables us to distinguish essential from peripheral accounting theories and practices and thereby allows us to predict which of them are and which of them are not likely to remain valid in the future. In responding to the challenges from the neighboring areas in business and economics, it is crucial to perceive whether the need for a change in accounting theories and practices lies in the essentials or the peripherals from the viewpoint of the structure of accounting measurement. Second, this is important from a pedagogical standpoint. By understanding the essense of accounting measurement before facing the numerous details of accounting practices, the student will be able to organize and comprehend the details much better. Third, by understanding accounting measurement in its most compact form, we can compare it with measurement systems in other fields of science. Such a comparison will allow us to integrate into accounting desirable methods observed in other fields and vice versa. Such interdisciplinary exchanges of ideas can be made only after our understanding of accounting measurement is reflected in a relatively simple set of concepts and structures. This book was written with these possibilities for improving accounting theories and practices in mind.

Acknowledgments. A portion of this book is based on four published papers: Ijiri [1965b][1], [1966a], Ijiri and Jaedicke [1966a], and Ijiri, Jaedicke, and Knight [1966][2].

I am indebted to the coauthors of the latter two papers, Professors R. K. Jaedicke and K. E. Knight of Stanford University, for their valuable contribution to these papers as well as their permission to reproduce them in this book. Permission from the American Accounting Association, publisher of the above four papers, is also acknowledged.

Professors W. W. Cooper of Carnegie Institute of Technology and C. T. Horngren of Stanford University as well as Messrs. B. C. Eaves and J. C. Kinard, who are doctoral candidates at Stanford University, reviewed the entire manuscript and gave me a number of helpful comments. I am especially indebted to Professor Cooper, who, in addition to reviewing the final manuscript, provided me with continual stimuli and encouragement throughout the whole endeavor crystallized in this book. His numerous valuable comments and suggestions have resulted in a marked improvement in the manuscript.

A number of people reviewed a portion of the manuscript and gave me helpful comments. In particular, my colleagues at Stanford University and doctoral candidates who have taken my accounting seminar over the

---

[1] All references in the book are listed in the bibliography at the end in alphabetical order by author's name and chronologically when by the same author. They are identified in the text by the name(s) of the author(s) and by the year of publication. In the case of more than one article published by the same author(s) in the same year, a letter suffix is used to identify the article.

[2] Chapter 7 is a reproduction of Ijiri and Jaedicke [1966a, pp. 475–83] with some modifications. Sections 1, 3, 4, and 5 of Chapter 8 contain a partial reproduction of Ijiri, Jaedicke, and Knight [1966] with some modifications. Here, of course, I only am responsible for any changes from the original papers. Ideas in Ijiri [1965b] and [1966a] are refined and reorganized, and presented, in part, in Chapters 3, 4, 5 (Section 4), and 6 (Section 1). Verbatim quotations from these two papers have been made throughout these chapters without specific identification. Appendix B, Section 4 as well as Chapter 6, Section 2 are based on Ijiri [1965d], which had been submitted to *Econometrica* before this book was written. However, their decision on publication had not been reached when this preface was written.

last three years have been an important source of comments and suggestions on various parts of this book. I only regret that individual acknowledgment to them is practically impossible.

Financial support by the Ford Foundation, made through the Graduate School of Business, Stanford University, and by the Office of Naval Research, made through the project directed by Professor K. J. Arrow at the Institute for Mathematical Studies in the Social Sciences, Stanford University, is gratefully acknowledged.[3]

I am also thankful to the people at Prentice-Hall who contributed to the production of this book, including Miss Pamela Fischer for her copy editing and Mr. J. F. Beggs for his art work. I am especially indebted to Miss Fischer for her excellent copy editing, which resulted in a great improvement in the manuscript.

My greatest debt is, however, first to my wife, Tomo, who, in addition to typing the entire manuscript, cheerfully shared the strain of book writing, and second to our daughter, Lisa, who would have enjoyed more attention from her father otherwise.

YUJI IJIRI

February 1967

[3] Ijiri [1965b] mentioned above was originally prepared for the Office of Naval Research with its financial support. The other four papers mentioned in Footnote 2 as well as Ijiri [1964a] and [1966c], which are incorporated in Appendix B and Chapter 5, respectively, were originally prepared as Ford Foundation working papers with its financial support.

Contents

3 AXIOMS OF CONTROL, QUANTITIES, AND EXCHANGES 68

4 AXIOMATIC STRUCTURE OF HISTORICAL COST VALUATION 86

5 CAUSAL DOUBLE-ENTRY AND MULTIDIMENSIONAL BOOKKEEPING 100

6 THE LINEAR AGGREGATION COEFFICIENT AND THE IDENTIFIABILITY OF ACCOUNTING VALUATION 116

THE FOUNDATIONS OF
ACCOUNTING MEASUREMENT

A Mathematical,
Economic, and
Behavioral Inquiry

CHAPTER ONE

Representation, Language, and Measurement

Accounting is a system for communicating the economic events[1] of an entity. Communication is based primarily on quantitative information. Therefore, our study is directed toward understanding the substance of the economic events of an entity and the rules of quantifying them as well as the relationship between accountants and users of accounting information.

The economic events of an entity must be represented by an organized set of symbols which are suitable for communication. Furthermore, the representation must follow certain rules so that the economic events can be inferred from the symbols. It is therefore important for us to understand some basic problems of all representation processes. Our inquiry into the foundations of accounting measurement starts from this point.

[1] Here the economic events are to be interpreted broadly to include not only internal events of the entity but also external events that affect the economic activities of the entity. Also we shall use the term "economic events" of an entity to mean the economic status of an entity as well as its changes. This definition of accounting is essentially the same as the one given by the American Accounting Association [1966], but it is expressed here more compactly.

1. PRINCIPALS AND SURROGATES

In our daily life we often encounter things which we use or things which we are interested in only insofar as they represent something else. For example, we use maps only because they represent sections of the earth's surface. We obey traffic lights only because they represent the legal right-of-way at intersections. Train schedules are useful providing they represent the actual arrival and departure time of the trains. A president of a company or of a nation can act for it only insofar as he has the capacity to represent it. When we see a movie, we are not concerned with the series of pictures per se but with the story that the series of pictures represents.

Among numerous other examples, perhaps the one which is most common is language. A language is a means of representing phenomena in the real world. For example, the sentence, "XYZ Company lost a million-dollar government contract," is of no use to us if it has nothing to do with whether XYZ Company actually lost a million-dollar government contract. Similarly, we rely upon the sentence, "The firm's debt has doubled over the last two years," only insofar as we are confident that it represents the fact that the firm's debt has actually doubled. To give a more typical accounting example, a firm's financial statement is useful not because it gives us any comfort or pleasure in itself but because it represents the financial position and the operating results of the firm.

We call things or phenomena that are used to represent other things or phenomena *surrogates*[2] and things or phenomena that are represented by surrogates *principals*. For the above examples, the principals and the surrogates are as outlined in Table 1.1. They illustrate that principals are things we are primarily concerned with, whereas surrogates are things we are concerned with only insofar as we can determine the principals from them. In general, we have no interest in maps, stoplights, train schedules, etc., if we know that they have no relationship to the principals that they are supposed to represent.[3]

However, the same phenomenon may be a principal and a surrogate simultaneously. For example, we may see a map from an artistic viewpoint, in which case the map is a principal in itself; we may have a special interest in the colors of a particular stoplight, in which case the stoplight is a principal; or we may be attracted by the way in which the numbers are arranged in a train schedule, in which case the train schedule is the object of our concern. Similarly, the personality of a president may become the focus of our attention regardless of whether he represents the company or the nation; the artistic aspect of a movie may become the object of critiques; the way in which a person pronounces the sentences, "XYZ

---

[2] To surrogate is to substitute or to put in the place of another.
[3] See Hayakawa [1964, Chapter 2] for his discussion of maps and territories.

TABLE 1.1　Principals and Surrogates

PRINCIPALS	SURROGATES
Earth's surface	Maps
Right-of-way	Stoplights
Actual arrival and departure time of trains	Train schedules
A company or a nation	The president
A story	A movie
The fact that XYZ Company actually lost a million-dollar government contract	The statement, "XYZ Company lost a million-dollar government contract"
The fact that the firm's debt has doubled over the last two years	The statement, "The firm's debt has doubled over the last two years"
The financial position and the operating results of a firm	Financial statements of the firm

Company lost a million-dollar government contract" or "The firm's debt has doubled over the last two years," may be of special interest as in speech training; the format of financial statements may draw accountants' attention apart from the contents of the statements.

Therefore, whether given phenomena are principals or surrogates depends entirely upon whether we are interested in the phenomena per se or whether we are interested in the phenomena that are represented by the phenomena in question. The same phenomenon may be a principal for one person and a surrogate for another, or a principal at one point in time and a surrogate at another for use by the same person, or a principal for one use and a surrogate for another use by the same person at the same time.

Furthermore, there are not only surrogates of principals but also surrogates of surrogates, surrogates of surrogates of surrogates, and obviously various other levels. For example, the statement, "I heard someone say that today's newspaper shows a picture of the plant of XYZ Company being flooded," is a surrogate of a statement, "Today's newspaper shows a picture of the plant of XYZ Company being flooded," which is a surrogate of a picture of the plant being flooded, which in turn is a surrogate of the actual plant being flooded. If we are primarily concerned with the plant, the plant being flooded is the principal and we rely upon the above original statement only insofar as we are confident that it represents this principal.

We use surrogates basically because we need 1) to discriminate principals and 2) to communicate the results of this discrimination to other persons (interpersonal communication) or to ourselves at a later time (intrapersonal communication by means of recording). If we are indifferent about discriminating principals, there is no need for us to have principals represented by surrogates. For example, for those who are indifferent about discriminating various possible financial positions of a firm, the firm's balance sheet will have no significance. Similarly, for those who do not care about the right-of-way, stoplights are not of any use. On the other hand, if everybody can observe and understand principals by himself, there is no need for another person to translate them by using surrogates. Similarly, if the principals are expected to be available at any future time with no added costs, there is also no need to keep a record of the principals by means of surrogates. Therefore, surrogates that are used in our life are always easier to use in communicating with others and/or easier to keep for future reference than the principals which the surrogates represent.

Before we proceed further, it is important to recognize the fact that the products of an accounting system are always surrogates; they are useful only because they represent principals, i.e., the economic events of an entity. This point can never be overemphasized. Had the products of accounting systems been useful in themselves, as various consumer products are, the theory of accounting would have been entirely different.

2. REPRESENTATION

The principal-surrogate relationships used in accounting are very complicated ones as we shall see in later chapters. However, in order to understand complicated relationships it is often effective to start with the most primitive relationship. Since it is difficult to find a useful example in accounting of such a primitive relationship, we shall use an example which almost all of us encounter in our daily life.

Let us consider four traffic situations based on right-of-ways at an intersection, as shown in Table 1.2. Other factors such as the number of cars in the intersection or the size of the intersection may also be of interest

TABLE 1.2 Traffic Situations

Situation A: North-south traffic may proceed.
        East-west traffic may not.

Situation B: North-south traffic may proceed with caution.
        East-west traffic may not.

Situation C: East-west traffic may proceed.
        North-south traffic may not.

Situation D: East-west traffic may proceed with caution.
        North-south traffic may not.

to the driver, but they are considered to be different matters. Our primary concern here is that a driver wants to discriminate these four traffic situations, and we want to help him to do so by means of surrogates.

If a driver in north-south traffic or a driver in east-west traffic wants to know simply whether he may proceed or not, we need to use only two objects as surrogates, such as a green light and a red light or simply a light on and a light off. On the other hand, if the driver wants to know whether he may proceed, may proceed with caution, or may not proceed, we need an additional object, e.g., a yellow light. If he wants to discriminate all four situations so that he can be ready before he is allowed to proceed, we must provide him with a set of four objects. Therefore, the number of objects that are needed as surrogates depends entirely upon how finely or how coarsely the principals have to be discriminated. Of course, the use of more surrogates than necessary produces a satisfactory result, although it may not be efficient to do so.

Furthermore, many other things may be used as surrogates providing they are distinguishable. For example, instead of red, yellow, and green lights, we may use $\times$, $\triangle$, and $\bigcirc$ signs or flags of three different countries. Similarly, the existence and nonexistence of an object may be used as two different surrogates, e.g., red, red and green, and green may be used in place of red, yellow, and green.

Finally, the driver must understand not only what surrogates are used for but also how they are related to the principals, i.e., he must understand the representation rules. Unless he does, the surrogates are of no use in discriminating the principals.[4]

Apart from communication and behavioral problems such as these, representation presents the purely analytical problem of *identifiability*. Suppose that a driver in north-south traffic wants to know whether he may proceed, may proceed with caution, or may not proceed. Since there are three principals to be discriminated, we prepare three surrogates such as red, yellow, and green lights and apply the representation rules in Table 1.3. Note that if the driver in north-south traffic sees a red light

TABLE 1.3   A Traffic-Light Representation I

Situation A (north-south go) ——————— Green
Situation B (north-south caution) ——————— Yellow
⌈Situation C (east-west go) ———————⟩ Red
⌊Situation D (east-west caution)⟍

[4] Perhaps the most dramatic example of a person learning the connection between principals and surrogates is the experience of Helen Keller. She had known about objects and had been able to spell words with her fingers, but she had not understood that a word meant an object. After a long period of struggle by her teacher, Annie Sullivan, finally there came the moment when she realized the connection. See Keller [1905, pp. 23–24] for her own description of this exciting moment.

he is unable to know whether Situation C or Situation D exists, even though he knows that one of them must exist. However, he is not bothered by this since, in this case, he is not interested in discriminating Situations C and D, providing the two situations can be discriminated from the rest. (We are assuming that he cannot see the stoplight for east-west traffic.)

Suppose, instead, that the same principals are represented by the same surrogates but in a slightly different way as in Table 1.4. If this is the repre-

TABLE 1.4   A Traffic-Light Representation II

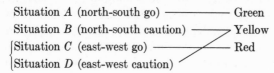

Situation A (north-south go) ——————— Green
Situation B (north-south caution) ————→ Yellow
⎰Situation C (east-west go) ——————— Red
⎱Situation D (east-west caution)

sentation rule, the driver in north-south traffic is unable to know whether he may proceed with caution or may not proceed if the light is yellow—he cannot make the desired discrimination of the principals. Notice that this is true even if he understands the representation rule perfectly. As mentioned earlier, this is a purely analytical problem which exists independently of other behavioral problems that will be discussed later.

Let us call a representation of principals by surrogates a *perfect representation* if a desired discrimination of principals can be made by discriminating surrogates (as in the representation in Table 1.3) and an *imperfect representation* if a desired discrimination of principals cannot always be made by discriminating surrogates (as in the representation in Table 1.4).

Table 1.5 is another example of imperfect representation. Here, Situ-

TABLE 1.5   A Traffic-Light Representation III

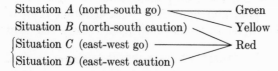

Situation A (north-south go) ——————— Green
Situation B (north-south caution) ————— Yellow
⎰Situation C (east-west go) ——————→ Red
⎱Situation D (east-west caution)

ation A (north-south go) is connected with both green and yellow. This means that the situation is represented sometimes by a green light and sometimes by a yellow light. In other words, a green light and a yellow light "mean" the same thing. Such redundancy in the use of surrogates does not affect the identifiability of the principals. However, this representation is imperfect because Situation B cannot be discriminated from Situations C and D. Still another example of imperfect representation is Table 1.6. A yellow light and a red light are used to discriminate Situ-

TABLE 1.6   A Traffic-Light Representation IV

Situation A (north-south go) ⟶ Green
Situation B (north-south caution) ⟶ Yellow
⎰Situation C (east-west go) ⟶ Red
⎱Situation D (east-west caution)

ations C and D, which need not be discriminated, whereas Situations A and B, which must be discriminated, are represented by the same surrogate, a green light, making the desired discrimination impossible.

On the other hand, Table 1.7 is an example of perfect representation.

TABLE 1.7   A Traffic-Light Representation V

Situation A (north-south go) ⟶ Green
Situation B (north-south caution) ⟶ Red
⎰Situation C (east-west go) ⟶ Purple
⎱Situation D (east-west caution) ⟶ Yellow

It is not conventional to represent Situation B (north-south caution) by a red light. However, from the viewpoint of identifiability, the important point is whether the desired discrimination of principals is possible and not whether the representation is commonly used.[5] Still another example of a perfect representation is Table 1.8. If the color of the stoplight is

TABLE 1.8   A Traffic-Light Representation VI

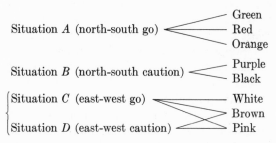

green, red, or orange, Situation A is identified. If it is purple or black, Situation B is identified. If it is white, Situation C is identified. However, if the color of the stoplight is brown or pink, it is not possible to identify

---

[5] " 'But "glory" doesn't mean "a nice knock-down argument," ' " Alice objected. 'When *I* use a word,' Humpty Dumpty said in rather a scornful tone, 'it means just what I choose it to mean—neither more nor less.' 'The question is,' said Alice, 'whether you *can* make words mean so many different things.' 'The question is,' said Humpty Dumpty, 'which is to be master—that's all.' "—Carroll [1872, p. 274].

whether Situation C or Situation D exists. But it is possible to identify that either one of the two situations must exist, or, stating the matter differently, neither Situation A nor Situation B exists. Since this is all that is to be identified, the representation is perfect.

How can we recognize whether a representation is perfect or imperfect? Since such recognition provides a basis for later discussions, let us analyze it in some detail; a more rigorous and complete treatment using set theory is given in Appendix B for readers who are interested in this topic.[6]

In deciding whether a representation is perfect or not, the particular characteristics of principals and surrogates are irrelevant. For example, instead of the eight colors used for the stoplight in the representation in Table 1.8 a set of any eight symbols may be used. The four traffic situations may be replaced by four types of assets. The important fact is that n principals which need to be discriminated to a given extent are represented by using m surrogates under a given rule of representation, where m may be greater than, equal to, or less than n.

Let us consider the case where n principals, denoted $p_1, p_2, \cdots, p_n,$ are represented by n surrogates, $s_1, s_2, \cdots, s_n$. Suppose that each of the n principals has to be discriminated from the rest. Then, obviously, a representation is perfect if and only if each principal is represented by one and only one surrogate and each surrogate is used to represent one and only one principal, i.e., the representation is perfect if and only if it makes a one-to-one correspondence between n principals and n surrogates. It is equally easy to see that if the number of surrogates is fewer than n, there is no representation which is perfect assuming that all n principals need to be discriminated. If there are more than n surrogates, we can simply select n surrogates and leave the remaining surrogates idle.

Suppose that the set of n principals is placed in k classes ($k \leq n$) so that each principal belongs to one and only one class. This is called a *partition* of the set into k classes. Suppose further that we need not discriminate principals in the same class providing we can identify the class to which a principal belongs. In the above example of traffic situations, Situations A, B, C, and D are placed into three classes ($A:B:C, D$), i.e., Class I consists of Situation A only, Class II Situation B only, and Class III Situations C and D, between which a discrimination need not be made. Let us also assume that each class contains at least one principal so that we can avoid a trivial class which contains no principal. Then, clearly we need at least k surrogates to represent the principals perfectly. In this case, a representation is perfect if and only if each principal is represented by at

---

[6] Appendix B discusses this topic from the viewpoint of aggregation. However, the concept of perfect aggregation defined there in terms of partitions of a set is totally analogous to the concept of perfect representation.

least one surrogate and none of the surrogates are used to represent principals that belong to different classes.

Table 1.9 is an example of a perfect representation of twelve principals

TABLE 1.9　A Perfect Representation

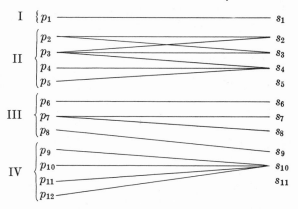

in four classes. In this example, the surrogates s_5 and s_{11} are not used. Note that each principal is represented by at least one surrogate and none of the surrogates is used to represent principals that belong to different classes. However, modifications of this representation such as those in Table 1.10

TABLE 1.10　Imperfect Representations

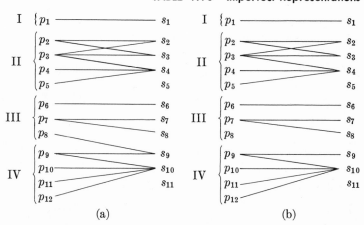

make it imperfect. In Example (a), Surrogate s_9 is used to represent both Principals p_8 and p_9, which belong to different classes. Hence, when Surrogate s_9 is transmitted to a receiver, he will be unable to determine whether the corresponding principal belongs to the third class or the fourth class.

In Example (b), no surrogate will be transmitted if the principal is p_8, hence the receiver will be unable to identify the occurrence of this principal.

Therefore, a convenient method of checking whether or not a representation is perfect is the following. For each class i, list all the principals that belong to the class. Call the list X_i. (For example, $X_3 = [p_6, p_7, p_8]$.) Then, list all surrogates that are used to represent the principals in X_i. Call this list Y_i. (For the examples in Tables 1.9 and 1.10(a), $Y_3 = [s_6, s_7, s_8, s_9]$, and for the example in Table 1.10(b), $Y_3 = [s_6, s_7, s_8]$.) Finally, list all principals that are represented by the surrogates in Y_i. Call this list X_i'. (For the examples in Tables 1.9, 1.10(a), and 1.10(b), $X_3' = [p_6, p_7, p_8]$, $X_3' = [p_6, p_7, p_8, p_9]$, and $X_3' = [p_6, p_7]$, respectively.) If $X_i' = X_i$ for every i, the representation is perfect. If $X_i' \neq X_i$ for any i, the representation is imperfect. Thus, the example in Table 1.9 is perfect since $X_i' = X_i$ for each of the four classes, as can be easily verified; but the two examples in Table 1.10 are both imperfect since $X_3' \neq X_3$.

Whether a representation is perfect or imperfect is not the property of a given representation rule per se. It depends on the partition of the set of principals. For example, if the partition is such that the set of twelve principals is classified into three classes—p_1 to the first class, p_2 through p_5 to the second class, and p_6 through p_{12} to the third class—then the representation in Table 1.10(a), which was formerly imperfect, becomes perfect. However, it is easy to see that the representation in Table 1.10(b) is imperfect no matter what the partition is since X_i' is always unequal to X_i for Class i which contains p_8.

The accounting examples in Tables 1.11, 1.12, and 1.13 may be of

TABLE 1.11   An Accounting Example of Perfect Representation I

PRINCIPALS (ASSETS)   SURROGATES (WORDS)

I   { Asset A
      Asset B ————————————— Current assets
      Asset C

II { Asset D ————————————— Fixed assets
      Asset E

TABLE 1.12   An Accounting Example of Perfect Representation II

PRINCIPALS (ASSETS)   SURROGATES (WORDS)

I   { Asset A ————————————— Cash
      Asset B ————————————— Marketable securities
      Asset C

II { Asset D ————————————— Land
      Asset E ————————————— Building

TABLE 1.13   An Accounting Example of Imperfect Representation

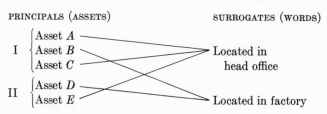

PRINCIPALS (ASSETS)   SURROGATES (WORDS)

further help in clarifying the nature of representation. The first two examples show perfect representation based on the partition shown on the left. The third example is imperfect since the desired discrimination cannot be attained from knowledge of the locations of the assets under the above representation.

In judging the usefulness of accounting information, the perfectness of the representation rule relative to the classification that a user of accounting information wants is an important issue. We will not be ready to discuss this in detail, however, until we have studied more complicated representations involving subjects and predicates in the next section.

It should also be pointed out here that the fact that a representation is imperfect does not necessarily mean that it is totally useless. A user of surrogates such as those in Table 1.10(a) can achieve the desired discrimination all the time except when the surrogate transmitted is s_9, in which case he may still be able to identify whether the corresponding principal belongs to the third class or to the fourth class by collecting additional information. This is fortunate for those who design accounting information systems since if an imperfect representation were totally useless, it would be virtually impossible to develop any workable accounting information system. This point will also be discussed in more detail later when users of accounting information come into our picture.[7]

3. LANGUAGE

Let us now consider a special type of representation—representation by means of a language, which is the most commonly used method. In

---

[7] See also Appendix B for the concept of satisfactory aggregations and reasonable aggregations, which may be interpreted in terms of representations. A representation is said to be satisfactory under a given decision function if it leads to the same decision as the one that would be reached by using a perfect representation. A representation is called reasonable under given decision and outcome functions if it leads to the same outcome as the one that would be obtained by using a perfect representation. See also Chapter 6, where the degree of identifiability of accounting information is characterized by means of the linear aggregation coefficient.

this section, we shall investigate the way in which a language represents principals.

Consider a variety of items stored in a warehouse and consider various ways of representing them. We may make miniature copies of the items and place them in a miniature warehouse in the same way as that in which they are actually located. We may take pictures of the inside of the warehouse. We may verbally describe the situation in the warehouse. We may list all the items in the warehouse, identifying them by names and quantities. Or we may represent the situation in the warehouse simply by a statement, "Inventories $360,500; warehouse $8,650,000 less accumulated depreciation, $3,587,100." These are all surrogates of the principal, which is, in this case, the physical or economic situation in the warehouse. What are the differences, if any, between representation by language and representation by, for example, pictures?

Consider possible ways of expressing the situation in the warehouse in English. As everyone who has studied English grammar knows, a sentence, in general, consists of a subject and a predicate. In other words, in expressing a principal we must capture some objects in the principal and then describe the properties of the objects by means of predicates. For example, we may say, "This warehouse is big. The inside is completely air-conditioned, and about ten warehousemen are working all the time"; or, "It is a clean warehouse. Inventories are well organized so that any item can be delivered with minimum effort"; or "There are 500 boxes of wine whose value is $10,000, 100 boxes of Scotch whose value is $30,000. . . ."

Compare this with representing the principal by drawing pictures. Here we do not have to identify any objects at all. All we have to identify are different colors, lines, etc. Actually our visual perception of the inside of the warehouse is a continuous whole. But language forces us to identify some relatively self-contained and independent portions of the whole as objects and then describe their properties. Such screening is necessary since any expression in (written) English is a finite sequence of twenty six letters plus a few other symbols, such as commas and periods, and unless the whole can be identified by finite classes of objects and their properties, it is not expressible in English. Therefore, for example, it is very difficult for us to express in English exactly what is shown in an abstract painting, in which the identification of objects is hardly possible.[8]

How, then, do we become able to identify objects in a continuous whole? Imagine a wave in an oscillograph. It is a continuous curve changing its shape all the time. Nevertheless, we can sense the independence of a

[8] In his discussion of the logic of infinity, Poincaré [1913, p. 63] states ". . . I would propose that we be guided by the following rules: 1. Never consider any objects but those capable of being defined in a finite number of words . . . ."

subshape within the wave if the subshape appears frequently in the middle of various other subshapes.[9] Typically, this happens when the subshape "moves." For example, in the series of waves in Figure 1.1, we sense a "movement" of Subshape A, even though, as everybody experiences at a seashore, nothing may actually be moving. If we have sensed such a movement of Subshape A for a long time, we suspect that there may be

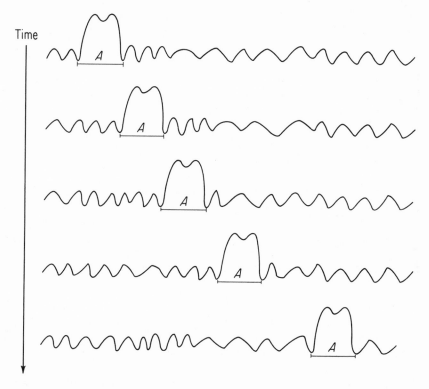

Fig. 1.1. Shapes and Subshapes

something which makes Subshape A independent of the rest. Then, later, we consider Subshape A to be independent of the rest even when there is no movement associated with A. Once we recognize this, we begin to describe Subshape A by saying, "There is A," "A is moving from left to right," "A is staying right in the middle," etc.

[9] More precisely, the subshape is "internally dependent and externally independent." It is internally dependent since we can judge from a part of the subshape its remaining part. It is externally independent since the subshape appears along with many other shapes.

Identification of objects in a continuous whole is important in the compilation of accounting information. The environment of an entity and its economic activities are in a sense comparable to a wave or to a picture and its changes. It is a continuous whole. However, because of the limitations imposed by language, we must arbitrarily pick out some portions of it, identify them as objects, and then describe their properties. As we shall see in the following chapters, we represent the economic events of an entity in accounting not by such a method as taking pictures but by identifying the economic resources of the entity as objects and by describing their properties and their changes.

Such conversion into finite categories can also be observed for the properties of objects. For example, the color of an object is actually of an infinite variety. However, since our language is finite, we cannot represent an infinite variety. Therefore, the color range is grouped into a finite number of color classes and the object is considered to have one of these colors. Thus, a whole principal is converted into a finite set of objects whose properties are also classified into a finite variety.

Furthermore, we can consider, for example, each one of the colors in the finite color set (blue, yellow, red, etc.) as an object. Thus, the fact that the color of the wine is red can be described as "the (color) relation between the wine and red," and we can argue whether such a relation holds or not. Similarly, we may say that the relations between paper and white, paper and yellow, paper and blue hold if the color of the paper in question is white, yellow, or blue, respectively.

Thus, we may say that a language represents phenomena in the real world, first by classifying them as objects and relations among the objects and second by expressing the objects and the relations with symbols. Namely, each principal, which may be considered analogous to a complicated three-dimensional picture (or four-dimensional including the time dimension), is screened by the person doing the transmitting into a set of objects and a set of relations among the objects before he expresses it by symbols. Then, according to a predetermined representation rule, he relates objects and symbols which stand for objects, and relations and symbols which stand for relations.

To make this argument more concrete, suppose that the fact that the warehouse contains wine is to be represented by words. First, the total three-dimensional situation is screened into two objects—the warehouse and wine—and one relation between the two objects—the relation that the former contains the latter. Second, symbols are attached to each object and each relation. Obviously, there are a number of ways of doing this. Table 1.14 is a list of a few possible symbols. In the first example, the warehouse is represented by a symbol WH, wine is represented by a

TABLE 1.14   Symbols for Objects and Relations

| ACTUAL OBJECTS AND RELATIONS | SYMBOLS FOR ACTUAL OBJECTS AND RELATIONS | | | |
	Example 1	*Example 2*	*Example 3*	*Example 4*
Warehouse	WH	□	X	"The warehouse"
Wine	WN	○	Y	"Wine"
Containment	⊃	Place the latter inside the former	$P(\ ,\ )$	"Contains"
The entire expression	$WH \supset WN$	◻	$P(X, Y)$	"The warehouse contains wine."

symbol WN, and the containment relation is represented by a symbol ⊃, which, by the representation rule, is supposed to be placed immediately after the symbol for the container and immediately before the symbol for the content. In the second example, the two objects are represented by geometric figures and the containment relation is represented by the geometric relation between the two figures. In Example 3, the two objects are represented by symbols X and Y and the containment relation is represented by $P(\ ,\ )$ where the symbol for the container is placed immediately before the comma and the symbol for the content is placed immediately after the comma. The last example shows a way in which the situation may be expressed in ordinary English.

Compare this with the simple representation method discussed in the previous section. Let us go back to the traffic example. The four principals are north-south go, north-south caution, east-west go, and east-west caution. These four situations are represented by four surrogates, e.g., colors of the stoplights, assuming that all four principals must be discriminated from each other. Furthermore, in representing the principals by the surrogates we did not have to know anything about the particular characteristics of each principal as long as we can discriminate each one of them from the rest.

In expressing these principals by words, this is no longer true. First we must list all objects that appear in any of the four principals to be discriminated. We have two objects, north-south traffic and east-west traffic. Also we must list all relations among the objects that appear in any of the four principals to be discriminated. We have two relations, "may proceed" and "may proceed with caution." These are relations in the sense that we can say whether or not the relation holds for a given object or a given set of objects. Compared with the containment relation which takes two objects, e.g., the warehouse and wine, the relations "may proceed" and "may proceed with caution" take only one object, e.g., north-south traffic or east-west traffic.

Next, we assign symbols to each object and each relation. Table 1.15

TABLE 1.15   Symbols for Objects and Relations II

ACTUAL OBJECTS AND RELATIONS	SYMBOLS FOR ACTUAL OBJECTS AND RELATIONS			
	Example 1	*Example 2*	*Example 3*	*Example 4*
North-south traffic	NS	$\triangle$	U	"North-south traffic"
East-west traffic	EW	$\triangledown$	V	"East-west traffic"
May proceed	$\Uparrow$	$=$	$R(\ )$	"May proceed"
May proceed with caution	$\uparrow$	$-$	$S(\ )$	"May proceed with caution"

lists examples of such assignments. In the first example, the two objects are represented by the symbols NS and EW and the two relations are represented by arrows which are attached immediately to the right of the symbol for the object for which the relation holds. In the second example, the triangles represent the two objects, with a bar or a double bar on top of the triangle representing the object for which the relation holds. In Example 3, the symbols U and V are used for the two objects, and the symbols $R(\ )$ and $S(\ )$ are used for the relations; the symbol for the relevant object is placed inside the parentheses. Finally, the fourth example shows the way in which the objects and the relations are expressed in English. Thus, Situation A, where north-south traffic may proceed, can be represented by NS $\Uparrow$, $\bar{\bar{\triangle}}$, $R(U)$, or "North-south traffic may proceed," depending upon which set of symbols and which representation rules are adopted. Similarly, Situation B, where north-south traffic may proceed with caution, can be represented by NS $\uparrow$, $\bar{\triangle}$, $S(U)$, or "North-south traffic may proceed with caution," again depending upon the symbols and the representation rule used.

Notice how this method reduces the number of symbols. If we have 1,000 objects and 1,000 relations of one object each, we have 1,000,000 principals that may be discriminated by using 2,000 symbols, whereas in the elementary representation discussed in the last section we would need 1,000,000 symbols as well as a representation rule which connected 1,000,000 principals to 1,000,000 symbols. If, with the new method, we have 1,000 objects and 1,000 relations of two objects each (e.g., the containment relation), we have 1,000,000 possible combinations for each relation and, therefore, 1,000,000,000 principals that can be discriminated by only 2,000 symbols. This is why we can represent an enormous number of principals with a relatively small vocabulary.

As a final point in our discussion of language, note that in English grammar words for objects are called nouns and words for relations are called verbs. Other parts of speech such as adjectives and adverbs expand exponentially the number of principals that can be discriminated. Since our purpose is to achieve a better understanding of measurement and accounting language, we shall not go into the analysis of ordinary language further, except for a brief remark about one point in syntax. In the above relations, "may proceed" and "contain," we noted that the former takes only one object whereas the latter takes two. We may distinguish the two by calling the former a *one-variable relation* or a *one-place predicate* and the latter a *two-variable relation* or a *two-place predicate*. Other examples of one-place predicates are "_____ exists," "_____ moves," "_____ smiles," "_____ stands"; other examples of two-place predicates are "_____ is greater than _____," "_____ is older than _____," "_____ is the father of _____," "_____ belongs to _____." There are, of course, three-place predicates, such as "_____, _____, and _____ form a trio," "_____ is a child of _____ and _____"; four-place predicates such as "_____ and _____ played against _____ and _____ in doubles"; and there are in general *n*-place predicates. This distinction is important in measurement, which will be discussed in the next section.

4. MEASUREMENT

Although language is a quite advanced method of representation, the methods of representation used in accounting are much more complicated and systematic. At the beginning of this chapter, it was stated that communication of the economic events of an entity is primarily based on quantified information. Therefore, in order to understand the representation methods in accounting, we must first understand the characteristics of measurement in general.[10]

Measurement is a special language which represents real-world phenomena by means of numbers and relations among numbers that are predetermined within the number system. To do this is nothing new since numbers are symbols and we have already discussed the use of symbols to represent objects and relations among objects. However, the use of relations among numbers that are predetermined within the number system is something new since it is not observable in ordinary language.

---

[10] For the recent emphasis on the measurement aspect in accounting, see, e.g., Devine [1962, Chapter 10], [1966], Bierman [1963], Anton [1964], Chambers [1965], [1966], Jaedicke, Ijiri, and Nielsen [1966].

Suppose that a firm deals with only one product, which is stored in the firm's warehouse, and we are concerned with the changes in the inventory level. The inventories at the end of January, February, March, and April are represented by the symbols I_1, I_2, I_3, and I_4, respectively. These are symbols for objects—which are inventories at various months' ends. We are now concerned with the relative differences in the inventory levels for these months. There are twenty-four different orderings of these four objects, assuming no two inventory levels are the same, as we can easily verify by Table 1.16. These are the twenty-four principals we want

TABLE 1.16   Ordering of Four Inventory Levels

1. $I_1 > I_2 > I_3 > I_4$	13. $I_3 > I_1 > I_2 > I_4$
2. $I_1 > I_2 > I_4 > I_3$	14. $I_3 > I_1 > I_4 > I_2$
3. $I_1 > I_3 > I_2 > I_4$	15. $I_3 > I_2 > I_1 > I_4$
4. $I_1 > I_3 > I_4 > I_2$	16. $I_3 > I_2 > I_4 > I_1$
5. $I_1 > I_4 > I_2 > I_3$	17. $I_3 > I_4 > I_1 > I_2$
6. $I_1 > I_4 > I_3 > I_2$	18. $I_3 > I_4 > I_2 > I_1$
7. $I_2 > I_1 > I_3 > I_4$	19. $I_4 > I_1 > I_2 > I_3$
8. $I_2 > I_1 > I_4 > I_3$	20. $I_4 > I_1 > I_3 > I_2$
9. $I_2 > I_3 > I_1 > I_4$	21. $I_4 > I_2 > I_1 > I_3$
10. $I_2 > I_3 > I_4 > I_1$	22. $I_4 > I_2 > I_3 > I_1$
11. $I_2 > I_4 > I_1 > I_3$	23. $I_4 > I_3 > I_1 > I_2$
12. $I_2 > I_4 > I_3 > I_1$	24. $I_4 > I_3 > I_2 > I_1$

to discriminate. Suppose that actually the inventories in April are the largest, the inventories in February are the second, the inventories in March are the third, and the inventories in January are the smallest. This relation may be represented symbolically by

$$(1.1) \qquad (I_4 > I_2 > I_3 > I_1)$$

where ($>$ $>$ $>$) is a symbol for a four-variable relation.

However, suppose that we have already established an ordering relation for a set of symbols, R, E, L, A, T, I, O, N, and S, so that

$$(1.2) \qquad R > E > L > A > T > I > O > N > S$$

Then, we can take advantage of our predetermined relation among these symbols instead of establishing a new one and simply say that the quantity of the inventories at the end of April or the quantity of I_4, or simply $Q(I_4)$, is R; the quantity of I_2 or $Q(I_2)$ is E; the quantity of I_3 or $Q(I_3)$ is L; and the quantity of I_1 or $Q(I_1)$ is A. Then, by referring to the relation in (1.2) among the symbols, we can immediately identify the ordering of the inventory levels in each of the four months. Of course, there are a number of other assignments that we can make to show the same ordering. Table 1.17 is a small list of such assignments. Any one of these assignments

TABLE 1.17   Assignments of "Numbers"—Measurement

ASSIGNMENT OF "NUMBERS"

	Example 1	Example 2	Example 3	Example 4	Example 5
$Q(I_4)$	R	T	E	R	A
$Q(I_2)$	L	I	A	A	T
$Q(I_3)$	T	O	T	I	I
$Q(I_1)$	O	N	N	S	O

makes it possible for us to identify correctly which one of the twenty-four principals we have on hand.

An advantage of this method of representation becomes clear when we add the inventories at the end of May, I_5. Then, the number of principals to be discriminated becomes 120 ($= 24 \times 5$). If we use the ordinary language method, we have to transmit a new five-variable relation such as

$$(1.3) \qquad I_4 > I_2 > I_3 > I_5 > I_1$$

However, if we are using "numbers" and if the previous assignment of "numbers" is, for example, the one given in the first example in Table 1.17, i.e., $Q(I_1) = O$, $Q(I_2) = L$, $Q(I_3) = T$, $Q(I_4) = R$, then we can simply transmit a new number $Q(I_5) = I$ and the relation in (1.3) can easily be derived by "decoding" these "numbers" with the relation given in (1.2). This is especially useful when we have a long list of observations from the past to which we want to add new observations from time to time, still indicating the ordering of all the observations.

From this analysis let us now generalize the process involved in measurement. Although we used an ordering as an example, there are a number of other relations among objects that may be expressed by means of assigning numbers to the objects. Furthermore, as is obvious from the above example, the use of arabic numbers is not necessary in measurement. The crucial point in measurement is the following. As in representation by language, we have a set of objects and a set of relations among the objects by which we want to discriminate the principals. We represent the objects by a set of symbols. For example, the actual inventories at the end of January may be represented by I_1 or by the phrase, "January inventories," etc. However, in measurement, the method by which the relations among objects are represented is different from the method used in ordinary language. We first choose a special set of symbols called numbers for this particular purpose and establish a relation among the numbers. We then choose a number and assign it to the symbol for the object as if the object

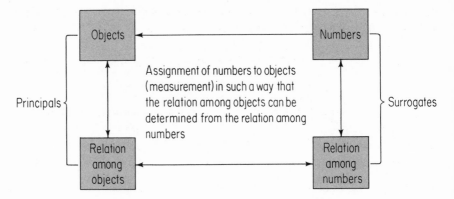

Fig. 1.2. The Measurement Process

had a property represented by the number which is independent of the properties that other objects have. This assignment of numbers to objects is called *measurement*. Thus, for example, we say, "The quantity of the January inventories is O, the quantity of the May inventories is I." Although these measures may appear to be independent of each other, it is important to realize that the purpose of measurement is to represent a given relation (or given relations) among objects by the predetermined relation (or relations) among the numbers. This point is clarified further by Figure 1.2 and Table 1.18.

TABLE 1.18   An Example of the Measurement Process

PRINCIPALS		SURROGATES		
RELATION AMONG OBJECTS	OBJECTS	SYMBOLS FOR OBJECTS	ASSIGNMENT OF NUMBERS	RELATION AMONG NUMBERS
	Actual inventories at the end of—			
April	April	I_4	R	R
$\vee$				$\vee$
February	February	I_2	L	L
$\vee$				$\vee$
March	March	I_3	T	T
$\vee$				$\vee$
May	May	I_5	I	I
$\vee$				$\vee$
January	January	I_1	O	O

Symbol for the relation among objects (or the property of objects): $Q(\ )$

Expression as the result of measurement: $Q(I_4) = R$, $Q(I_2) = L$, etc.

Before we proceed further, let us take another example in order to understand clearly what we mean by a relation. Suppose that the average balance of cash was greater in the year 1, denoted by C_1, than in the year 2, denoted by C_2, and was greater in the year 2 than in the year 3, denoted by C_3. The relation among the objects can be expressed pairwise as in Table 1.19 since the relation "greater than" is a two-variable relation.

TABLE 1.19
A Two-Variable Relation

P

$\langle C_1, C_2 \rangle$
$\langle C_2, C_3 \rangle$
$\langle C_1, C_3 \rangle$

Here, the relation holds if and only if the ordered pair is in List P. Since there are nine different ordered pairs that may be made from three objects, there are six other ordered pairs that are not in P. Let us list them as in Table 1.20 and call this List $\tilde{P}$. Since every possible ordered pair of the

TABLE 1.20
A Complementary List

$\tilde{P}$

$\langle C_1, C_1 \rangle$
$\langle C_2, C_1 \rangle$
$\langle C_2, C_2 \rangle$
$\langle C_3, C_1 \rangle$
$\langle C_3, C_2 \rangle$
$\langle C_3, C_3 \rangle$

three objects is either in P or in $\tilde{P}$, we say that the set of all possible ordered pairs, denoted by U, is partitioned into P and $\tilde{P}$. This is true for any relation no matter how many variables it has. If the relation has n variables, we still have a set U of all possible ordered n-tuples of objects that is partitioned into P and $\tilde{P}$ based upon whether the relation holds for a given ordered n-tuple of objects. Thus the relation is completely characterized by List P, which includes all ordered n-tuples of objects for which the relation holds; hence we may say that the purpose of measurement is to determine the content of List P.

Such a list can also be made for numbers based on a given relation among the numbers. Suppose, for example, that we use four numbers,

10, 50, 76, and 90, and consider a relation, less than, among these four numbers. Table 1.21 is List S of all such ordered pairs of the numbers.

**TABLE 1.21   A List for the
Relation Among Numbers**

S

$\langle 10, 50 \rangle$
$\langle 10, 76 \rangle$
$\langle 10, 90 \rangle$
$\langle 50, 76 \rangle$
$\langle 50, 90 \rangle$
$\langle 76, 90 \rangle$

Table 1.22 is a complementary List $\tilde{S}$ of all ordered pairs of the numbers for which the less-than relation does not hold.

**TABLE 1.22
A Complementary List**

$\tilde{S}$

$\langle 10, 10 \rangle$	$\langle 76, 76 \rangle$
$\langle 50, 10 \rangle$	$\langle 90, 10 \rangle$
$\langle 50, 50 \rangle$	$\langle 90, 50 \rangle$
$\langle 76, 10 \rangle$	$\langle 90, 76 \rangle$
$\langle 76, 50 \rangle$	$\langle 90, 90 \rangle$

We now want to assign the numbers to the objects in such a way that whether or not the relation P holds for an ordered pair of objects $\langle x, y \rangle$ can be identified solely from whether or not the relation S holds for the corresponding ordered pair of numbers $\langle a, b \rangle$, where a is the number assigned to the object x and b is the number assigned to the object y. Table 1.23 lists ex-

TABLE 1.23   Examples of Measurement

OBJECTS (AVERAGE CASH BALANCE)	ASSIGNMENT OF NUMBERS TO OBJECTS			
	Example 1	Example 2	Example 3	Example 4
C_1	10	10	50	10
C_2	76	50	76	50 or 76
C_3	90	76	90	90

amples of such an assignment. The reader may verify that the condition above is satisfied by any of these assignments of numbers to the objects. In the last example, the average cash balance in the second year is measured as 50 at one time and as 76 at another time. Notice that this does not create any problem since we are interested in the relation stated in Table 1.19. Of course, it is not conventional to represent a greater-than relation among objects by a less-than relation among numbers. This is deliberately done here to emphasize the point that any List S may be used, providing List P may be derived both from List S and from the assignment of the numbers to the objects. Furthermore, a greater-than relation among numbers and a greater-than relation among objects are entirely different things which have no a priori relationship other than that they are often used together.

As mentioned earlier, the relations among objects and among numbers may involve more than two elements. Consider a set of all ordered quadruples $\langle x_1, x_2, x_3, x_4 \rangle$, where each element x_i represents the average balance of cash in some year. We proceed as before and select those quadruples which satisfy certain requirements, calling the set of all such quadruples P. For example, we may include in P only those quadruples where the difference between x_1 and x_2 is the same as the difference between x_3 and x_4. In the above cash-balance example, we may include in P a quadruple $\langle C_1, C_2, C_2, C_3 \rangle$, meaning that the increase (or decrease) in the cash balance between the year 1 and the year 2 is equal to the increase (or decrease) in that between the year 2 and the year 3. List P also includes such quadruples as $\langle C_1, C_1, C_1, C_1 \rangle$, $\langle C_1, C_1, C_2, C_2 \rangle$.

We then develop a relation among the numbers in such a way that the relation among the objects may be identified from the relation among the numbers when the objects are measured properly. For example, we may include in S those quadruples of the four numbers 10, 50, 76, and 90 (i.e., $\langle a_1, a_2, a_3, a_4 \rangle$) which satisfy the condition that $a_1 - a_2 = a_3 - a_4$. List S includes, therefore, $\langle 10, 50, 50, 90 \rangle$ and $\langle 90, 50, 50, 10 \rangle$ in addition to such quadruples as $\langle 10, 10, 10, 10 \rangle$, $\langle 10, 10, 50, 50 \rangle$. Then, it is easy to see that either of the assignments in Table 1.24 achieves the desired result.

TABLE 1.24　Another Example of Measurement

OBJECTS (AVERAGE CASH BALANCE)	ASSIGNMENT OF NUMBERS TO OBJECTS	
	Example 5	*Example 6*
C_1	10	90
C_2	50	50
C_3	90	10

Note that if we adopt the assignment given in Example 6, the greater-than relation that was discussed earlier can no longer be identified by the less-than relation since $\langle C_1, C_2 \rangle$ is in P in Table 1.19 but the corresponding ordered pair of numbers $\langle 90, 50 \rangle$ is not in S in Table 1.21. If we are interested in identifying both relations, "greater than" and "equality of pair differences," then Example 5 is the only proper measurement.

This latter case involves an important problem in measurement. So far we have discussed the representation of only one relation P among a given set of objects by using one relation S among a given set of numbers. However, quite often we want to represent more than one relation among objects by more than one relation among numbers. In addition, we want to do this by assigning just one number to each object. For example, we assign 10 to C_1, 50 to C_2, and 90 to C_3. Then, as discussed above, we can identify the greater-than relation among objects by the less-than relation among the numbers assigned to the objects, and in addition we can also identify the relation "equality of pair differences among objects" by the relation "equality of pair differences among numbers" assigned to the objects. Thus, in this case, two principal relations are represented by two surrogated relations with a single assignment of numbers to objects.

Notice that there are many relations among numbers that may be used to represent a relation among objects. In addition to the well-known two-variable relations, "greater than" (_____ > _____), "less than" (_____ < _____), "equal to" (_____ = _____), "greater than or equal to" (_____ $\geq$ _____), "less than or equal to" (_____ $\leq$ _____), etc., there are a number of three-variable relations, such as the relations for addition (_____ + _____ = _____), for subtraction (_____ − _____ = _____), for multiplication (_____ $\times$ _____ = _____), for division (_____ $\div$ _____ = _____), and for exponentiation (_____ ‾‾‾ = _____). Furthermore, there are numerous other functions which may be used as relations such as the relations for logarithm (log _____ = _____); for sine (sin _____ = _____); for the function $f(x) = 2x$ or half as large (2 $\times$ _____ = _____); for the function $f(x, y, z) = 5xy + z$ or (5 $\times$ _____ $\times$ _____ + _____ = _____). Also there are numerous one-variable relations such as the relation for positive integers (_____ > 0); the relation for numbers less than 10 (_____ < 10); the relation for even numbers (_____ $_{\mathrm{mod}\ 2}$ = 0), where mod 2 means the surplus after dividing by 2; the relation for numbers in the range of 1.2 to π inclusive (1.2 $\leq$ _____ $\leq$ π). For each one of these n-variable relations (n being the number of _____'s used in defining the relation), there is a corresponding unique List S of all ordered n-tuples of numbers which satisfy the relation. Since we are now considering the case where there is more than one relation among the numbers, let us represent each relation by S with a subscript in order to distinguish that relation from the rest, e.g., S_1, S_2, and S_3, where S_1 stands for the less-than relation, S_2 for the equality relation, and S_3 for the relation "twice as large."

By the same token, we may have several relations among the objects that we want to represent—for example, "greater than," "equal to," and "three times as large," among inventories at two points in time to be represented by using three relations among numbers. We can then devise List P for each relation among the inventories and identify them by means of a subscript, e.g., P_1, P_2, and P_3, where P_1 stands for the greater-than relation, P_2 for the equality relation, and P_3 for the relation "three times as large."

Now we can generalize from these observations the following definition of perfect measurement. We have a set X of objects x, and k relations $P_1, P_2, P_3, \cdots, P_k$ among the objects in X. We also have a set N of numbers n, and k relations $S_1, S_2, \cdots, S_k$ among the numbers in N. We want to represent each one of the k relations among the objects by a corresponding relation among the numbers, i.e., P_1 by S_1, P_2 by S_2, $\cdots$, P_k by S_k. We do this by assigning a number n in N to each object x in X. We want to do this in such a way that *if a relation among objects holds then the corresponding relation among the numbers assigned to the objects holds and if a relation among objects does not hold, then the corresponding relation among the numbers assigned to the objects does not hold.* A measurement is called a *perfect measurement* if it satisfies this condition.[11]

A perfect measurement does not necessarily exist for any pair of a relation P among objects and a relation S among numbers. For example, if P is a greater-than relation among objects and S is a relation for positive numbers, there is no perfect measurement since P is a two-variable relation whereas S is a one-variable relation. In general, P and S must take the same number of variables (unless some of the variables are held constant in one or both of the relations). However, to have the same number of variables is not enough to guarantee the existence of a perfect measurement. For example, if P is a greater-than relation among objects and S is an equality relation among numbers, there is no perfect measurement since S is symmetrical ($n_1 = n_2$ if and only if $n_2 = n_1$) and P is asymmetrical ($x_2 \not> x_1$ if $x_1 > x_2$).

Analyses of the relationship between a set of principal relations P_i's and a set of surrogated relations S_i's involve much more complicated problems than those described above. They have been primarily developed in the field of metamathematics, especially in the model theory. Therefore, readers who have a special interest in this topic should refer to works in

---

[11] See Appendix A, Section 4, for a more complete treatment of this subject by means of homomorphism and isomorphism between two relational systems.

this field.[12] The above analysis is intended only to give a brief introduction to the concepts of *model homomorphism and isomorphism*, which are essential for understanding the nature of measurement.[13]

5. SOME MISCONCEPTIONS ABOUT MEASUREMENT

The above analysis points out some significant misconceptions about measurement which are worth elaborating here. First, measurement is not concerned with a single object. It is concerned with relations among objects, although a number is assigned to an object and on the surface such an assignment looks as though it has nothing to do with the other objects involved. This point is clearly indicated in the examples we have discussed above. Measurement is like a telephone line which goes only to the central terminal but whose purpose is to make a connection with other parties. A number assigned to an object is meaningless unless it is compared with other numbers assigned to other objects and unless the relation among these objects is inferred properly from the relation among these numbers.

Second, as mentioned earlier, a simple assignment of numbers to objects does not convey anything unless it is specified which relation among numbers is used to represent which relation among objects. Unfortunately, this is not always done in current practice and confusion often occurs. For example, suppose that the measure of a property of Object A is 10 and the measure of the same property of Object B is 20. What can we infer from this about the relation between the two objects? Nothing, since we do not know which relation between the objects is represented by which relation between the numbers.

A good example is an efficiency measure of Cars A and B that someone has devised arbitrarily. The information that the efficiency measure of Car A is 10 and that of Car B is 20 does not mean anything, except possibly that the efficiencies of the two cars are different (simply because we are used to having the same measure if the property of the two objects is the same). We cannot say that Car B is more efficient than Car A since the relation "less than" among the numbers may be used to represent the relation "more efficient" among the objects. On the other hand, the two measures may indicate that Car B is half (or twice) as efficient as Car A,

---

[12] See, e.g., Robinson [1963], Addison *et al.* [1965]. See also Suppes and Zinnes [1963], Stevens [1959], Cohen and Nagel [1934], etc., which deal with the problems of measurement specifically. Finally, see Churchman [1961, Chapter 5], which discusses the teleology of measurement in detail.

[13] Model homomorphism and isomorphism are the bases of all scientific models. See the discussion by Chambers [1966, pp. 126–28] on this topic.

which makes sense if the efficiency is measured in terms of the total main-
tenance expenses. Or again, these efficiency measures may be multiplicative.
If the efficiency measure of Car C is 200, this may indicate that Car C
is as efficient as Car A and Car B combined, which makes sense if the
efficiency is measured in terms of the reciprocal of the probability of failing
to run in any given period. (The probability of Car C failing to run is equal
to the probability of both Cars A and B failing to run.) It is, therefore,
crucial in measurement to specify which principal relation is represented
by which surrogated relation.

The third misconception about measurement arises from the fact that
the measurement problem is often confused with the problem of comprehending phenomena in the real world. We cannot represent by numbers
phenomena which we do not know. The measurement problem is strictly a
representation problem which comes after the relations among objects are
clearly understood. Such comprehension of the relations among objects or,
more generally, comprehension of real-world phenomena can be gained
without any measurement system, although a measurement system can
certainly help us in studying the phenomena. This is especially important
in accounting measurement. A useful accounting measurement system can
never be developed unless efforts are made to comprehend the underlying
relations among business phenomena.

Related to this is another misconception about measurement. We tend
to consider the functional expressions of the underlying relations as being
independent of measurement, but actually the functional expressions and
measurement are two integrated parts of the same system. For example,
consider Galileo's law of a falling body, which is expressed as

$$(1.4) \qquad\qquad d = \tfrac{1}{2}gt^2$$

where d is the distance traveled by the falling body, g is the gravitational
constant, and t is the time elapsed since the body started to fall. Clearly
this functional expression is related to the way in which elapsed time is
measured since, for example, if the elapsed time is measured by the square
of the seconds[14] ($t = 1$ after 1 second, $t = 4$ after 2 seconds, $t = 9$ after 3
seconds, etc.), the expression must be modified to

$$(1.5) \qquad\qquad d = \tfrac{1}{2}gt$$

which may create the impression that the real relation represented by the

---

[14] Of course, such a measure of time does not satisfy requirements such as those
stated in Whitrow [1961, pp. 169–75] and will be of no practical use. This is only for
the purpose of illustrating the relationship between measurement and functional
expressions.

expression is linear. Figure 1.3 clarifies this point still further. The real relation shows that if the value of the independent variable is A, the value of the dependent variable is B. However, the independent variable is measured in such a way that the number C is assigned to the value A. Similarly, the dependent variable is measured in such a way that the number D is assigned to the value B. Thus in the expressed relation the independent variable whose value is measured as C is related to the dependent variable whose value is measured as D. Notice that those who observe only the expressed relation without knowing the measurement process can get an erroneous idea about the underlying relation that is represented by the expressed relation. They may think that the underlying relation is increasing when it is actually decreasing or that the underlying relation is linear when it is actually nonlinear.

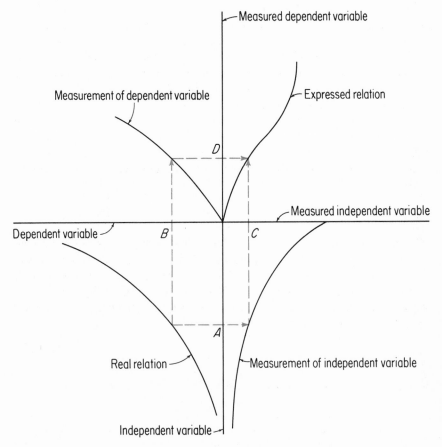

Fig. 1.3. Measurement and Functional Expression

The separation of those who measure and those who analyze the relations based on the measures is efficient, but it can also lead to confusion since the underlying relation can be understood only by comprehending the integration of measurement and functional expressions. This is not necessarily a serious problem in physics or engineering since physicists or engineers have complete control over both measurement and functional expressions, and if existing measures are not satisfactory in expressing observed relations among objects, a physicist can devise new measures and with such new measures he can revise his functional expressions. However, this is a serious problem in accounting where the measurers (the accountants) are separated from the users of the measures. The measurers must clearly understand what the users want and the users must clearly understand how the measurement system works. We shall discuss this relationship between accountants and users of accounting information in Chapters 6–8.

CHAPTER TWO

Duality of Values and Valuation

In order to examine the foundations of accounting measurement, we studied in Chapter 1 the essential characteristics of representation, language, and measurement. Although as we shall see in Chapters 3 and 4 the structure of accounting measurement is much more elaborate than the structure discussed in Chapter 1, the latter provides the methodological foundation for accounting measurement. In contrast to Chapter 1, this chapter discusses the substantive foundation of accounting measurement, namely the economic events of an entity.

It was stated at the beginning of Chapter 1 that accounting is a system for communicating the economic events of an entity. However, there is no reason why accounting could not deal with other principals such as purely engineering phenomena or purely behavioral phenomena. Actually, as a result of developments in management sciences as well as in information technology, the field of accounting may in the future be expanded to include many different kinds of noneconomic phenomena as principals. Nevertheless, it is unconventional at this time to regard such phenomena as principals to be represented and communicated in accounting. Since our objective here is to examine the foundations of measurement in current accounting practice, we shall limit our concern to the economic events of an entity.

These are identified in accounting by economic resources which the entity controls and by their changes. (We discussed in Chapter 1 the need for identifying objects in a continuous whole in order to represent them by a language.) Economic resources are things that benefit us and that we must make a sacrifice to obtain. These two aspects of economic resources will be analyzed in this chapter by a discussion of the basic nature of values.

This chapter, however, does not give a survey of the voluminous literature on the theories of values. Just as the previous chapter gives the essense of the concept of model isomorphism in the simplest way without requiring any background in this topic, this chapter provides the core of the concept of values and valuation without requiring any previous knowledge. Therefore, discussions of the historical development of the theories of values are altogether eliminated.[1] Instead, three significant aspects of values and valuation are emphasized, namely, 1) the duality of values, 2) the transformation from a utility differential to a monetary differential, and 3) valuation as a representation of causal networks. These three points, which will be discussed in the first three sections of this chapter, are essential for understanding the nature and properties of accounting valuation. Then the analyses will be related to various accounting valuation methods in the last section of this chapter.

1. THE DUALITY OF VALUES

Let us start at the beginning. Consider a man living alone in a cottage in a wood. He is hungry, but he has nothing to eat. He knows that he can go out, collect nuts, crack them, and eat them to satisfy his hunger. But he must force himself to do this since he prefers staying in the cottage and lying down to going out and collecting nuts. Therefore, he balances the *benefit* (pleasure of satisfying his hunger) and the *sacrifice* (pain of labor) which will result from his activity of collecting nuts.

If we observe him collecting nuts, we explain it rationally by saying that he considers the benefit to be greater than the sacrifice. Actually, the man may not be conscious at all of the sacrifice and the benefit resulting from the activity. Or he may for some reason engage in the activity although he considers the sacrifice to be greater than the benefit. However, in order to explain human behavior rationally, we state that a man engages in an activity because he evaluates the benefit to be greater than the sacrifice.

The sacrifice that a man expects to make and the benefit he expects to receive from engaging in an activity stem from physiological and psycho-

---

[1] For a more detailed analysis of the theory of values as well as studies on its historical development, see Whitaker [1904], Urban [1909], Stuart [1918], Laird [1929], Knight [1951], Kaulla [1936], Lamont [1955], Blaug [1962], Rothenberg [1966], etc.

logical pain and pleasure.[2] An increase in pain or a decrease in pleasure is considered a sacrifice; a decrease in pain or an increase in pleasure is considered a benefit. A man has a variety of pain and pleasure. However, since we interpret a man's activity to result from his comparison of the various kinds of pain and pleasure he expects to receive from his activity, they are assumed to be comparable. Therefore, it makes sense to talk about the difference between the benefit and the sacrifice, or the utility and the disutility, that a man expects to result from his activity. We shall call this difference a *benefit-sacrifice differential* or more simply a *utility differential*. We may then say that the utility differential triggers a man's activity.[3]

Since various kinds of pain and pleasure are considered comparable, it is convenient for us to assume that pain and pleasure can be measured in units such as *utils*, which stands for utility. For example, we may say that the man in the cottage considers the degree of hunger pain to be 5 utils and the degree of labor pain to be 3 utils. This positive utility differential initiates his activity of collecting nuts. Of course, this does not mean that the man in the cottage actually has such numbers in mind when he decides to collect nuts. The numbers are surrogates designed to help us represent our rational explanation of human behavior.[4]

If a positive utility differential initiates a man's activity, how can we rationally explain the termination of his activity? Why does the man in the cottage not continue to collect and eat nuts if a positive utility differential exists? We explain this by assuming that a marginal sacrifice increases and a marginal benefit decreases as the level of the activity increases. Consider the labor pain of the man in the cottage. The first unit (e.g., a pound) of nuts may be collected easily, but each additional unit of nuts becomes more difficult for him to collect. That is, the degree of marginal sacrifice (labor pain) increases as he collects more nuts. Therefore, if we plot the sacrifice (in utils) per unit of nuts collected, it looks like Line S in Figure 2.1. On the other hand, consider the hunger pain that is eased by eating a unit quantity of nuts. The first unit may make a significant contribution by reducing the hunger pain. However, as the man eats more, the

---

[2] See Bentham [1789], which analyzes pain and pleasure in considerable detail. Here we shall take them as given and proceed to our analysis of values.

[3] The familiar concept of *consumers' surplus* is included in this concept of utility differentials. See Marshall [1961, Book III, Chapter 6] for the former concept.

[4] The measurement of utility has been an important topic in economics and in psychology. Readers who are interested in the mathematical properties of utility measures, such as additivity of measures and transitivity of preferences, should see von Neumann and Morgenstern [1953], Stigler [1950], Luce [1959], etc. Luce [1959] develops an axiomatic structure of a utility measure particularly. See also Adams [1960] for the analysis of Bernoullian utility theory. Incidentally, Jevons [1871] credits Hutcheson [1742] with the first attempt to treat pain and pleasure in a definitely quantitative manner.

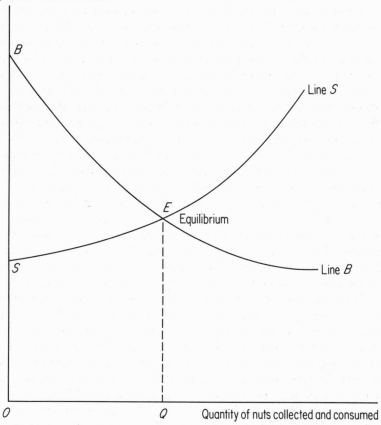

Fig. 2.1.   Marginal Sacrifice and Benefit

contribution becomes less and less. Thus if we plot the benefit (in utils) per unit of nuts consumed it looks like Line B in Figure 2.1. Notice that when the man has collected and eaten Q units of nuts his sacrifice to obtain an extra unit quantity of nuts becomes greater than the benefit he can obtain from eating the nuts that are collected. Therefore, at this level his activity of collecting and eating nuts is terminated.

Now consider the total sacrifice of obtaining the Q units of nuts measured in utils of labor pain that had to be suffered. This is represented by the area $OQES$. The total benefit from consuming the Q units of nuts measured in utils of hunger pain that were relieved by eating the nuts is represented by the area $OQEB$. If the area $OQES$ is 3 utils and the area $OQEB$ is 5 utils, then he has a utility differential, represented by the area EBS, of 2 utils from this activity. Of course, the activity volume has to be determined with respect to a given time period, e.g., a day, a week, a month. However, because of this saturation phenomena there is a limit to the activity volume in any given period.

From Figure 2.1, we can draw the curves for the total amount of sacrifice and the total amount of benefit. They are shown in Figure 2.2. Note that at Q, where the activity is terminated, the utility differential is maximum. Therefore, we explain the fact that the man stopped collecting and eating nuts at Q by saying that his utility differential was maximum at that quantity and that any increase or decrease in the quantity was not beneficial to him.

The above analysis is applicable regardless of whether or not the activity is the acquisition and consumption of goods such as nuts.[5] However, if the activity is aimed at acquiring and consuming certain goods or services (i.e., economic resources), which we shall simply call goods, the

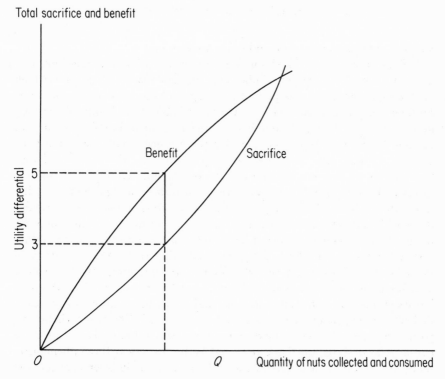

Fig. 2.2.   Total Sacrifice and Benefit

[5] Note that in psychology human behavior is explained by such concepts as homeostasis, tensions, drives, etc., which do not involve objects, whereas in economics human behavior is analyzed with more object orientation.

sacrifice and the benefit, or the disutility and the utility, of the activity are attributed to the goods. The evaluation of an activity is transformed into the evaluation of the goods that the activity is aimed at acquiring and consuming. The utility and disutility of an activity are attributed to goods as if they were intrinsic properties of the goods. This shift from a subject-oriented to an object-oriented argument is convenient since goods are easier to conceive of than pain and pleasure. However, it is very important to recognize that it is personal pain and pleasure which give rise to the concept of values.

As a result of such attribution, we now consider the properties of goods in terms of the sacrifice it requires for us to obtain them and the benefit they provide us. We think that goods demand a sacrifice and provide a benefit because we recognize a causal relationship among the sacrifice, the goods, and the benefit, represented by

$$\text{Sacrifice} \rightarrow \text{Goods} \rightarrow \text{Benefit}$$

where $\rightarrow$ indicates the cause-and-effect relationship.

What then is the basis for our recognition of causal relationships? The eighteenth-century philosopher David Hume made a significant attack on the materialists on this point by saying that our notion of causality is nothing more than repeated observations of one event being followed by another event. "Motion in one body is regarded upon impulse as cause of motion in another. When we consider these objects with the utmost attention, we find only that the one body approaches the other; and that the motion of it precedes that of the other, but without any sensible interval. It is in vain to rack ourselves with *further* thought and reflecting upon this subject. We can go no *further* in considering this particular instance."[6] For example, since the man has collected nuts on numerous occasions in the neighborhood of his cottage, he assumes that he can obtain nuts by going outside his cottage and collecting them; namely, after repeated observations that his effort is followed by obtaining nuts, he assumes that his effort is the cause of his obtaining nuts. Similarly, since the man has eaten nuts on numerous occasions and his hunger pain is always satisfied after eating them, he assumes that eating nuts is the reason his hunger pain is satisfied. Of course, he does not know the ultimate reason for these causal relationships, but he knows that he has observed these phenomena many times. From these observations, he makes a bold inference that the

---

[6] Hume [1739, Book I, Part III]. Bunge [1963] discusses various problems involved in causality. See also Simon [1957, Chapters 1 and 3] on casual ordering and identifiability. For a discussion on the means-ends relationships from the accounting standpoint, see Chambers [1966].

next time he goes out and makes an effort to collect nuts he will be able to obtain nuts and that the next time he eats nuts his hunger pain will be satisfied; that is, he applies the inference rule that phenomena in the future will be similar to phenomena he has observed in the past. Actually, when he goes out the next time he may not be able to find any nuts at all, or when he eats nuts the next time he may become sick rather than satisfying his hunger pain.

A man applies the inference rule not only timewise for predicting phenomena in the future but also spacewise for inferring phenomena in other places in the past, present, or future. For example, the man in the cottage assumes that he can collect nuts anywhere by going out and looking for them under trees and that he can satisfy his hunger pain by eating nuts even after he has moved into an entirely new area. Thus, he assumes nuts will be of value regardless of where he is.

This space-time inference rule is so fundamental to our behavior that we may define it as the *similarity assumption* of human behavior—the assumption that unknown phenomena are similar to known phenomena, unknown in terms of space and time and known in terms of a man's direct or indirect experiences. Obviously, this is the only sensible assumption that a man can make in dealing with unknown phenomena since the assumption that unknown phenomena are dissimilar to known phenomena does not help him face unknown phenomena.

The similarity assumption may be stated in terms of regularity (or laws or rules, etc.) as the assumption that the regularity that has been observed in known phenomena will also be observed in unknown phenomena. For example, the man in the cottage recognizes a regularity in the phenomena of eating nuts in the sense that eating nuts is always followed by a decrease in his hunger pain, and he assumes that this regularity will be applicable in the future or in other places.

The regularity may be probabilistic. For example, if in the past the man has been successful in finding nuts under trees 80 per cent of the time, he assumes that this probabilistic regularity is also applicable in the future or in other places, i.e., he expects that the probability of his being able to find nuts under trees will be 0.8 regardless of time and place.

In order to recognize regularities in the phenomena a man observes, he must classify them. If he classifies phenomena poorly, he may not be able to find any regularity at all. His classification system is set up so that he can find the maximum degree of regularity in the phenomena he observes, and he adjusts his classification system if he finds that another method will improve the degree of regularity in the phenomena. However, at the very basic level, his classification system is based on identities which he perceives. Since he can recognize the identity or similarity of colors, shapes, sounds, smells, tastes, etc., he naturally classifies objects or phenomena according to their effect on his perception. Therefore, he puts all objects with a specific color and shape into a class and calls them nuts. As he gains more experience, he classifies objects or phenomena according to their effect on senses other than his sight. For example, he puts two kinds of nuts in the same class even though their colors are entirely different because both have the same effect upon his taste. He can further expand the concept and develop a class for food, including in it various objects which may be totally different from the standpoint of perception. However, functionally they have one thing in common—they are edible.[7]

When classifying phenomena according to function, however, we must be careful, especially when using such terms as food, house, materials, and fixed assets. According to Hume, the statement, "Motion in one body is the cause of motion in another upon impulse, because the force in the former is transferred to the latter," does not make any sense since the concept of force is something we have created after observing the impact of two bodies many times in order to express the phenomena more conveniently. That is, the term force is a consequence of observing the impact many times and cannot be the reason for it. Similarly, we have observed objects falling many times in the past. As a result we have created the concept of gravity as a short expression for this phenomena. Therefore, it does not make any sense to say that objects fall because there is gravity. The same thing is true for concepts such as utility and value. What is precisely meant by the statement that Goods A have utility is that we have observed on numerous occasions that consumption of goods in the class to which Goods A belong is always followed by the satisfaction of a need of the man who consumes it. The statement that A has utility is simply a short way of describing the observation above.

We now come to the central issue in the concept of values. Notice that nuts have utility in the sense that they provide a benefit, but they also have disutility in the sense that they demand a sacrifice. Therefore, the dual aspect of an activity—the benefit and the sacrifice—is transformed into the valuation of goods in terms of their utility and disutility. It is obviously incorrect to say that a man is concerned with only the benefit or only the sacrifice in engaging in an activity since the activity is a result of his balancing the benefit and the sacrifice. By the same token, it is incorrect to say that a man is concerned only with the utility of goods or the disutility of goods. He is actually concerned with both.

[7] Eddington [1929] states, "Everything known about the material world must in one way or another have been inferred from these stimuli transmitted along the nerves. . . . Mind is the first and most direct thing in our experience; all else is remote inference." (p. 34 and p. 37.)

If the degree of labor pain to obtain a pound of nuts is 3 utils, a pound of nuts may be evaluated as 3 utils based on its disutility. If the degree of hunger pain relieved by eating a pound of nuts is 5 utils, a pound of nuts may be evaluated as 5 utils based on its utility. Can we say which is the value of a pound of nuts, 3 utils or 5 utils? The answer is no, as is clear from the above argument. Each number describes only one side of the coin.

Value is, in this sense, a dual concept. In order to describe the value of goods properly, we must provide either a pair of numbers representing utility and disutility or a number representing utility differential if the measurement is such that differences in utils are meaningful.

The dichotomy of the utility and the disutility of goods may be further clarified if we consider reversing the direction of the time flow as we do when we turn movie films in the opposite direction. Then, the decrease in hunger pain as a result of consuming nuts becomes an increase in hunger pain as a result of creating nuts and the increase in labor pain as a result of collecting nuts becomes a decrease in labor pain as a result of throwing nuts away! Clearly, then, the utility of nuts becomes disutility and the disutility of nuts becomes utility when the time flow is reversed.[8] Therefore, utility and disutility are essentially dual aspects of the same thing.[9,10]

In order to distinguish measurement of the utility and measurement of the disutility of goods G, let us define their *sacrifice value*, denoted by $s(G)$, to be a measure of their disutility (in other words a measure of the sacrifice necessary to obtain the goods) and their *benefit value*, denoted by $b(G)$, to be a measure of their utility (in other words, a measure of the benefit the goods provide). Also, let us define the *net value* of goods G,

---

[8] Of course, these are not time-reversible changes. The above argument points out the fact that the basis for the duality of value essentially lies in the two directions of time, past and future. See d'Abro [1950, Chapter 19] for a discussion on the principle of entropy to explain the difference between reversible and irreversible changes.

[9] Jevons [1905, p. 9] states: "It is surely remarkable that, while economists have had so much to say about utility and commodities, they have seldom, if ever, used terms for the contrary notions. Perhaps our attention is more fixed on the utility which we desire to secure than the disutility from which we are trying to escape."

[10] The duality of values has always been stated in economic analyses in terms of use value versus exchange value. (See, e.g., Smith [1776, Book I, Chapter 4], Marx [1906, Book I, Chapter 1]. Even Aristotle had distinguished the two as discussed in Marx [1906, Book I, Chapter 1].) However, the latter is a transformation of the former since an exchange is a means to obtain eventual benefits or use value. In the duality of a benefit value versus a sacrifice value, we cannot say one is a transformation of the other. One is rather a diametrical opposite of the other. (See also Walsh [1926, p. 15], where four kinds of values are discussed, i.e., use value, esteem value, cost value, and exchange value.)

denoted by $d(G)$, to be a measure of their utility differential.[11] For example, for a pound of nuts G we have

(2.1) $$s(G) = 3 \text{ utils}$$

(2.2) $$b(G) = 5 \text{ utils}$$

(2.3) $$d(G) = 2 \text{ utils}$$

Then we may say that, under the rationality assumption, if the man seeks G, $d(G)$ is positive; if the man is indifferent with respect to acquiring G, $d(G)$ is zero; and, if the man avoids seeking G, $d(G)$ is negative.

2. EXCHANGES

Let us go back to the causal chain for the man in the cottage. We state it in Figure 2.3 together with util measures. Here, S stands for a sacrifice, G for goods, and B for a benefit.

So far we have analyzed the simplest situation, involving only one man. Now let us introduce another man into our analysis of values. Let us call the man in the cottage Adams and the man just introduced Brown. Brown is a fisherman. Every day his hunger pain amounts to 70 utils, and in order to satisfy it he eats a pound of fish. However, to obtain a pound of fish he must sacrifice labor pain amounting to 40 utils. Notice that since the degree of pain is a purely personal matter the utils for Adams are not comparable to the utils for Brown. We shall denote by utils$_A$ and utils$_B$ the utils of Adams and the utils of Brown, respectively.

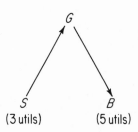

S B
(3 utils)   (5 utils)

Fig. 2.3. A Causal Chain in One-Man Society

One day the two men meet and Adams proposes to trade a pound of nuts for a pound of fish; Brown agrees. Adams evaluates his need that is satisfied by eating a pound of fish to be 7 utils$_A$, while Brown evaluates his

---

[11] Compare these with cost, selling price, and margin of merchandise. We will discuss later the accounting implication of these concepts in more detail.

need that is satisfied by eating a pound
of nuts to be 80 utils$_B$. As a result of
the exchange, Adams gains 2 utils$_A$
$(7 - 5)$, while Brown gains 10 utils$_B$
$(80 - 70)$ in benefit values; the sacrifice values are the same as before for
both Adams and Brown. Figure 2.4
represents the causal chain for Adams
(solid arrows) and Brown (broken
arrows). G_1 is a pound of nuts and G_2
is a pound of fish. S stands for a sacrifice and B for a benefit as before, with
subscripts A and B for Adams and
Brown, respectively.

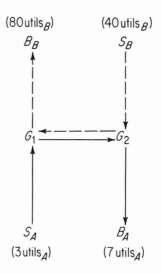

Fig. 2.4.   A Causal Chain in Two-
Man Society

From the viewpoint of Adams,
the sacrifice value of G_1, $s_A(G_1)$, is
3 utils$_A$ and the benefit value of G_2,
$b_A(G_2)$, is 7 utils$_A$. However, what
are the sacrifice value of G_2 and the
benefit value of G_1? Note that insofar
as the effort of exchanging a pound of nuts for a pound of fish is negligible,
a pound of fish may be obtained by the same amount of effort on the part
of Adams as that required for him to obtain a pound of nuts. Therefore,
we can set $s_A(G_2) = s_A(G_1)$; namely, we can impute the sacrifice value of
G_2 from the sacrifice value of G_1.

Similarly, since the exchange is assumed to be effortless, a pound of
nuts can relieve the same amount of pain (or bring the same amount of
pleasure) as a pound of fish does. Therefore, we can impute the benefit
value of G_1 from the benefit value of G_2, i.e., we can set $b_A(G_1) = b_A(G_2)$.
Thus we have

(2.4) $$s_A(G_1) = s_A(G_2) = 3 \text{ utils}_A$$

(2.5) $$b_A(G_1) = b_A(G_2) = 7 \text{ utils}_A$$

In this exchange of nuts and fish, we recognize what we may call an
exchange slack, i.e., Adams gave more nuts than were necessary to induce
Brown to give him a pound of fish and Brown gave more fish than was
necessary to induce Adams to give him a pound of nuts. For Adams,
suppose that 0.6 pound of fish satisfies 5 utils$_A$ of need. Then Adams is
willing to trade a pound of nuts for 0.6 pound of fish or more. Similarly,
for Brown, suppose that 0.7 pound of nuts satisfies 70 utils$_B$ of need. Then,

Brown is willing to trade a pound of fish for 0.7 pound of nuts or more. Thus, Adams gave 0.4 pound of nuts over and above what was necessary and Brown gave 0.3 pound of fish over and above what was necessary. How this exchange slack is actually divided between the two depends upon the bargaining process. We shall discuss this point later in more detail.

Now let us add a third man to our picture. The third man, Clark, is a hunter. He hunts rabbits for his own meals. His degree of labor pain to get a rabbit is 100 utils$_C$ whereas his degree of pain relieved from eating a rabbit is 150 utils$_C$. (The subscript C denotes that the number of utils is Clark's personal evaluation.)

Suppose the three men, Adams, Brown, and Clark, get together and decide to trade their goods in such a way that Adams gives Clark a pound of nuts, Brown gives Adams a pound of fish, and Clark gives Brown a rabbit. For Adams a pound of fish has a benefit value of 7 utils$_A$ as before; for Brown a rabbit has a benefit value of 90 utils$_B$; and for Clark a pound of nuts has a benefit value of 200 utils$_C$. Therefore, Brown and Clark are better off as a result of this three-man exchange, while Adams is exactly as well off as he was in the previous two-man exchange. In Figure 2.5, G_1 is a pound of nuts, G_2 is a pound of fish, G_3 is a rabbit; S stands for a sacrifice, and B for a benefit. Here, for Adams, we can set the sacrifice values and the benefit values of G_1 and G_2 in the same way as before. The only difference

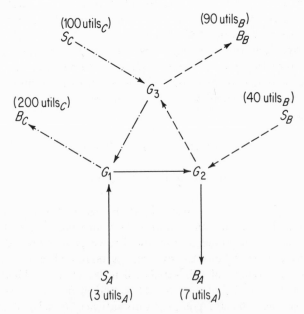

Fig. 2.5. A Causal Chain in Three-Man Society

is that in the present case in order to have an exchange without any extra effort on Adam's part, both Brown and Clark must cooperate and trade their goods as agreed whenever Adams wants to have fish, whereas before only Brown's help was necessary. Contrary to the previous exchange, the buyer of the pound of nuts is not the same person as the seller of the pound of fish.

Since it is rather awkward for the three to get together every time someone wants to have his goods exchanged, the men agree to introduce money.[12] Now the situation has changed as in Figure 2.6, where M stands

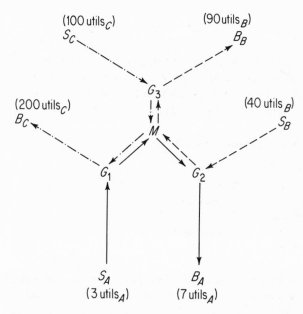

Fig. 2.6. A Causal Chain in an Exchange with Money

for money. It is assumed that everyone has agreed to exchange his goods for \$1. Now Adams can sell a pound of nuts to Clark for \$1 and then whenever he wants to eat fish he can buy a pound of fish from Brown in exchange for \$1. Therefore, from Adam's standpoint \$1 of money has a sacrifice value of 3 utils and a benefit value of 7 utils, just as a pound of nuts and a pound of fish have, i.e.

$$(2.6) \qquad s_A(G_1) = s_A(M) = s_A(G_2) = 3 \text{ utils}$$

$$(2.7) \qquad b_A(G_1) = b_A(M) = b_A(G_2) = 7 \text{ utils}$$

---

[12] See Smith [1776, Book I, Chapter 4] for the history of the introduction of money.

However, this new factor, money, has created another way of evaluating goods, i.e., by means of the amount of money for which the goods can be purchased or sold. Let us denote this monetary value of goods G_1, G_2, and G_3 by $m(G_1)$, $m(G_2)$, and $m(G_3)$. In this example, we have

$$(2.8) \qquad m(G_1) = m(G_2) = m(G_3) = \$1$$

Furthermore, we now have a variety of ways of measuring goods and money. Let us reproduce the causal chain for Adams in Figure 2.6 and state it as

$$(2.9) \qquad S \to G_1 \to M \to G_2 \to B$$

If we assume as before that no additional effort is required in going through the causal chain, then each of the five elements are equivalent under any valuation. These five elements may thus be measured in five different ways; each of them has the values in Table 2.1. For example, a pound of fish

TABLE 2.1   Various Measurement Bases

MEASUREMENT BASIS	MEASURE
S: Sacrifice value	3 utils
G_1: Value in nuts	1 pound (nuts)
M: Monetary value	$1
G_2: Value in fish	1 pound (fish)
B: Benefit value	7 utils

may be evaluated as 3 utils of labor pain, 1 pound of nuts, $1, etc., or $1 may be evaluated as 1 pound of nuts, 3 utils of labor pain, or 7 utils of hunger pain, etc.

3. UTILITY DIFFERENTIAL AS THE SOURCE OF PROFIT

A peculiar thing happens if we expand the causal chain to include profit-making activities by Adams. Suppose that Adams sells nuts and, by the money thus obtained, buys a bushel of grain from a fourth man, Davis, not for his own consumption but to sell to another man, Evans, for a profit. Here there is the same saturation factor as discussed before which stops Adams from making an unlimited amount of profit. If Adams tries to buy more grain, he must pay more money per unit in order to induce Davis to sell more since Davis' labor pain per unit of grain is increased as more grain is demanded. (See Line S in Figure 2.1.) Therefore, Adams' marginal cost curve is given by Line C in Figure 2.7. On the other hand, if Adams tries to sell more grain, he must sell it for less money per unit in order to induce Evans to buy more since Evans' hunger pain relieved by consuming a unit of grain is decreased as more grain is consumed. (See Line B in Figure 2.1.) Therefore, Adams' marginal revenue curve is given by Line R in Figure 2.7. Thus, after buying and selling Q units of grain, it

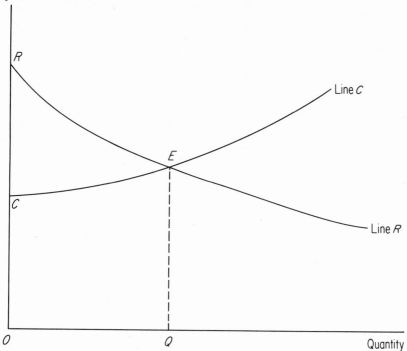

Fig. 2.7.   Marginal Revenue and Marginal Cost

does not pay for Adams to continue the trade. In other words, his activity volume is limited to Q units in any given period. The total amount of money paid by Adams for Q units of grain is represented by Area $OQEC$, and the total amount of money received by Adams for selling Q units of grain is represented by Area $OQER$.

Now let us consider a new causal chain for Adams. He starts with S, which represents his labor pain, and obtains a primary product, nuts, represented by G_p, which in turn he sells to obtain money M. He then purchases grain, denoted by G_e (e for exchanges), in order to sell it for more money M', with which for his own consumption he purchases fish, denoted by G_c (c for consumer goods), to satisfy his need B. Thus the causal chain is

$$(2.10) \qquad S \rightarrow G_p \rightarrow M \rightarrow G_e \rightarrow M' \rightarrow G_c \rightarrow B$$

The difference between M' and M represents the profit from the activity. Let us analyze where it comes from. First, consider the relationships among the following variables for Davis: 1) Total amount of sacrifice or pain in utils necessary to produce and sell a given quantity of grain, denoted by S; 2) sales quantity of grain, denoted by Q; 3) total amount of money received for the grain, denoted by M; 4) total amount of benefit in utils obtained from spending the money thus received and consuming the goods purchased with the money, denoted by B. Then, the relationships

Fig. 2.8.   Basic Relationships Among S, Q, M, and B I

between S and Q, Q and M, and M and B may be represented by the three diagrams in Figure 2.8. The first diagram shows the relationship between labor and products. As Davis expends more effort the quantity of products produced and sold will increase but at a decreasing rate. Stating the matter differently, for each additional unit of the product, more utils of labor are required of Davis. This diagram, therefore, represents the same phenomenon as the one represented by Line S in Figure 2.2, except that the horizontal and vertical axes are reversed. The second diagram in Figure 2.8 shows a simple relationship between the quantity sold and the money received, assuming that the price of the product is a constant. This assumption is made for the sake of simplifying the illustration and is not crucial in our analysis. The third diagram in Figure 2.8 shows the relationship between the amount of money received and the benefit obtained from consuming goods purchased with the money thus received. We shall assume that Davis will spend his money in the most efficient way, so the curve here represents the maximum benefit that Davis can obtain for a given amount of money. As the amount of money increases the benefit obtained from the money also increases but at a decreasing rate. This diagram may be compared with Line B in Figure 2.2 except that the variable on the horizontal axis is given here in terms of the amount of money, while it is in terms of the quantity of goods in Figure 2.2.

Let us put all three diagrams together in Figure 2.9 to create a fourth relationship, i.e., a relationship between the total sacrifice S and the total benefit B. The curve in the lower right-hand corner of the figure is obtained

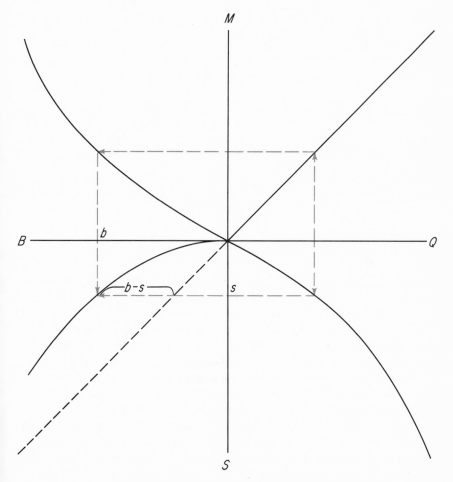

Fig. 2.9. Relationship Between S and B I

by turning 90° clockwise the first diagram in Figure 2.8. The line in the upper right-hand corner is the same as that in the middle diagram in Figure 2.8. The curve in the upper left-hand corner is obtained by turning 90° counterclockwise the third diagram in Figure 2.8. The curve in the lower left-hand corner is obtained by tracing the three curves for every point on the axis for the total sacrifice S as shown by a sample point s. Then, it is clear that the difference between the curve thus obtained and the 45° line is the utility differential $b - s$ for Davis expressed in utils and that he should produce and sell at the point where $b - s$ is maximum.

Let us next do the same thing for Evans. Since he is a purchaser of grain while Davis is a seller, we approach this in the entirely opposite way, starting with the benefit and moving toward the sacrifice as shown in

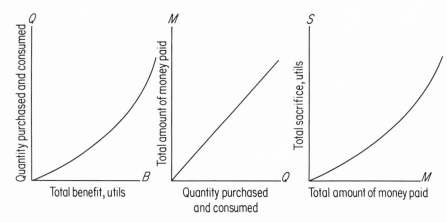

Fig. 2.10. Basic Relationships Among S, Q, M, and B II

Figure 2.10. The first diagram in the figure shows that in order to satisfy a util of need Evans must consume more grain as his consumption increases, or, stating the matter differently, an increase in the quantity of grain brings more benefit to Evans but at a decreasing rate. The middle diagram is the same as the middle diagram in Figure 2.8. The last diagram shows that in order to obtain \$1 he must work harder as the amount of money increases, or, stating the matter differently, an increase in labor brings more money to Evans but at a decreasing rate. We shall assume that Evans will obtain money in the most efficient way, so the curve here represents the minimum sacrifice that Evans must make in order to obtain a given amount of money. The curves in the first and the third diagram correspond to Line B and Line S, respectively, in Figure 2.2, when the necessary adjustments are made as discussed for Figure 2.8.

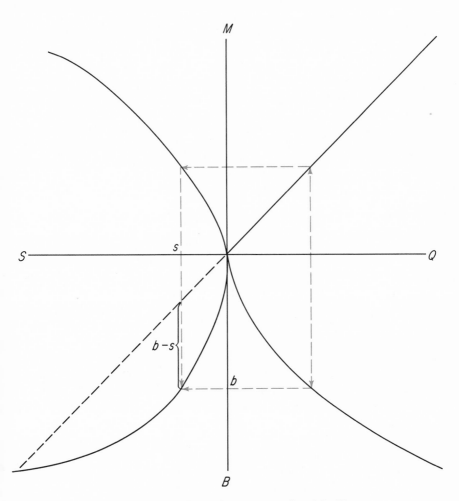

Fig. 2.11. Relationship Between S and B II

We then combine these three diagrams (Figure 2.11) and create the fourth curve in exactly the same way as we created the curve for Davis. Note that compared with Figure 2.9, which is for Davis, the axes for total benefit and total sacrifice have been interchanged. Now the difference between the curve thus obtained and the 45° line is the amount of the utility differential $b - s$ at various levels of the total sacrifice. Evans then should purchase grain at the point where $b - s$ is maximum.

Let us now superimpose Figure 2.11 on Figure 2.9 (see Figure 2.12) in order to analyze the relationship between the behavior of Davis and

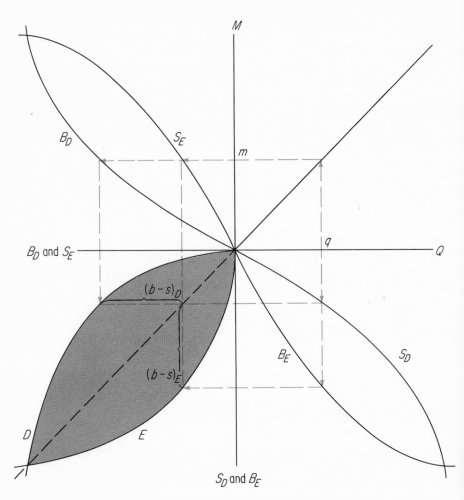

Fig. 2.12. Interaction of a Buyer and a Seller

Evans. The shaded area in the lower left-hand corner represents the personal utility differential which may be shared by Davis and Evans. Let us for a moment set Adams aside and consider the direct trade between Davis and Evans. Notice that if Davis and Evans agree to trade q units of grain for m dollars, Davis will obtain the utility differential of $(b - s)_D$ and Evans will obtain the utility differential of $(b - s)_E$ as a result of the trade. If Davis and Evans have equal "power" in the trade, they try to choose q so that they can each obtain the maximum net benefit; as a result the price is adjusted so that the quantity of grain which is optimum for Davis to sell is also the optimum quantity for Evans to purchase.

Although in the above example the price of grain is set in such a way that both Davis and Evans can enjoy the utility differential, this may not be the case because of the relative social power of the two. For example, Davis may dominate Evans in setting the price (i.e., Davis acts as a monopolist) and the only thing that Evans can do is decide the quantity he wants to buy in exchange for the specified amount of money. The maximum amount of money that Davis can charge in this case and still induce Evans to buy a given quantity of grain may be obtained from Figure 2.13. Since under the rationality assumption Evans is willing to buy and consume grain as long as any utility differential exists, the breakeven sacrifice-benefit line for Evans is represented by the 45° line in the lower

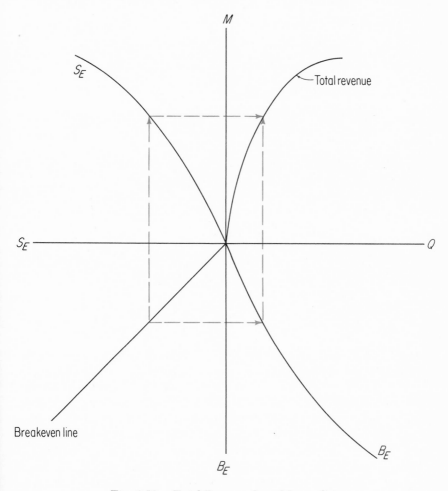

Fig. 2.13. Total Revenue for a Monopolist

left-hand corner of the figure. Then, the total revenue curve for Davis is obtained by tracing the three curves for every point on the Q axis as shown for a sample quantity. For this total revenue curve, Davis' sacrifice-benefit curve is changed from the broken line to the solid line in Figure 2.14. Thus, the personal utility differential which was previously shared by Davis and Evans is now enjoyed only by Davis. (Notice a change in the shaded area compared with that in Figure 2.12.)

Let us next consider a breakeven selling price for Davis, assuming that Evans is a monopsonist. Then, the total cost curve for Evans is

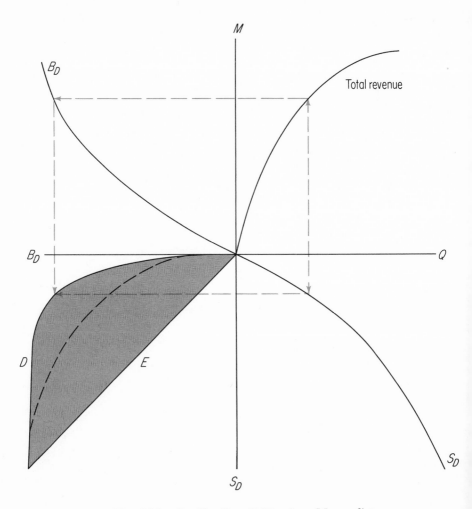

Fig. 2.14. Sacrifice-Benefit Line for a Monopolist

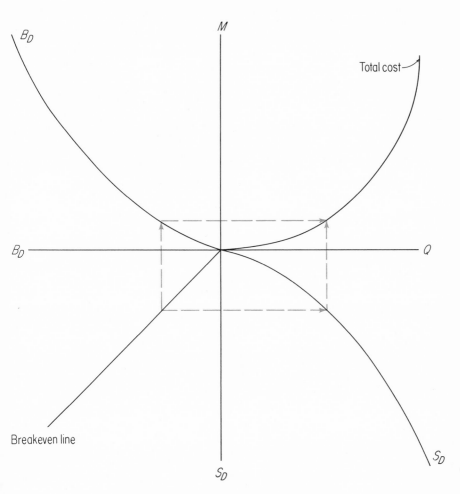

Fig. 2.15. Total Cost for a Monopsonist

derived as given by the total cost line in Figure 2.15. Superimposing this figure on Figure 2.13, we obtain Figure 2.16. Compare this figure with Figure 2.12 and notice that the personal utility differential shown by the shaded area in Figure 2.12 is now transformed into a monetary differential (i.e., profit), which is represented by the shaded area in Figure 2.16. Davis is willing to sell grain at any price above the total cost curve and Evans is willing to buy grain at any price below the total revenue curve. How the monetary differential (total revenue minus total cost) will be allocated between the two depends, therefore, entirely on their relative social power.

Furthermore there is no reason why this monetary differential should

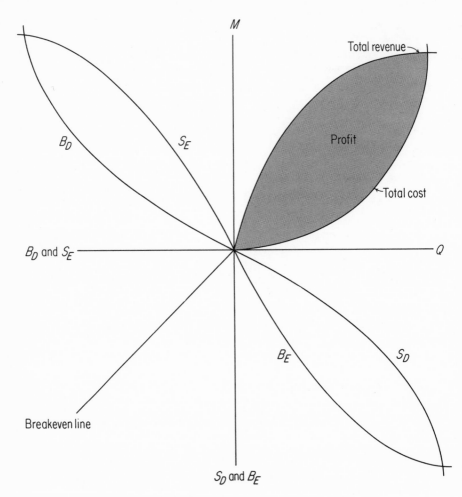

Fig. 2.16.   Breakeven Total Revenue and Cost Curves

be allocated between the two. For example, if Adams has social power over Davis and Evans (the power may come from the ignorance of the latter two or Adams' special knowledge of technology or other social advantages), then he can buy grain from Davis in exchange for the money indicated by the total cost curve and then sell it to Evans receiving the money indicated by the total revenue curve. In this way Adams can realize the monetary differential represented by the shaded area in Figure 2.16 as profit based on his activity, $M \rightarrow G_e \rightarrow M'$.

It is clear, therefore, that profit essentially comes from various forms of personal utility differentials. If no exchanges are involved, as was the case when Adams collected nuts for his own consumption, the personal utility differential represented by Area EBS in Figure 2.1 is enjoyed only by the person who originates the utility differential. Exchanges make personal utility differentials a social property subject to reallocation among the members of the society, and the reallocation process depends entirely upon the relative social powers of the members of the society.

Notice that just as utility differentials provide impetus for our activities, monetary differentials, or profit as their realization, provide impetus for our economic activities. This is natural because monetary differentials are simply a transformation of utility differentials in which the latter are made visible in the form of excess money. Furthermore, the utility differentials and their transformations (monetary differentials) given in Figure 2.16 do not disappear in any economic system. Technology determines the amount of these differentials, while the economic system determines how they should be allocated among the members of the society.[13]

Now that we understand the source of profit, we can discuss an important issue in the monetary valuation of goods and services. Suppose that Adams buys a bushel of grain for \$1 and sells it for \$2. What is the monetary value of the bushel of grain? We can answer this question very easily. In the process

$$(2.11) \qquad\qquad S \;\;\rightarrow\;\; G \;\;\rightarrow\;\; B$$
$$\text{\small(3 utils)} \qquad\qquad \text{\small(5 utils)}$$

that was discussed earlier we noted that the value of G may be expressed in two ways—one based on sacrifice, i.e., $s(G) = 3$ utils, and the other based on benefit, i.e., $b(G) = 5$ utils. Because the utility differential is the reason for our obtaining and consuming G, the value of G must be dual and it needs to be expressed as a pair as discussed earlier, i.e.

$$(2.12) \qquad\qquad v(G) = (3 \text{ utils}, 5 \text{ utils})$$

where $v(G)$ stands for the value of G. Namely, a single value for $v(G)$ is incomplete because value is a dual concept in itself.

Similarly in the process

$$(2.13) \qquad\qquad M \rightarrow G \rightarrow M'$$
$$\text{\small(\$1)} \qquad\qquad \text{\small(\$2)}$$

---

[13] See Newman [1965] for a more elaborate analysis of exchanges starting from an axiomatic structure of utility. Our discussion here is intended to give only a brief outline of the relationship between utility differentials and monetary differentials.

the monetary value of G, denoted by $m(G)$, must be expressed by a pair of numbers, i.e.

$$(2.14) \qquad\qquad m(G) = (\$1, \$2)$$

the first element representing the sacrifice value of G in monetary units and the second element the benefit value of G in monetary units. Thus, the question, "Is the value of the grain \$1 or \$2?" cannot be answered unless it is restated in a way such as "Is the sacrifice value of the grain \$1?", "Is the benefit value of the grain \$2?", or "Is the value of the grain (\$1, \$2)?", or "Is the net value of the grain \$1?" In all four cases the answer is yes.[14]

4. INSEPARABILITY, MULTIPLICITY, AND INSTABILITY OF CAUSAL NETWORKS

So far we have discussed the causal relationships among labor, goods, money, and need only in terms of a causal chain, e.g., $S \to G_p \to M \to G_e \to M' \to G_c \to B$. However, this is only an explanation of the very basic nature of values. Actual causal relationships are not so simple as this. There are three factors which complicate them. First, there may be more than one cause and more than one effect as we observe in the production process, where multiple factors are used to produce a product or multiple joint products are produced from a single factor. Second, there may be many alternative ways to obtain a given amount of goods or money. Third, the causal relationships may change over time. We shall investigate each of these points below.

Multiple causes or effects bring quite complicated problems.[15] A basic case may be presented as follows:

$$(2.15) \qquad
\begin{array}{c}
\qquad\quad G_a \to M'_a \\
\qquad\quad \nearrow \qquad {\scriptstyle(\$6)} \\
M \to G_e \\
{\scriptstyle(\$5)} \qquad \searrow \\
\qquad\quad G_b \to M'_b \\
\qquad\qquad\qquad {\scriptstyle(\$4)}
\end{array}$$

This causal network (tree) shows joint products G_a and G_b, which are produced from G_e. If M is \$5 of money, then the sacrifice value of G_e is

---

[14] See Mattessich [1964] for the duality in accounting from the viewpoint of dual classifications. Contrary to his emphasis on classificational duality in accounting, our emphasis is on causal duality. The distinction between the two is discussed in Chapter 5.

[15] See Bunge [1963] for the discussion of multiple causation and other problems involved in isolating a portion of a causal network.

$5, but what are the sacrifice values of G_a and G_b? Unfortunately, there is no logical reason why the $5 should be allocated in a particular way. The only convenient bases of allocation that exist within this causal network are the benefit values of G_a and G_b. For example, if M'_a and M'_b represent $6 and $4, respectively, then the benefit values of G_a and G_b are $6 and $4, respectively. Hence, the sacrifice value of $5 may be allocated to G_a and G_b in proportion to their benefit values, i.e., $3 to G_a and $2 to G_b. However, there is no logical reason why the sacrifice value should be allocated in proportion to the benefit values since the sacrifice value and the benefit value represent two entirely different aspects of the goods as we observed in Section 1. Practically speaking, however, since this method allocates the utility differential among the goods in proportion to their benefit values, it is often adopted in dealing with joint products. It is equally practical to set the sacrifice value of G_b equal to its benefit value, $4, and allocate the remaining sacrifice value ($1) to G_a, which is done in dealing with by-products. Similarly, if G_b may be obtained in an alternative way by paying $1, then we may set the sacrifice value of G_b equal to $1 and allocate the remaining sacrifice value ($4) to G_a. There are many such examples in accounting when dealing with indirect costs, costs of fixed assets that are to be allocated over many periods, etc.

On the other hand, an allocation problem arises for the benefit values where multiple factors are used as in the following basic case:

(2.16)
$$
\begin{array}{c}
M_a \to G_a \\
{\scriptstyle (\$3)} \qquad \searrow \\
\qquad\qquad G_e \to M' \\
\qquad \nearrow \qquad {\scriptstyle (\$10)} \\
M_b \to G_b \\
{\scriptstyle (\$2)}
\end{array}
$$

There is no problem in determining the benefit value of G_e in this case. It is $10 since M' represents $10 of money. However, the benefit values of G_a and G_b cannot be determined unless some allocation method is specified, e.g., benefit values are to be determined in proportion to sacrifice values.

Note that there is no problem in determining the sacrifice value of G_e in (2.16) or the benefit value of G_e in (2.15). The sacrifice value of G_e in (2.16) is $3 + $2 = $5, while the benefit value of G_e in (2.15) is $6 + $4 = $10, assuming, of course, the additivity of monetary values. However, in the following situation, both the sacrifice values of G_b and G_c and their benefit values cannot be determined.

(2.17)
$$
\begin{array}{c}
\qquad\qquad G_b \\
\qquad \nearrow \qquad \searrow \\
M \to G_a \qquad\qquad G_d \to M' \\
{\scriptstyle (\$5)} \qquad \searrow \qquad \nearrow \qquad {\scriptstyle (\$10)} \\
\qquad\qquad G_c
\end{array}
$$

There is no basis for allocating the sacrifice value of \$5 and the benefit value of \$10 unless we use factors outside this causal network. Actual causal networks that we observe in business are naturally far more complicated than this, and so we have to use external factors as a basis for allocating sacrifice values and benefit values.

We have this ambiguity in the allocation of sacrifice and benefit values because valuation is a surrogate of a causal network,[16] and, unless the network is a simple one, valuation alone cannot represent it. For example, the causal network in (2.17) is the principal we want to represent by a surrogate. To indicate the fact that there is a causal chain between M (m dollars of money) and goods G_a, i.e., to represent a causal chain $M \to \cdots \to G_a$, we state as a surrogate that the sacrifice value of G_a, denoted by $s(G_a)$, is m dollars. Similarly, to represent a causal chain $G_d \to \cdots \to M'$, we state as a surrogate that the benefit value of G_d, denoted by $b(G_d)$, is m' dollars. However, in order to state the value of G_b or G_c in the network of (2.17), we must separate G_b from G_c in the network. Of course, we can determine the sacrifice and benefit values of (G_b and G_c), but if the network is so complicated that G_b and G_c are used for different purposes we are forced to separate them in order to continue using the valuation system. Notice, however, in the principal relation given by the network of (2.17) G_b and G_c are not separable, and, as we discussed in Chapter 1, a surrogate relation cannot create a principal relation. Therefore, the valuation method of representing a causal network necessarily involves an artificial separation of elements in the network.

Another characteristic of the representation of a causal network by valuation is that the measure derived from the valuation is additive, i.e., the measure (or the amount) of (M_1 and M_2) is equal to the sum of the measure of M_1 and the measure of M_2. This additivity of a value measure is used to represent a portion of a network that forms a tree, such as

(2.18)

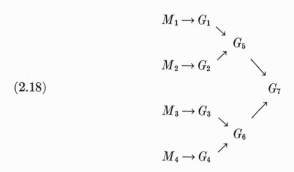

[16] More precisely a directed network. See Berge [1958], Charnes and Cooper [1961], etc. for the mathematical analysis of directed networks.

or

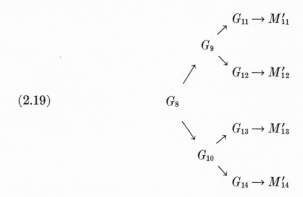

(2.19)

The tree in (2.18) can be suitably represented by the additivity of a sacrifice-value measure and the tree in (2.19) can be suitably represented by the additivity of a benefit-value measure. Therefore, $s(G) = m$ means that the causal network has a tree coming into G whose branches start with M's with the sum of their quantities (amounts) equal to m. Similarly, $b(G) = m'$ means that the causal network has a tree going out from G whose branches end with M'''s with the sum of their quantities equal to m'. Of course, $s(G)$ and $b(G)$ do not tell us how many branches there are in the tree. (There may be just one, in which case it is a causal chain.)[17]

Although there are still problems of separability and allocation of values as discussed above, valuation problems are far simpler when the causal network is unique, i.e., when there are no alternative ways of obtaining or disposing the goods or money involved. Unfortunately, however, most of the causal networks we observe in business are not unique, and this is why valuation problems become extremely complicated. To understand the problem of alternative causal networks, we must make a distinction between a class of objects and a particular object in the class. Take, for example, a bushel of grain, denoted by G. We may be concerned with the valuation of a bushel of grain G in general or with the valuation of particularly identified grain (e.g., grain in a specific box) whose volume is a bushel. We shall denote by $\bar{G}$ goods with particular identification. If the causal network is unique, the value of $\bar{G}$ is equal to the value of G all the time. However, as soon as we introduce alternative causal networks, this identity ceases to exist. Suppose, for example, a bushel of grain G may be obtained in many different ways and may be used in many different

---

[17] See Chapter 3 for a more detailed discussion of the additivity of quantity measures.

ways, e.g.

$$\text{Chain 1: } (\$m_1) \; M_1 \to \cdots \to G \to \cdots \to M_1' \; (\$m_1')$$

$$\text{Chain 2: } (\$m_2) \; M_2 \to \cdots \to G \to \cdots \to M_2' \; (\$m_2')$$

(2.20) $\cdots\cdots\cdots\cdots\cdots\cdots\cdots\cdots\cdots\cdots\cdots\cdots\cdots\cdots\cdots$

$$\text{Chain } n\colon (\$m_n) \; M_n \to \cdots \to G \to \cdots \to M_n' \; (\$m_n')$$

If a particular bushel of grain $\bar{G}$ is obtained and sold by following Chain 1, then we can say $s(\bar{G}) = m_1$ and $b(\bar{G}) = m_1'$. However, what are the sacrifice and benefit values of a bushel of grain G in general? Should $s(G)$ be the minimum value of $m_1, m_2, \cdots, m_n$ and $b(G)$ be the maximum value of $m_1', m_2', \cdots, m_n'$? Should $s(G)$ be the maximum value of $m_1, m_2, \cdots, m_n$ and $b(G)$ be the minimum value of $m_1', m_2', \cdots, m_n'$ to make a "conservative" valuation? Or should $s(G)$ and $b(G)$ be some kind of weighted average of $m_1, m_2, \cdots, m_n$, and $m_1', m_2', \cdots, m_n'$, respectively, using, for example, frequencies of occurrence as weights?[18]

So far as there are alternative causal networks pertaining to G, we cannot say which causal network should be used in the valuation of $\bar{G}$ since this depends entirely upon which causal network we are interested in. However, we can at least select one particular causal network among the numerous networks and give it a distinction. This is the causal network by which $\bar{G}$ is actually obtained and disposed. No matter how many causal networks there may be, this particular one is uniquely defined. Let us call this network the *factual causal network* pertaining to $\bar{G}$ and the valuation of $\bar{G}$ based on the factual network the *factual valuation*, while calling the rest of the causal networks pertaining to G *imputed causal networks* and a valuation of $\bar{G}$ based on an imputed causal network an *imputed valuation*. Of course, whether or not a causal network and a valuation based on the causal network are factual depends upon which goods $\bar{G}$ we are concerned with. As we shall discuss in the next section, factual valuation plays an important role in accounting valuation.

A problem closely related to this choice of alternative causal chains is the effect upon valuation of a time dimension in a causal network. Consider two causal chains, both of which may be expressed as $M \to G \to M'$, but

---

[18] This also involves the issue of the additivity of values in the sense that if G_1 may be obtained by Chain 1 and G_2 may be obtained by Chain 2, while (G_1 and G_2) may be obtained by Chain 3, we would want to have their sacrifice and benefit values to be additive, i.e., $m_3 = m_1 + m_2$ and $m_3' = m_1' + m_2'$. In general, this is of course not necessarily true.

one of which takes a longer time than the other to complete. If we represent the difference in the length of time by the difference in the length of arrows, the two causal chains may be written

$$(2.21) \qquad\qquad M \to G \to M'$$

and

$$(2.22) \qquad\qquad M \longrightarrow G \longrightarrow M'$$

Then, the question is, "Are $s(G)$ and $b(G)$ the same for G in both chains?" Take the benefit value of G. Since G can be converted into M faster in (2.21) than in (2.22), we feel that G in (2.21) has a higher benefit value than G in (2.22). Similarly, we feel that the sacrifice value of G in (2.22) is higher than the sacrifice value of G in (2.21) since we consider that somehow we have sacrificed more to obtain G in (2.22) than G in (2.21). This extra sacrifice or benefit is ordinarily converted into interest on money. Thus, for the causal chain in (2.22) we substitute

$$(2.23) \qquad\qquad M \to M_p \to G \to M'_p \to M'$$

where the portion $M_p \to G \to M'_p$ has the same length as the causal chain in (2.21) and M_p represents M plus interest on M during the period $M \to M_p$ and M'_p represents M' minus the discount on M' during the period $M'_p \to M'$. Then the portion $M_p \to G \to M'_p$ may be equated with $M \to G \to M'$ and the problem is reduced to choosing alternative causal networks as was discussed earlier. An accounting valuation that emphasizes this aspect of the problem from the viewpoint of benefit values is a proposal to evaluate goods based on the present value of the future service potential of the goods. Of course, the same idea may be applied to the sacrifice value of goods as well.

In addition to the inseparability and the multiplicity of causal networks which have been discussed, there is a third factor which complicates the valuation problem—that is, the instability of a causal network. When a causal network that has been applicable to past phenomena is not expected to be applicable to future phenomena because of a change in the environment, there is a choice between the use of a causal network that was applicable in the past as a basis of valuation and the use of a causal network that is expected to be applicable in the future. Stating it more generally, there is a choice between an *ex post* valuation and an *ex ante* valuation. An *ex post* valuation is a valuation of goods $\bar{G}$ based on a factual or an imputed causal chain pertaining to G (which is equivalent to $\bar{G}$) that is assumed to have been applicable at the time $\bar{G}$ was obtained or disposed. An *ex ante* valuation is a valuation of goods $\bar{G}$ based on an estimated causal chain that is expected to be applicable in the (immediate) future in obtaining G or in disposing of $\bar{G}$ or G. That is, if a valuation is based on what has actually happened or what could have happened, it is called an *ex post* valuation; and if it is based on what is actually supposed to happen or what could happen, it is called an *ex ante* valuation. This distinction becomes important when, as is ordinarily the case, because of changes in the environment, some causal networks that have been applicable are not expected to be applicable in the future and new causal networks which have not been applicable in the past are expected to be applicable in the future.

Thus, we have discussed three major problems which make valuation ambiguous and difficult. 1) The *inseparability* of elements in a causal network; 2) the *multiplicity* of a causal network involving a particular element; and 3) the *instability* of a causal network over time. No wonder so many different valuation methods and value-allocation methods have been proposed in accounting!

5. SIGNIFICANCE OF HISTORICAL COST VALUATION

Let us classify some accounting valuation methods based on the above analysis. Consider the sacrifice value of particular goods $\bar{G}$. It may be based on the factual causal network that actually brought $\bar{G}$. This is the *historical cost valuation*. It may also be based on a causal network that is expected to be most applicable in the (immediate) future in obtaining G, which is equivalent to $\bar{G}$. This is the *replacement cost valuation*. On the other hand, the benefit value of $\bar{G}$ may be based on the factual causal network by which $\bar{G}$ was actually disposed of. This is called a *realized value* of $\bar{G}$. Of course, this cannot be determined until $\bar{G}$ is actually disposed of and, in the case of the monetary valuation with which we have been concerned, money has actually been received. We determine the benefit value of $\bar{G}$ when $\bar{G}$ is still on hand, by an estimated factual causal network, i.e., a causal network that is expected to be most applicable in disposing of $\bar{G}$. This is called a *a realizable value* of $\bar{G}$.[19] These valuation methods may be organized as in Table 2.2.[20] The valuation of $\bar{G}$ based on the factual causal

---

[19] See Bedford [1965] for the distinction between realized and realizable values. Vatter's fund concept, i.e., a fund as a collection of service potentials that have been brought together for some functional purpose [1947, p. 18], is also centered on the benefit values of resources, although an emphasis is placed on the collective power of resources.

[20] Notice that the dichotomy between the valuation methods based on the sacrifice value and those based on the benefit value is closely related to the dichotomy between the labor theory of value and the utility theory of value. In this sense, we disagree with Canning's statement [1929, p. 198] that accountants subscribe to no theory of value but only to theories of valuation.

TABLE 2.2   A Classification of Accounting Valuations

	SACRIFICE VALUE	BENEFIT VALUE
EX POST	Historical cost	Realized value
EX ANTE	Replacement cost	Realizable value

network is an *ex post* valuation, while the valuation of $\bar{G}$ based on an expected causal network is an *ex ante* valuation, although there are many other kinds of *ex post* and *ex ante* valuations.[21]

The four kinds of valuation have one thing in common—they are based on the factual causal network or a causal network that most closely approximates the factual causal network. They are different from other valuation methods that are based on opportunity costs or opportunity benefits since the latter emphasize the optimality of a causal network; namely, here we evaluate $\bar{G}$ based on what we could have done had we acted optimally in the past in the case of an *ex post* valuation or based on what we expect to be able to do if we act optimally in the future in the case of an *ex ante* valuation. On the other hand, we may evaluate $\bar{G}$ based on the most conservative estimate, i.e., guaranteed maximum cost or guaranteed minimum benefit. A valuation of assets based on their immediate liquidating value may be considered an example of this since such valuation normally produces a guaranteed minimum benefit value of the assets in a firm.

Among all these various valuation methods, how can we select one as the "best"? There is no answer to this question. It may be possible to say that for a particular use of accounting information, one valuation method is better than another. But an overall selection seems to be impossible. As we mentioned earlier, valuation is a surrogate designed to represent underlying causal networks, and since the causal network itself is inseparable, multiple, and unstable, any one valuation is not likely to satisfy all needs. We shall investigate the problems involved in selecting a particular valuation method in later chapters. (See Chapters 6–8.)

However, among various valuation methods, there is one which is unique in terms of its practicality in measurement, i.e., the valuation method based on historical costs. Notice that the valuation of goods $\bar{G}$ based on the factual causal chain that actually involves $\bar{G}$ has an advantage over other methods in the sense that it is unique and certain. If we base our valuation on another method, regardless of whether it is an *ex post* valuation or an *ex ante* valuation, we cannot be certain that the causal network could have been followed (*ex post* valuations) or can be followed

---

[21] Edwards and Bell [1961] classify the six concepts of values and costs into 1) exit values (expected values, current values, and opportunity costs) and 2) entry values (present cost, current cost, and historic cost).

(*ex ante* valuations) because we have never actually observed such a causal network to be applicable to the particular goods $\bar{G}$ in question. We merely apply the similarity assumption, which was discussed earlier, and say that a causal network has been observed many times in the past, therefore, we can reasonably assume that the same network could have been applied to the phenomena in our unknown past—unknown in the sense that this is a purely hypothetical past, which we have never actually experienced. There is no way of being sure that we would have obtained the expected result if we had actually decided to follow the network to obtain and dispose of $\bar{G}$ because there might have been an unexpected reaction of the environment to our selection of the network. A similar argument holds for an *ex ante* valuation.

This is not true for a factual causal network and a factual valuation. Since this is the network by which $\bar{G}$ was actually obtained or disposed, we have already "gone through" the path $M \rightarrow \cdots \rightarrow \bar{G} \rightarrow \cdots \rightarrow M'$. This network is, therefore, in our known past. It is not just one of many possible networks concerning $\bar{G}$ but is the unique one in the sense that it is the chosen alternative.[22]

From this viewpoint, valuations based on historical cost and realized value have advantages over all other valuation methods including valuations based on replacement cost and realizable value.[23] (See Table 2.2.) However, in order to apply the realized value method, we must wait until goods are actually disposed of, whereas we often want to evaluate goods on hand. This makes the realized value basis practically unsuitable. Thus, historical cost valuation has an advantage over all other valuations in this regard.

Of course, there is a problem of identifying and interpreting the unique causal network by which goods $\bar{G}$ are actually obtained or disposed of. Furthermore, the inseparability problem still exists even in historical cost valuation and some external factor, e.g., realizable values, must be brought in as a basis of allocation when joint products (in a broader sense) are involved. However, we can at least avoid the multiplicity and the instability problems associated with causal networks if we adopt historical cost valuation.

[22] It may seem as though an optimum causal network has this uniqueness property. However, we must remember that there are numerous unchosen alternatives, and we are unable to take all of them into account in determining optimality. Therefore, optimality can de defined only on one subset of all possible alternatives and ambiguity remains in determining which subset to select.

[23] In this regard, the realizable value basis has the advantage of being less ambiguous than other methods except the historical one in the sense that it is an estimated factual valuation and whether our estimate was correct can be verified later as realizable values become realized values. There is no way of verifying values based on any other methods since they are derived from hypothetical activities.

If we classify accounting into *equity accounting* and *operational accounting*, depending upon whether or not accounting data are used to solve conflicting interests, historical cost valuation plays an important role in equity accounting. This is because, contrary to the case in operational accounting, where the accountants' objective is primarily to provide useful data for users, in equity accounting accountants must develop and operate an accounting system in the most objective, consistent, and unambiguous manner since the data they provide directly affect the way in which conflicting interests are solved, as in income tax accounting or in divisional accounting involving transfer of goods and services among divisions.

Our society needs some valuation system to regulate various conflicts among parties involved in business activities. In choosing criteria for such regulation, uniqueness and stability should be the most important virtues for a valuation system to have, just as they are for a legal system. We shall investigate the current practices of historical cost valuation in particular in Chapter 4, after discussing the foundations of accounting valuation in general in the following chapter.

CHAPTER THREE

Axioms of Control, Quantities, and Exchanges

In the previous two chapters we explored the methodological and substantive foundations of accounting measurement. In particular, we noted that the purpose of accounting is to communicate the economic events of an entity, which are identified by economic resources controlled by the entity and their changes. In this chapter we will explore three axioms of accounting that are essential for achieving this purpose—the axiom of control, the axiom of quantities, and the axiom of exchanges.

1. CONTROL

Accounting is not concerned with economic resources in general but only those which are under the control of a given entity. Therefore, we must specify which entity we are concerned with.[1] Accounting does not exist for a simple collection of individuals such as a mob unless such a collection is considered to constitute an entity. (A holding company is an example of a collection of companies recognized as an entity.) Similarly, accounting does not represent economic resources which are not under the

[1] Paton [1922, pp. 472–73] states, "To start with, *the existence of a distinct business entity* is something which the accountant almost universally assumes.... Accordingly, it is convenient for him to assume that this enterprise or business situation has a distinct existence, that it constitutes a real institution through which flows a stream of values and in the operation of which several, perhaps many individuals have a part."

control of any entity, such as minerals on the moon (unless the moon itself is considered an entity). Of course, the entity need not be limited to individual and legal entities such as corporations and estates. Divisions of an organization may be considered entities if they are given control over resources by the administrative rules of the organization, as they are in responsibility accounting.[2]

Since the control relationship between the entity and its resources is the basis of accounting, we must have *control criteria* by which we can determine whether each resource is under the control of the entity. In conventional accounting legal ownership is the control criterion. Therefore, resources that are not owned by an entity are not, in general, considered to be under its control even though they are under its control in other respects, as in the case of rented machines.[3] Of course, the syntax of accounting language is not affected by the types of control criteria that are used. We may expand the relationship to include control based on various other factors such as location, possession, and physical attachment, and still be able to represent it in accounting language.

However, regardless of which control criteria are used, we should be able to divide the set of all resources uniquely into the portion which is under the control of the entity and the portion which is not under its control. We call resources under its control the *assets*[4] of the entity or we call them the *property set* of the entity if we want to emphasize the point that we are concerned with the entire assets of the entity.

Before we proceed further, an important extension of the concept of control must be noted since it has materially affected the syntax of accounting language by introducing the concept of negative assets. This is the extension of the control concept to include expected control over resources. Suppose that an entity does not have control over a resource at the present moment under the given control criteria, but it expects that the resource will be put under its control in the future. In conventional accounting, some resources such as these are recognized as assets of the entity under rigid conditions. For example, when goods are delivered to a

---

[2] Devine [1962, Chapter 13] analyzes this as "the unit problem" from a broader viewpoint which includes the accounting periods.

[3] Although there are various degrees of control, a basic issue is whether the entity has a sufficient degree of authority to decide use or disposition. See Cooper [1949] for the concept of control retention as an important consideration in the theory of the firm. See also Fisher [1906] on the concept of property as "the right to the uses of wealth."

[4] Sanders, Hatfield, and Moore [1938, p. 58] defines assets as follows: "The assets of a business comprise all its properties of resources. In general, three conditions apply to the listing of items as assets, (1) that the business in question *own* them, (2) that the business has acquired them at a *cost*, and (3) that they are of *value* to the business." In our analysis, (1) corresponds to the control concept and (2) and (3) correspond to the sacrifice value and the benefit value of economic resources.

customer who has not paid yet, the entity expects to receive cash in the future. In this case, the entity is allowed to recognize control over the cash even though it may actually not receive it. On the other hand, conventional accounting does not recognize goods to be received in the future as assets of an entity even if the contract has been signed. (If money has been paid for the goods, it is treated as advance payment, not as "future goods.")

Since the concept of control is extended in this way to include resources that the entity expects to receive (gain control over) in the future, it can also be extended to include resources that the entity expects to deliver (lose control over) in the future, thus giving rise to the concept of negative assets. Again, in conventional accounting some resources are recognized as negative assets of the entity under rigid conditions. For example, when goods are received from a supplier whom the entity has not paid but to whom the entity expects to deliver cash in the future, the entity is allowed to recognize its negative control over the cash. On the other hand, conventional accounting does not recognize goods to be delivered in the future as negative assets of an entity even if the contract has been signed.

Later we shall discuss the conditions under which the entity's control may be extended over future assets (positive or negative) in conventional accounting. However, let us now analyze the relationships between proper control and extended control and between positive assets and negative assets.

Assume that control criteria have been given for a certain entity and that we have determined that Resources a, b, and c are under its control. They are called *present assets* since control over them presently exists. In the future the entity expects to receive Resources d, e, f, and g and expects to deliver Resources a, b, d, and f. (See Figure 3.1.) Of course, judgments on receipt or delivery are based on the control criteria specified earlier. The control criteria applied to present assets must be the ones applied to future assets. If the control criterion is legal ownership, the receipt or delivery of future assets must be judged by the same criterion and not, for example, by the physical location of the assets.

However, of the future receipts or deliveries which fulfill the control criteria, only those which meet *recognition criteria* are recorded as changes in the assets as we observed above when discussing control in conventional

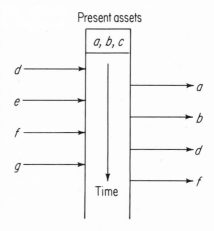

Fig. 3.1. Present Assets and Their Changes

accounting. If the receipts of Resources d and e and the deliveries of Resources a, d, and f are recognized, the assets of the entity under the extended control concept can be classified in three categories as shown in Table 3.1. Two aspects of the extended concept of assets should be noted from the table. First, there are no present negative assets. The control criteria tell either that the resource is presently under the control of the entity or that it is not under its control. There is no such concept as negative control of present assets since negative assets exist only after we extend the control concept to *future assets*. Second, Resource f appears only in the negative-asset group. Logically, the entity cannot forego control of a resource over which it never had control. However, as Figure 3.1 clearly shows, this occurs because the recognition criteria did not cover the receipt of Resource f. Thus, when we quantify these resources later it is possible that liabilities (negative cash) will exceed cash and receivables combined (positive cash).

The extended concept of assets in conventional accounting is, therefore, based on the control criteria and the recognition criteria. It consists of positive assets and negative assets as shown in Table 3.1. In the subse-

TABLE 3.1 Extended Concepts of Assets

	POSITIVE ASSETS	NEGATIVE ASSETS
FUTURE ASSETS	d, e	a, d, f
PRESENT ASSETS	a, b, c	

quent discussions, we shall always assume the extended concept of assets. Whatever the control criteria and the recognition criteria may be, the crucial point is that we can determine at any point in time the positive assets and the negative assets of the entity.

This ability to determine assets helps us understand the concept of income. The income of an entity between two points in time is defined as the difference between the assets of the entity at those two points. Here, the distinction is made between income and the quantification of income, which are often confused in theories of economics and accounting. In many cases, two different income "concepts" vary only in their valuation methods. Income (principal) and the quantification of income (surrogate) are two different things, and they should be clearly separated in theory. For example, if one has a plot of land on January 1, and the same land plus a building on December 31, the building is his income during the year. How to represent the building by means of a number is a problem which exists apart from the definition of income. The building may be represented differently, but different representations do not make the income itself different.

This concept is consistent with the Hicksian concept of income—"the maximum value which he can consume during a week, and still expect to be as well off at the end of the week as he was at the beginning." (Hicks [1946, p. 172].) Even though Hicks defined income as value, the underlying concept is clearly free of any quantification. The man can "consume" the building and still be as well off at the end of the year as he was at the beginning. In other words, he can restore the original position even after "consuming" the building.

In this case the income consists only of a building; in general, however, it consists of an *increment* and a *decrement*. An increment is the set of all resources that are assets of the entity at the end of the period but were not assets at the beginning of the period. A decrement is the set of all resources that were assets of the entity at the beginning of the period but are not assets at the end of the period. For example, if the man's assets at the end of the year consist of the building only, then his income I during the year is an increment I^+, the building, and a decrement I^-, the land. The original asset position may be restored if he "consumes" the building and "produces" the land.

If an entity has positive and negative assets, its income is defined as follows. If the beginning assets A_b are positive assets (a, b, c) and negative assets (c, d, e) and the ending assets A_e are positive assets (a, g) and negative assets (d, h), then the income I during the period is an increment $I^+ = (g:h)$ and a decrement $I^- = (b, c:c, e)$, i.e., from

$$(3.1) \qquad A_b = (a, b, c:c, d, e)$$

and

$$(3.2) \qquad A_e = (a, g:d, h)$$

we obtain

$$(3.3) \qquad I = \{(g:h)^+, (b, c:c, e)^-\}$$

where a colon separates positive assets and negative assets. In order to restore the beginning asset position, the entity must consume $(g:h)$ and produce $(b, c:c, e)$, where "consumption" of negative assets means fulfilling or canceling obligations, and "production" of negative assets means generating them by making commitments to deliver certain resources.

Thus, the basic idea behind the Hicksian concept of income is a change in the assets of an entity, making income a derivative of assets. Hence, we can determine income whenever we can determine the assets of an entity at two points in time.

Assets and income defined in this way may be represented by various methods. The most primitive method is denotation, of which (3.1)–(3.3) are examples. It is, of course, very laborious and, in most cases, impossible to list resources individually. This is especially true for future assets because we may not know specifically which resource the entity is going to receive or deliver. Therefore, we must shift our attention to the classification and the quantification of resources in each class. This will be done in the next section. After classification and quantification, the assets and income of an entity can be represented by listing pairs of a class name (i.e., a connotation[5]) and a quantity instead of by listing the assets and income individually. This is the representation of assets and income by quantities. Of course, these quantities need not be commensurable. For example, if the assets A of an entity are

(3.4) $A = \{$Cash, \$100; gasoline, 150 gallons; machines, 3 units$\}$

it is not assumed that the quantities can be aggregated into one measure. When these quantities are aggregated into one measure

(3.5) $A = \$520,486$

we have represented assets and income by using only one number. This is the third and the most advanced method. We shall discuss it in later chapters.

2. QUANTITIES

Let us now consider the first step in a quantitative representation of assets and income. Note that in the previous section assets and income were identified and represented by symbols *individually* without any indication of quantity. This individuality of resources must, however, be replaced in business transactions by the broader concept of *resource classes* since we do not purchase or sell goods (except special goods such as antiques) by individual identification. We order 500 light bulbs, 10 desks, 10 chairs, 100 bushels of wheat, 150 gallons of gasoline, etc., with specifications which identify the class of the goods we want to buy, but we are not particularly interested in which goods we receive as long as they meet the specifications. In this way, we communicate our *indifference to* certain resources; by this we mean we are not concerned with choosing among

---

[5] See, e.g., Cohen and Nagel [1934] for the distinction between denotation and connotation.

such resources since the differences between them are not essential to us. For example, we are indifferent to two machines with different serial numbers providing both meet the same specifications.

In order to shift from individual resource identification to resource-class identification, we have to be able to define quantities. An order to deliver gasoline which meets certain specifications does not make sense unless the quantity to be delivered is specified. This is not true in the case of individual resource identification. An order to deliver "the gasoline in this drum" is a completely unambiguous order. Thus, classification and quantification go together.

In the following discussion, we shall be concerned only with resources in a given class (e.g., gasoline with a given specification) and only with one quantity measure (e.g., volume of gasoline in gallons) in order to understand the nature of a quantity measure.

Let us first distinguish between a quantity measure and a quantity. A quantity measure is a method or, more rigorously, a function; by applying it to a particular set of objects we obtain a number which is called a quantity. An analogy to a machine may help. A quantity measure is a machine (or a scale) which takes a set of objects as input and generates a number —a quantity—as output. We shall use the term *sets* to denote the things to be measured in order to conform to accepted terminology in mathematics. Therefore, instead of saying the volume of gasoline in Tank A, we shall simply say the quantity of Set A.

For any given set of objects to be measured, a quantity measure must yield a unique number to avoid ambiguity. If a scale provides different numbers for the same set of objects, we are not sure which is the proper weight. Of course, in reality an error of measurement always exists, but for the sake of our theoretical investigation of the nature of quantity measures, we assume that such error is negligible and that every set of objects has a unique quantity derived from a given quantity measure.

Quantities are always nonnegative. For example, a scale does not show negative weight. Of course, we may use a negative sign with a quantity to mean an opposing property of the set of objects, but this is part of the applications or uses of quantities and not part of their definition.

We now come to two fundamental properties of quantities: the additivity of quantities and the indifference to sets of objects with the same quantity. First, quantities must be additive, i.e., the quantity of Set A and Set B together must be equal to the sum of the quantity of Set A and the quantity of Set B, providing there are no objects that commonly belong to Sets A and B. For example, if $q(A)$ is the volume of gasoline in Tank A and $q(B)$ is the volume of gasoline in Tank B, then we must have

(3.6) $$q(A \text{ and } B) = q(A) + q(B)$$

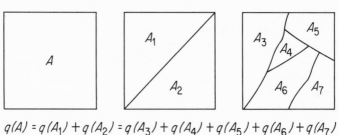

$$q(A) = q(A_1) + q(A_2) = q(A_3) + q(A_4) + q(A_5) + q(A_6) + q(A_7)$$

Fig. 3.2. Additivity of a Quantity Measure

providing, of course, no portion of the gasoline is common to Tanks A and B. Stating the matter differently, the quantity of a whole must equal the sum of the quantities of all its parts.[6] Figure 3.2 clarifies this point further. In it, the quantity of A (e.g., the weight of Plate A) is equal to the sum of the quantities of all its parts no matter how we divide it. This assures us that the quantity of 1,000 gallons of gasoline is 1,000 no matter how we divide them and measure them part by part. Thus any portion of the set may be measured independently from the rest. This is the most important property of quantities. If quantities were not additive, we could not consider the quantities themselves properties of a set of objects. For example, Sets A, B, and C are disjoint, i.e., have no common parts; the weight of A is 30 pounds; B, 20 pounds; C, 10 pounds. If, however, the weight of A and B is 55 pounds and of A and C is 35 pounds, we cannot consider 30 pounds to be the property of Set A since when it is added to B it increases the total weight by 35, whereas when it is added to C it increases the total weight by 25. In other words, the weight of A is dependent upon the environment (the existence or nonexistence of Set B or Set C) and can no longer be considered the property of A per se. This additivity condition requires also that since A may be trivially partitioned into its own set A and an empty set $\emptyset$

(3.7) $$q(A) = q(A) + q(\emptyset)$$

Thus, the quantity of an empty set must always equal zero.[7]

    [6] See the additivity axiom and the related discussions on the additivity of value in Churchman [1961, Chapter 9]. In measure theory, a measure must be countably additive whereas (3.6) guarantees only that the measure is finitely additive. However, this leads to a discussion that is too technical for this book; readers who are interested in pursuing this more rigorously are referred to literature on measure theory such as Halmos [1950], Royden [1963].

    [7] However, this does not mean that the quantity of a nonempty set could not be equal to zero. In measure theory, a quantity measure which always produces zero as a quantity of a set of objects is also considered a legitimate measure. On the other hand, in measure theory $q(A)$ can be positively infinite, in which case (3.7) does not imply $q(\emptyset) = 0$. Hence, the latter is included in the definition of a measure in measure theory. See, again, Halmos [1950] and Royden [1963].

The second fundamental property of quantities is that we are indifferent to two sets of objects if and only if their quantities are the same. We order, e.g., 10 gallons of regular gasoline, because we are indifferent as to which particular gasoline we get, providing it is regular and has a volume of 10 gallons. If we are not indifferent to sets of objects in a given class whose quantities are the same, then we should not have classified these objects in the same class.

Of course, the decision to be indifferent or not to given sets of objects is a personal judgment with which everyone might not agree. However, the environment of an entity roughly determines the kinds of classifications and quantity measures considered acceptable. For example, among scrap dealers scrap is traded by weight, although it may contain many different metals which we are not indifferent to. Retailers in general have many more classifications for goods than wholesalers have because consumers are concerned with finer points than retailers are concerned with. In any case, a quantity measure must be supported by some concept of indifference, or *Gleichgültigkeit* as Hegel calls it.[8]

We now define a quantity measure and a quantity more rigorously as follows:

A *quantity measure* q is a function which assigns to each set A of objects in the class for which the measure is defined a unique nonnegative number called a *quantity* of A, denoted by $q(A)$, in such a way that the following two conditions are satisfied.

Condition 1: The quantities are additive; namely, the quantity of a whole is always equal to the sum of the quantities of all its parts.

Condition 2: We are indifferent to any two sets A and B of objects in the class, denoted by $A \simeq B$, if and only if their quantities are the same, i.e., $q(A) = q(B)$.[9,10]

A quantity measure is called a *natural quantity measure* if its output is always a natural number $(0, 1, 2, \cdots)$. It is called a *rational quantity*

[8] "Quality is primary and immediate determinateness; quantity is such determinateness as has become indifferent to Being." Hegel [1812, Volume I, Book I, Section 2, p. 198].

[9] The requirement of indifference here may be too strict from a practical viewpoint since we have a margin of error which is discussed in the literature in terms of "just noticeable difference (jnd)" (see, e.g., Torgerson [1958]). However, Condition 2 is a good approximation of our empirical behavior in regard to quantities.

[10] Since the equality of quantities is reflexive $[q(A)=q(A)]$, symmetrical $[q(A)=q(B)$ implies $q(B)=q(A)]$, and transitive $[q(A)=q(B)$ and $q(B)=q(C)$ imply $q(A)=q(C)]$, the indifference must also fulfill these conditions, i.e., $A \simeq A$; $A \simeq B$ implies $B \simeq A$; and $A \simeq B$ and $B \simeq C$ imply $A \simeq C$. (See Appendix A for a more rigorous analysis of these concepts.) In addition, since a quantity measure is additive $[q(A)=q(B)$ and $q(C)=q(D)$ imply $q(A$ and $C)=q(B$ and $D)$, assuming A and C have no joint part and neither have B and $D]$, the indifference must also be additive, i.e., $A \simeq B$ and $C \simeq D$ imply $(A$ and $C) \simeq (B$ and $D)$ under the same assumption.

measure if its output is always a rational number, i.e., a number expressible as a ratio of two natural numbers $(0, 2, 5.5, \frac{1}{3}, \frac{492}{7}, 129.6549, \text{etc.})$. In the same way, the outputs of *real quantity measures* are always real numbers, including irrational numbers such as $\sqrt{2}, \sqrt{3}, \pi$. In accounting, we rarely deal with irrational numbers; hence, we shall not find it necessary to discuss real quantity measures. On the other hand, a natural quantity measure is clearly insufficient in accounting since fractional quantities do occur frequently. Therefore, in the following discussions, we shall assume that the quantity measures are always rational.

Let us consider Bottles A and B, each containing milk. The quantity of milk in A, $q(A)$, is 1.2 quarts and the quantity of milk in B, $q(B)$, is $\frac{4}{3}$ quarts. Precisely what do these numbers mean? We can immediately say that B contains more milk than A does, but these numbers represent also a principal relation that is far more complicated than this.

Let us assume that there are a number of green bottles each containing milk and that we are indifferent to milk in Bottle A and milk in any one of the green bottles. Similarly, let us assume that there are a number of white bottles each containing milk and that we are indifferent to milk in Bottle B and milk in any one of the white bottles. Now, by Condition 2 we are indifferent to the entire milk in m green bottles, denoted by mA, and the entire milk in n white bottles, denoted by nB, if and only if $q(mA) = q(nB)$, i.e., the quantities of milk are the same. However, $q(mA) = m \cdot q(A)$, i.e., the quantity of milk in m green bottles is equal to m times the quantity of milk in one green bottle, based on the additivity of quantities expressed in Condition 1, and similarly $q(nB) = n \cdot q(B)$. Therefore, we are indifferent to milk in m green bottles and milk in n white bottles if and only if $m \cdot q(A) = n \cdot q(B)$. Stating this as a theorem,

Theorem: $mA \simeq nB$ if and only if $m \cdot q(A) = n \cdot q(B)$

Therefore, if $q(A) = 1.2$ and $q(B) = \frac{4}{3}$, we are indifferent to milk in ten green bottles and milk in nine white bottles since $10 \times 1.2 = 9 \times \frac{4}{3}$.

In general, for any two rational quantities $q(A)$ and $q(B)$, it is always possible to find a pair of natural numbers m and n so that $m \cdot q(A) = n \cdot q(B)$. This is true because by definition $q(A)$ and $q(B)$ can be expressed as ratios of natural numbers, e.g., $q(A) = a/b$ and $q(B) = c/d$, where $a, b, c,$ and d are all natural numbers, in which case $m = bc$ and $n = ad$ clearly satisfy $m \cdot q(A) = n \cdot q(B)$. If m and n satisfy the requirement, km and kn for any natural number, k, also satisfies the requirement. In any case, we can now divide the basic ability to measure the quantity of a set of objects into two categories: 1) the ability to count[11] and 2) the ability

---

[11] Note that counting is the most fundamental quantitative procedure of science. See Lenzen [1938].

to recognize indifference to sets of objects. With these we can establish a set of natural numbers m and n so that $mA \simeq nB$, and from this we can construct quantities so that $m \cdot q(A) = n \cdot q(B)$. Of course, we need a unit set whose quantity is defined to be 1 in order to determine $q(A)$ and $q(B)$ uniquely. However, any nonempty set can be used as a unit set without affecting the conditions for a quantity measure. For example, a length of fabric may be measured in inches, feet, or yards, but the principal relations represented by the quantities are not affected by the choice of a unit.

If we have to develop a real quantity measure, we need more advanced abilities than the two mentioned above, and in addition it is very difficult to indicate exactly what kinds are necessary. This is why we decided to work with rational quantity measures in addition to the fact that irrational numbers rarely appear as quantities in accounting.

In order to represent assets and income by means of a set of quantities we must first place all homogeneous resources into one class and define a quantity measure for that class, where *homogeneity* is determined by means of the indifference to resources in the class providing the quantity is the same. If a resource has no other resources with which it is homogeneous, as in the case of antiques, we provide a class for that resource only and assign an arbitrary positive number, e.g., 1, to the quantity of the resource. When we have assigned all resources to classes, the assets of an entity can be represented by an ordered set of quantities. For example, if the assets of an entity at time t are placed into two classes, cash and wheat, with the quantities 10,000 and 4,000 respectively, then the assets of the entity at time t, denoted by A_t, are

$$(3.8) \qquad\qquad A_t = (10{,}000,\ 4{,}000)$$

with the understanding that the first element in the vector represents the amount of cash in dollars and the second element the amount of wheat in bushels. Suppose further that at a later time t' the assets of the entity become

$$(3.9) \qquad\qquad A_{t'} = (15{,}000,\ 6{,}000)$$

Then the assets of the entity have increased during the time interval t to t' by

$$(3.10) \qquad\qquad A_{t'} - A_t = (5{,}000,\ 2{,}000)$$

This is the income of the entity for that period as represented by a set of quantities. If, instead, $A_{t'}$ is given by

$$(3.11) \qquad\qquad A_{t'} = (12{,}000,\ 3{,}000)$$

then the income during the time interval t to t', denoted by $I_{t'-t}$, is

(3.12) $\qquad I_{t'-t} = A_{t'} - A_t = (2{,}000,\ -1{,}000)$

If A_t and $A_{t'}$ contain negative assets, new classes are established for them and their quantities are placed next to the quantities of the positive assets with a colon separating them, as in (3.1)–(3.3). Thus the representation of assets and income by means of quantity measures is necessarily multi-dimensional since assets are not always homogeneous across classes. In a later chapter we shall consider the extent to which we can develop an accounting system based on multiple quantity measures.

3. EXCHANGES

In addition to the axioms of control and quantities, there is a third axiom which is at least as important a foundation of accounting measurement. This is the axiom of exchanges. Without the ability to recognize an exchange—a cause-and-effect relationship between things foregone and things obtained—we cannot even define what economic resources are. (See our discussion of values in Chapter 2.) In a sense, the economic activities of an entity are a sequence of exchanges of resources—the process of giving up some resources to obtain others. Therefore, we have to not only keep track of increases and decreases in the resources that are under the control of the entity but also identify and record which resources were exchanged for which others. For example, in Figure 3.1 present assets and their changes are identified. In order to record exchanges we must relate resources obtained (simply called an *increment*) to resources foregone (a *decrement*). An example of such identification of exchanges is shown in Figure 3.3. Here, Increment d is combined with Decrement b, Increments e and f with Decrement a, and Increment g with Decrements d and f. Such exchanges may occur through market transactions or through production processes within the entity. Since the essential characteristics are the same in either case, we shall treat both under the single concept of exchanges.

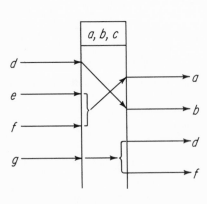

Fig. 3.3.   Exchanges of Resources

How can we make such combinations of increments and decrements? What are the bases of doing so? We have already investigated the fundamental part of the judgment-making process involved here in Chapter 2 in terms of the similarity assumption as well as in Chapter 1 in terms of the recognition of the independence of an object. However, a further discussion of this topic based on another analogy may be useful here.

Consider the following sequence of letters

(3.13)   *ihlkxyzilowxyzsrxyzkiaffljsxyzeqwohrbqgt*

Although at first there seems to be no regularity in the way in which the letters appear, as we go through the sequence we realize that the letters *xyz* are always a group. Furthermore, this group appears in the middle of many other letters. That is, the group of letters *xyz* is the maximum group containing *x*, *y*, and *z* which appears repeatedly since if we add any other letter to the group, e.g., *s*, this is no longer true.

For convenience, let us call any group of letters, not necessarily contiguous, a *configuration*[12] and a configuration with the above properties, i.e. internally dependent and externally independent, a *complete configuration*. It is harder to recognize a configuration in which the letters are not contiguous as in the following example, where *xy··z* is a complete configuration.

(3.14)   *ihlkxyilzowxysrzxykizaffljsxyeqzwohrbqgt*

The chances of detecting such a complete configuration increase as the sequence is made longer. Once a complete configuration is detected, it can be communicated to others, who are saved from going through the same laborious process to find it as the original person did.

With more experience in observing and studying the sequence of letters, we are able to detect configurations which are not quite complete, i.e., *partially complete configurations*. For example, if *A* is always followed by *D*, although *D* can occur without *A*, we consider Configuration *AD* as a group although it is not complete since *D* occurs elsewhere without *A*.

Furthermore, if Configurations *AD*, *BD*, and *CD* occur frequently, we assume that *A*, *B*, and *C* have something in common, and so we develop Concept *α* and Configuration *αD*. Here, *α* is not a specific group of letters but is a way of representing *A*, *B*, or *C*. Similarly *D* may be replaced by

---

[12] We may adjoin vertically a number of letter sequences such as (3.13) and consider two-dimensional (time-and-space) configurations.

Concept β if, for example, αD, αE, αF, and αG occur frequently. Here β indicates D, E, F, or G. Obviously, the process can be continued to higher levels of abstraction, i.e., concept of concept, concept of concept of concept, etc.[13]

In business we have a sequence of events analogous to the sequence of letters above. In it we recognize a group of events as a unit because they are internally dependent and externally independent—they always occur together and the group as a whole occurs in the middle of various other events. If the events in the group include an increase as well as a decrease in the assets of the firm, we consider that the group involves the exchange of an increment and a decrement. Gradually, we become able to recognize partially complete groups of events. For example, if a firm sells inventories on account (Event A), we assume the buyer will pay the firm later (Event B) because the group of Events A and B has been observed many times in the past. However, occasionally we find a situation where B does not occur after A occurs; thus the group of Events A and B is not complete. Nevertheless, we continue to regard them as a group insofar as they occur together most of the time.

Actually, the concept of events itself already involves a considerable degree of abstraction. Events are constructed from more elementary factors and eventually from our basic perception and memory, based on internal dependency and external independency. Therefore, the association of Events A and B is more analogous to the configuration based on concepts than to the configuration based on perceptions.[14]

In any case, we base our recognition of exchanges on the unity of events—on finding two subgroups of events in a given group that are related to each other as a cause and an effect. In particular, we find these when we relax the unity of events to include partially complete groups. For example, after Events A and B have occurred we reason that Event B would not have occurred if Event A had not occurred. Of course, this does not mean that A is always followed by B. Goods may be delivered, but the payment may not occur. On the other hand, B may occur following any one of Events A_1, A_2, $\cdots$, A_n. The payment may be an advance, may be a refund or a loan, etc. Suppose we are certain that if B has occurred one of A in A_1, A_2, $\cdots$, A_n has occurred. Here, we assume that B could not have occurred without a reason, and we list all possible reasons for B. If one reason exists, we associate it with B. If more than one reason

---

[13] This is the way rationalists explain the origin of our knowledge. See Joad [1936, Chapter 4]. See also Hayakawa [1964, Chapter 10] on the process of abstraction in relation to language.

[14] See Kolmogorov [1956, pp. 3–5] for the concept of a *complex*, which supports events and their repetition.

exists, we investigate further (e.g., ask the payer whether the payment is for goods or is a refund of a loan) until the cause is uniquely determined.[15]

Since the basis for recognizing exchanges lies in grouping or associating events, there are situations where subgroups or supergroups of events are also recognized as unities. For example, Events A and B are grouped and Events C, D, and E are grouped, but Events A, B, C, D, E, and F are also grouped, i.e., we have $[(A, B), (C, D, E), F]$. If A involves foregoing Resource a and B involves obtaining Resource b, we assume that a and b are exchanged. Similarly, if C involves obtaining Resource c, D involves no changes in assets, and E involves foregoing Resource e, we assume that Resources c and e are exchanged. But what happens if also F involves foregoing Resource f? From the viewpoint of the larger grouping, Resources b and c are obtained in exchange for Resources a, e, and f, i.e., the cost of Resources b and c is Resources a, e, and f. But from the viewpoint of the smaller grouping, the cost of b is a, the cost of c is e, and Resource f is treated as a loss, i.e., an exchange with an empty incoming resource set.[16] Clearly this problem arises frequently in accounting in the form of indirect costs, which cannot be associated with any one of the activities but which are clearly associated with all of them as a group. In current accounting practices, such costs are either allocated to each activity by means of some allocation factors (full costing) or treated as period costs (direct costing). As shown in the above example, as we expand the grouping of events, more indirect costs or indirect benefits become directly associated with other changes in the assets.[17]

---

[15] Symbolically we can state this as

$$B \to (A \cup A_1 \cup A_2 \cdots \cup A_n)$$

where $\to$ means "imply" and $\cup$ means "or." Similar treatment may be given to the effect side, i.e.

$$A \to (B \cup B_1 \cup B_2 \cdots \cup B_m)$$

By doing this for all A_j's and B_j's and combining them

$$(A \cup A_1 \cup A_2 \cdots \cup A_n) \leftrightarrow (B \cup B_1 \cup B_2 \cdots \cup B_m)$$

where $\leftrightarrow$ means "imply and is implied" or "if and only if." Notice that if we develop concepts α and β, which represent events A, A_1, $\cdots$, A_n and B, B_1, $\cdots$, B_m, respectively, then $\alpha\beta$ is complete. Thus, although in the above situation we can say neither that A is necessary for B to occur (B can occur under other conditions) nor that A is sufficient for B to occur (B may not follow A), at the higher level of concepts we can say α is the necessary and sufficient condition for β.

[16] Similarly if F involves obtaining Resource f, f is treated as a gain, i.e., an exchange with an empty outgoing resource set.

[17] See the concept of relevant cost in Horngren [1965].

Why do we worry about exchanges or, more generally, groupings of events? Why do we not simply record increases and decreases of resources as they occur without going through the trouble of matching increments with decrements? Let us go back to the sequence of letters in (3.13). Since Configuration xyz appears frequently, the next time we observe x we expect that y and z will follow immediately afterwards. Suppose that the expectation is fulfilled many times. We then have confidence in such a prediction and use it as a basis for our planning. Actually, our belief that the regularity shown in the past will continue to work in the future, i.e., the similarity assumption, is the only basis on which we can predict the future.

This is the crucial characteristic of accounting measurement. If we simply record increases and decreases of resources, we can never predict what it takes to obtain particular resources. The concept of costs derived from the concept of exchanges is, therefore, the most essential element in accounting measurement. Without it, accounting measurement ceases to have its unique methodological characteristics.

4. AXIOMS

In this chapter we have investigated the three kinds of judgment necessary in accounting. They are judgments on control, quantities, and exchanges. We must be able to recognize among numerous economic resources which ones are controlled by the entity. We then must be able to classify resources and to define a quantity measure for each class so that we are indifferent to resources in a given class providing the quantity is the same. Finally, we must be able to recognize which resources are exchanged.

The ability to recognize control makes it possible for us to identify a set of the entire resources that are controlled by an entity. The ability to classify and measure resources in each class by its quantity measure makes it possible for us to represent the set of resources controlled by the entity by means of a set of quantities. Finally, as we shall see in the next chapter, the ability to recognize which resources are exchanged makes it possible for us to develop a value measure as an aggregation of the set of quantity measures.[18]

---

[18] These three abilities essentially stem from our ability to classify. See Littleton [1953, Chapter 3] and Sorter [1963], which emphasize classification in accounting. In this regard, Sorter [1963, Chapter 2] makes an interesting distinction in classifications. "A *class* represents a grouping by cause; a *category* is a grouping by effect and a *type* is a grouping by both cause and effect."

As we shall explain in detail in the next chapter, these three abilities are analogous to the five axioms in Euclidean geometry. All theorems in Euclidean geometry can be derived from the five axioms, and each one of the five axioms is necessary to do so. In other words, the five axioms are necessary and sufficient to derive all theorems. The same thing can be said about the three abilities discussed above. We cannot delete any one of them in order to derive any kind of accounting valuation that has been used or has been proposed. Furthermore, after these three factors have been determined, only a computational procedure which does not require an empirical judgment remains in the valuation procedure. We shall demonstrate this for historical cost valuation in the next chapter. This procedure also holds for other accounting valuation methods if we expand judgment on exchanges to include expected or contemplated exchanges. (See the discussion of imputed causal networks and estimated factual causal networks in Chapter 2.) Since these three factors are both necessary and sufficient to support accounting valuation, we may call them three axioms of accounting valuation.

Among various valuation methods, we singled out historical cost valuation in Chapter 2 because the underlying causal network is unique and stable. We shall, therefore, devote our analysis in the next chapter to historical cost valuation and develop for it an axiomatic system of valuation that approximates practices in conventional accounting.

CHAPTER FOUR

Axiomatic Structure of Historical Cost Valuation

Valuation based on historical costs, or simply historical cost valuation, is developed from exchanges that have actually taken place. In essence, if Asset A is exchanged for Asset B and if the value of A is quantitatively defined but the value of B is undefined, the latter is set equal to the former. If both values are defined, the difference between them is derived as the value gain or loss. If both values are undefined, then either the recording of the exchange is postponed until at least one of them is known or some supplementary methods of valuation are used. Under the historical cost valuation method, the values of all assets are determined in this way and the value of the entire assets of the firm is calculated by taking the difference between the sum of the values of all positive assets and the sum of the values of all negative assets. We shall state the valuation rules more rigorously in this chapter. Before we proceed, however, we must explain the method of analyses in this chapter as well as its development, especially the axiomatic approach to accounting measurement.[1]

---

[1] This first axiomatic approach appears to have been taken by E. L. Kohler. See the definition of axiom and related terms in Kohler [1952]. For other axiomatic approaches to accounting, see Churchman [1961, Chapter 13], Moonitz [1961], and Mattessich [1964].

1. AN AXIOMATIC APPROACH

Unlike some other attempts (e.g., of Moonitz and Sprouse[2]) our analysis in this chapter develops and elucidates a uniform approach to the conventional historical cost valuation system as such. That is, we take the conventional accounting system as given rather than *ab initio* seeking to prescribe what we think an accounting system should be. We then view the valuation system of conventional accounting as though it consisted of a set of axioms on one hand and a set of valuation rules on the other. These are extracted from conventional accounting in such a way that they are not only necessary but also sufficient to explain most of the principles and practices in it. Unfortunately, conventional accounting is a collection of many different principles and practices, which, in some cases, are mutually inconsistent. Hence, no systematic theories can describe all of them. Thus our attempt has been directed toward approximating conventional accounting by devising a relatively simple set of axioms and valuation rules, in the same manner that scientists in other fields have tried to develop a relatively simple set of concepts and theories in order to explain complicated phenomena to a satisfactory degree.

The set of axioms and the set of valuation rules developed in this chapter correspond to the set of axioms and the set of theorems (including lemmas and corollaries), respectively, in Euclidean geometry in the sense that if the set of axioms is granted, the valuation rules can be applied in a purely mathematical way without making any empirical judgment. Although the truth of the axioms cannot be proved (in the purely philosophical sense), they are empirically supported since they are abstracted from what accountants have been doing. In addition, the number of axioms is minimized to avoid redundancy. Thus, the set of axioms is necessary and sufficient to support the set of valuation rules. They are not a mere listing of concepts we think necessary for conventional accounting but are tied logically and mathematically to the set of valuation rules and hence to the whole valuation system.

Having explained our basic approach to historical cost valuation, we will review some basic concepts discussed in the previous chapter, add a few new concepts, state the set of axioms necessary to support historical cost valuation, and elaborate on the valuation rules.

Economic resources or simply resources are objects that have a sacrifice value and a benefit value. Under a given set of control criteria and a set of recognition criteria, the set of all economic resources that are controlled by a given entity, namely the assets of the entity, is determined. The assets of an entity consist of present assets and future assets. Present

[2] Moonitz [1961] and Sprouse and Moonitz [1962].

assets are the resources that are presently controlled by the entity under the given set of control criteria. Future assets are the resources that are expected to be put under the control of the entity in the future (future positive assets) or to be released from the control of the entity in the future (future negative assets). The recognition criteria, together with the control criteria, determine when such future resources are to be recognized as assets. Economic resources can be divided into a number of classes in such a way that a quantity measure is defined for each class. Each quantity measure is nonnegative and additive, and has the property that we are indifferent to the choice between any two sets of resources in a given class if and only if their quantities are the same. A class of objects with a nonnegative and additive measure is called a measurable class. A change in the assets of an entity (an increment or a decrement) is always matched with another change (a decrement or an increment) by means of an exchange. The increment and the decrement in an exchange may not occur simultaneously, and it is possible for one of them to be empty, in which case the exchange shows a gain or a loss of resources without a corresponding decrement or increment.

The definition of the control criteria used in historical cost valuation is immaterial as long as the present assets can be uniquely determined. However, in conventional accounting where historical cost valuation is used legal ownership is the basic control criterion. On the other hand, in historical cost valuation, future assets (positive or negative) are recognized as the assets of an entity if and only if they are exchanged for other assets which have been received or delivered in the past. In other words, we do not recognize an exchange between future resources until at least one of them is received or delivered. This recognition criterion based on actual exchanges is an important aspect of historical cost valuation. (There is an exception to this in conventional accounting when dealing with future cash. This will be explained in detail later.)

In order to carry out the historical cost valuation method, we must first be able to identify the assets of an entity. Then we must put the assets into a number of measurable classes so that they can be represented by a set of pairs—an account and a quantity. Finally, we must be able to identify exchanges as they take place. An exchange involves two sets of resources, an increment d^+ and a decrement d^-, where either one can be empty. All changes in the assets are partitioned into a set of pairs $[d^+, d^-]$; when all increments d^+'s and all decrements d^-'s in the set of pairs are added together to derive I^+ and I^-, respectively, we obtain the income $[I^+, I^-]$ for the period as described in the previous chapter.

Since we are going to impute the value of an increment from the value of a corresponding decrement, we must impose a constraint on the way in which all changes are partitioned. As we observed in Chapter 2, trouble arises if the increment consists of resources belonging to more than one class. For example, if Resources a and b are obtained in exchange for Resources c and d, we set the value of Resources a and b, denoted by $v(a$ and $b)$, equal to the value of c plus the value of d, $v(c) + v(d)$. In this case if a and b belong to the same class, they are homogeneous and can be measured by the quantity measure defined for the class. Therefore, we may allocate $v(c) + v(d)$ to a and b according to their relative quantities. However, if a and b belong to different classes, we must allocate $v(c) + v(d)$ by some arbitrary methods such as the ratio of the current market values of a and b. This is what we discussed as inseparability of a causal network in Chapter 2. An allocation of the cost of fixed assets over the periods of their lives is another example of this problem. Therefore, the decomposition of an exchange so that the increment belongs to one and only one class is necessary before we apply the valuation rules which will be described below. Let us call an exchange *simple* if the increment belongs to the same class and *compound* otherwise. We shall assume in the following discussions that all exchanges are simple. Also, since the order in which the exchanges take place affects the values we require that all exchanges be ordered according to the time of their occurrence, i.e., the occurrence of the receipt or the delivery of the resources, whichever comes first. The following three axioms summarize these points.

Axiom of Control: There exists a method by which resources under the control (present or future, positive or negative) of a given entity at any time t are uniquely determined at that time or later.

Axiom of Quantities: There exists a method by which all resources are uniquely partitioned into a collection of classes so that for each class a nonnegative and additive quantity measure is defined and so that we are indifferent to any two sets of resources in the same class if and only if their quantities are the same.

Axiom of Exchanges: There exists a method by which all changes in the resources controlled by a given entity up to any time t are identified at that time or later and are partitioned uniquely into an ordered set of pairs of an increment and a decrement, where the increment belongs to one and only one class.

2. VALUATION RULES

With this set of axioms, we develop valuation rules for historical cost accounting in the following way. Notice that by the axiom of control the sets of all assets of an entity is uniquely identified. As mentioned in Chapter 3, the entire assets (i.e. the property set) of an entity at time t, denoted by A_t, consists of present assets A_t^P, future positive assets A_t^{FP}, and future negative assets A_t^{FN}, i.e.

$$(4.1) \qquad\qquad A_t = [A_t^P, A_t^{FP}, A_t^{FN}]$$

Then the axiom of quantities enables us to express A_t in terms of an ordered array of numbers, i.e. a vector $(q_t^0, q_t^1, q_t^2, \cdots, q_t^k)$, where the superscripts identify classes to which resources in A_t belong and q_t^i ($i = 0, 1, 2, \cdots, k$) is the quantity of all resources in A_t that belong to the ith class. We shall denote this vector simply by q_t. Just as A_t consists of three parts A_t^P, A_t^{FP}, and A_t^{FN}, the vector q_t consists of three subvectors, q_t^P, q_t^{FP}, and q_t^{FN}, namely

$$(4.2) \qquad\qquad q_t = (q_t^P, q_t^{FP}, q_t^{FN})$$

each of q_t^P, q_t^{FP}, and q_t^{FN} consisting of an ordered array of quantities. Here, q_t is a surrogate of A_t in the sense that was discussed in Chapter 1 since it is developed to represent some properties of A_t. However, in many cases future assets in A_t are not specified individually but are described in terms of classes and quantities. Thus, although it may be possible to specify which resources are to be received or delivered in the future, normally it only matters how much of the resources in a given class is to be received or delivered. Furthermore, a sale is sometimes made of resources which do not exist at the time of the sale, in which case it is not possible to specify which resources are to be delivered. Therefore, by moving from the most primitive representation method, denotation, to a more advanced representuation method, connotation and quantification, we are able to expand the concept of assets itself.

By means of the axioms of control and quantities then, we can represent the assets of an entity by a set of quantities. Our task now is to define a method by which these heterogeneous quantity measures are converted into a homogeneous measure called a *value measure*. For this purpose, we first select a basic class and use the quantity measure defined for the class to generate a value. It is convenient to choose a class whose objects are often used in exchanges, but this is not essential from the viewpoint of valuation. We then state the two basic rules of valuation.

Basic Rule 1: The value of any set of (current and future) resources in the basic class is defined to be equal to its quantity as determined by the quantity measure for the class.

Basic Rule 2: The value of an empty set is defined to be equal to zero.

If cash is selected for the basic class, the value of any set of cash, regardless of whether it is cash on hand (current cash) or cash to be received or paid in future (future cash), is given by the quantity defined for the class, dollars. All receivables and payables as well as deposits and loans belong to the basic class. If gasoline is selected for the basic class, all receivables and payables of gasoline belong to the basic class.[3]

Then, we use the quantity measure defined for the basic class as the basis for the value measure to be used for all resources in various classes. In historical cost accounting, however, it is necessary first to specify the starting values of assets in each class. If Property Set A consists of resources in the basic class only, the values of resources are easily derived since for the basic class they are equal to the quantity of resources (Basic Rule 1) and for nonbasic classes they are zero (Basic Rule 2). If Property Set A includes nonbasic resources, then we must determine the values of the resources in each nonbasic class. Initial proprietary investments of nonbasic resources belong to this category. The values of such resources must be determined outside this valuation system by taking recourse to, for example, current market values, since the three axioms are capable of providing values for nonbasic resources only if they are obtained in exchange for other resources whose values have been determined by the time of the exchange. This will be discussed later with other cases in which current market values are used in conventional accounting.

Thus we have at the beginning of the period (at time $t = 0$) to which the valuation system is to be applied a set of quantities q_0^i and a corresponding set of values v_0^i determined for all resources in class i that are under the control of the entity. Namely, Property Set A_0 is represented first by

$$(4.3) \qquad\qquad q_0 = (q_0^0, q_0^1, \cdots, q_0^k)$$

and second by

$$(4.4) \qquad\qquad v_0 = (v_0^0, v_0^1, \cdots, v_0^k)$$

Here, we assume that Class 0 is the basic class; hence we have by Basic Rule 1

$$(4.5) \qquad\qquad q_t^0 = v_t^0 \qquad \text{for all } t$$

For example, suppose that a firm starts with \$12,000 cash and 2,000

---

[3] This is what Walras [1926, p. 161] calls *numéraire* (or standard commodity), in terms of which the prices of all the others are expressed.

bushels of wheat. If we select cash as the basic class, 2,000 bushels of wheat is evaluated, in terms of cash, by means of its current market value or some other factors, as, for example, $6,000. Then

(4.6)
$$q_0 = (12{,}000, \ 2{,}000)$$
$$v_0 = (12{,}000, \ 6{,}000)$$

where the first components in the vectors are for the cash class and the second components are for the wheat class. On the other hand, if we select wheat as the basic class and if $12,000 cash is evaluated in terms of wheat as, for example, 4,000 bushels, then

(4.7)
$$q_0 = (2{,}000, \ 12{,}000)$$
$$v_0 = (2{,}000, \ 4{,}000)$$

where the first components are for wheat and the second for cash.

As Property Set A_t changes over time by means of exchanges, its surrogate q_t also changes. Thus, we want to derive a method of changing v_t as q_t changes. We do this first by determining the value of the decrement $v(d^-)$ in an exchange $[d^+, \ d^-]$ and then by setting the value of the increment $v(d^+)$ equal to $v(d^-)$. However, if d^+ belongs to the basic class, a value gain or loss is calculated by taking the difference between $v(d^+)$, which is simply given by Basic Rule 1, and $v(d^-)$. For example, in the above case where cash is used as the basic class suppose that 1,000 bushels of wheat were obtained in exchange for $3,600 cash. Then, since the value of the decrement, $3,600 cash, is $3,600 by Basic Rule 1, we set the value of the increment, 1,000 bushels of wheat, equal to $3,600. We add and subtract $3,600 to and from the classes to which the increment and the decrement, respectively, belong. Thus after the exchange, *at* time $t = 1$

(4.8)
$$q_1 = (8{,}400, \ 3{,}000)$$
$$v_1 = (8{,}400, \ 9{,}600)$$

Suppose, further, that between times 1 and 2 the firm sold 1,000 bushels of wheat for $4,000 cash. We first determine the value of the decrement, 1,000 bushels of wheat, by allocating the value of all resources in the wheat class in proportion to the quantities. That is, the value of 1,000 bushels of wheat is

(4.9)
$$\$9{,}600 \times \frac{1{,}000}{3{,}000} = \$3{,}200$$

Then we ordinarily set the value of the increment equal to $3,200. However, in this case, its value is $4,000 according to Basic Rule 1 since it belongs to the basic class. Hence, we calculate a value gain by taking $v(d^+) - v(d^-)$, which is $800. We increase the value of the cash class by $4,000 and decrease the value of the wheat class by $3,200, obtaining

(4.10)
$$q_2 = (12,400, \; 2,000)$$
$$v_2 = (12,400, \; 6,400)$$

On the other hand, if wheat is used as the basic class, in the first exchange the value of the decrement, $3,600 cash, is

(4.11)
$$4,000 \times \frac{\$3,600}{\$12,000} = 1,200$$

and a value loss is $1,200 - 1,000 = 200$ bushels. After the exchange

(4.12)
$$q_1 = (3,000, \; 8,400)$$
$$v_1 = (3,000, \; 2,800)$$

In the second exchange, the value of the decrement, 1,000 bushels of wheat, is 1,000 bushels by Basic Rule 1. From this we impute the value of the increment, $4,000 cash. Thus, after the second exchange

(4.13)
$$q_2 = (2,000, \; 12,400)$$
$$v_2 = (2,000, \; 3,800)$$

Notice that value gains and losses are calculated at the time of sale if cash is used as the basic class and at the time of purchase if wheat is used as the basic class. In either case, the essence of historical cost valuation is not to recognize value gains or losses until the exchange is made with the resources in the basic class, i.e., until the cycle ends with the basic class. Before that time the values of resources are always recorded as being equal to the values of their predecessors in the cycle. This procedure stems from the realization principle in historical cost valuation.

If the decrement consists of resources belonging to more than one class, the values of the outgoing resources in each class are calculated separately and then their sum is used as the value of the decrement.

We shall now formally state these valuation rules.

Value Allocation Rule: Allocate the value of all resources in each class before the exchange to outgoing resources in the class and remaining resources in the class in proportion to their quantities. The sum of values allocated to outgoing resources in each class is the value of the decrement. Decrease the value of resources in each class by the value allocated to outgoing resources in the class.

Value Imputation Rule: If the resources in the increment belong to a nonbasic class, set the value of the increment equal to the value of the decrement. Increase the value of resources of the class by the value of the increment.

Value Comparison Rule: If the resources in the increment belong to the basic class, calculate a value gain or loss by subtracting the value of the decrement from the value of the increment.

The value allocation rule above is for the moving average method, but value allocation rules for other methods used in conventional accounting can be derived from it. For example, rules for FIFO or LIFO may be determined by using a set of ordered subclasses in each class with each subclass having a pair of a quantity measure and a value measure. Then, by specifying the order in which these subclasses are used for value allocation and by applying the above rule for the moving average method, we can derive rules for the FIFO or LIFO method.

When an exchange involves nonbasic future resources—resources in a nonbasic class that are to be received or delivered at some later time—the exchange must be modified before applying the above rules. To do this, consider the various combinations of an increment and a decrement shown in Table 4.1. If the exchange is between a present or basic future resource and another present or basic future resource, the exchange is recorded immediately. [Cases (1), (2), (4) and (5) in Table 4.1.] There is no

TABLE 4.1 Combination of an Increment and a Decrement

INCREMENT	Present	Basic future	Nonbasic future
Present	(1) Record	(2) Record	(3) Treat as advance receipt
Basic future	(4) Record	(5) Record	(6) Do not record
Nonbasic future	(7) Treat as advance payment	(8) Do not record	(9) Do not record

(Column header group: DECREMENT)

problem in determining the value of the decrement by applying the value allocation rule or Basic Rule 1 if the decrement is present or basic future resources. On the other hand, if the exchange is between future resources [Cases (5), (6), (8), and (9)], it is not recorded until either the increment or the decrement is actually received, except when the exchange is between basic future resources [Case (5)] in which case it is recorded as stated above. For example, even if a purchase order has been issued, it is the practice in conventional accounting not to make an entry until either goods have been received or cash has been paid [Case (8)]. On the other hand, if a note is issued by a customer who owes the firm, an entry is made immediately by increasing notes receivable and by decreasing accounts receivable [Case (5)]. Similarly, if a firm borrows money from a bank which, in turn, deposits the sum in the firm's account, the exchange is recorded immediately [Case (5)].

If in an exchange the increment is nonbasic future resources and the decrement is present resources [Case (7)], the exchange is modified so that it is between basic future resources as the increment and present resources as the decrement, where the increment has the same value as the decrement. When the nonbasic future resources (the original increment) are actually received, an exchange between them as the increment and basic future resources as the decrement is recorded. For example, suppose that a purchase order has been issued and cash has been paid but goods have not yet been received. The cash paid is recorded as an advance payment (a basic future resource) until goods are received instead of recording the increase of nonbasic future resources from the beginning. That is, instead of the entry [Dr. Future Inventories:Cr. Present Cash] we record [Dr. Future Cash:Cr. Present Cash], where future cash is the advance payment. Then, when goods are actually received, we cancel future cash by making an entry [Dr. Present Inventories:Cr. Future Cash]. This method avoids recording nonbasic future resources.

A similar treatment using an advance receipt account is given to an increment and decrement that are reversed—when present resources are the increment and nonbasic future resources are the decrement [Case (3)]. For example, if an order is sent from a customer with an advance payment, the cash received is treated as an advance receipt until goods are actually delivered to the customer, at which time a value gain or loss is calculated. Instead of the entry [Dr. Present Cash:Cr. Future Inventories] we record [Dr. Present Cash:Cr. Future Cash], and when the goods are actually delivered we record [Dr. Future Cash:Cr. Present Inventories] together with an entry for the value gain or loss. This is in line with the realization principle which recognizes value gain or loss only after inventories are delivered.

However, trouble arises when the increment is nonbasic present resources instead of basic present resources as in the above example since in such a case neither the value of the increment nor that of the decrement can be determined. For example, suppose that 100 barrels of crude oil are received in exchange for 1,000 gallons of gasoline to be delivered thirty days from now. The most likely treatment in conventional accounting is to use the replacement cost of the increment—the amount of cash which would be paid if the exchange were made with cash. In our system, however, we do not have a mechanism to generate such a replacement cost or any other market value. As an approximation we may use the average costs, at the time of the exchange, of goods on hand in the classes that the decrement belongs to. If the average costs are not defined for a class that the resources in the decrement belong to, we must look for other means of evaluating the decrement such as current market values. We will comment on this later when we discuss market values.

By means of these rules we can determine the value of the entire property set of an entity in the following manner. Since recording of non-basic future resources (positive or negative) is completely avoided, we have only present resources and basic future resources. The values of present resources, class by class, are determined by the three valuation rules stated earlier. We simply add them together to derive the total value of present resources. The values of basic future resources are defined by their quantities. Thus, the total value of the assets of an entity is the value of present assets plus the value of basic future positive assets less the value of basic future negative assets. The income figure for a period is the difference between the value of assets at the end of the period and the value of assets at the beginning.[4]

We emphasize that the concept of income in conventional accounting cannot be derived without the concept of assets (or the property set in our system) as we elaborated in Chapter 3. Income is an evaluation of the set of activities that have taken place during the given period of time. Unlike job evaluation or grading students' performances, however, in conventional accounting we do not evaluate activities as such but evaluate them by their effects on assets. The tendency toward stressing income determination in current accounting theories should not be misinterpreted to mean that income figures are derived as measures of activities without regard to how these activities affect assets. In addition, just as the speed of an object is derived from the difference in the positions of the object at

---

[4] From a mathematical standpoint, the axiom of control provides a set-valued function of time, $A = f(t)$, where A is a subset of a universal set U of all economic resources; the axiom of quantities provides a vector-valued function of sets, $q = g(A)$, where q is a vector of quantities; and the axiom of exchanges provides a mechanism by which we can produce a scalar-valued function of time, $m = h(t)$, where m is the net value of assets of the entity at time t.

two different points in time relative to the length of the time period, income is derived from the difference in the values of the property set at two different points in time relative to the length of the time period.

3. EXCEPTIONS

We shall now discuss principles and procedures used in conventional accounting that cannot be handled the same way in our system.

Market Values: The conventional accounting system that we have tried to approximate by our axiomatic valuation system is the one which is based upon such principles as historical cost, realization, and accrual. Therefore, we have neglected such concepts as current market values, replacement costs, and net realizable values. These enter conventional accounting systems and procedures as supplementary factors and in somewhat inconsistent ways. Some examples are 1) cost-or-market-whichever-lower method applied to inventory and marketable securities; 2) donated assets or assets obtained at unusually low prices; 3) initial proprietary investment involving noncash assets; 4) allocation of joint costs based upon current market values of joint products.[5]

Proprietary Investments: An exchange involving proprietary investment must be regarded as an exchange between current cash and future cash to be delivered at an indefinite time in order to operate the system developed here and to generate a measure that approximates the one generated by the conventional accounting system, even though proprietary investment is different from loans and other payables from the standpoint of legal claims against the entity. This interpretation is also consistent with the one which will be discussed in Chapter 5 in connection with causal double-entry.

Capital Surplus: An exchange involving capital surplus cannot be distinguished from an exchange involving earned surplus in our measurement system. However, the need for such a distinction comes from legal and managerial requirements for distributing income. It is a problem of allocation that arises after the total value gain has been determined.

---

[5] Note that in the axiom of exchanges we required that the set of incoming objects belong to a single class in any exchange to avoid this case. If an exchange involves incoming objects that belong to more than one class, the exchange must be decomposed before the valuation rules are applied to it. See the discussion on inseparability of a causal network in Chapter 2.

Reverse Exchanges: Our system also cannot handle an exchange made in order to cancel an exchange made earlier (sales return, purchase return, etc.). Recognition of such exchanges presupposes our ability to identify one exchange as the reverse of another. It is possible to set up an axiom to cover this, but reverse exchanges themselves are rather unimportant. Hence we have not included such an axiom in order to stress the most fundamental factors in conventional accounting.

4. SUMMARY

We have shown that if the set of three axioms—control, quantities, exchanges—is granted, we can generate, by a set of valuation rules, the value of a property set from a set of quantity measures by means of value imputations through exchanges. And, we can do this in a purely mathematical way without appealing to empirical judgment once the axioms are granted.

Furthermore, empirical support for this valuation system is clear and very plausible; loosely speaking, all that is required is that 1) the set of all resources under the control of the entity, i.e., the property set, can be identified; 2) the resources can be quantified based on indifference; and 3) the changes in the property set can be partitioned into a set of exchanges; or more simply, we can identify the things we have control over, the things which we are indifferent to, and the things that are exchanged.

Finally we want to emphasize that although valuation in monetary units has been considered a fundamental convention in accounting,[6] the basic theory of historical cost valuation is free from the choice of any basic class, i.e., *numéraire*, as shown in the above example in (4.6) through (4.13). We shall further discuss the use of nonmonetary measures in accounting in the next chapter where multidimensional accounting is elaborated in detail.

[6] See, e.g., Gilman [1939], American Accounting Association [1957].

CHAPTER FIVE

Causal Double-entry and Multidimensional Bookkeeping

In contrast to previous chapters, which discussed the measurement aspect of accounting, this chapter deals with the recording systems in accounting. In the first three sections we shall show that the double-entry system is closely related to historical cost valuation and that actually the former was devised to suit the latter. Then in the fourth section we shall discuss how the recording system based on double-entry can be extended to multidimensional accounting so that recording may be based on multiple quantity measures rather than on a single value measure.

1. CLASSIFICATIONAL DOUBLE-ENTRY AND CAUSAL DOUBLE-ENTRY

Since Pacioli's famous work, *Summa de Arithmetica, Geometria, Proportioni et Proportionalita* [1494], there have been so many studies of the double-entry bookkeeping system that there seems to be no need for further discussion. The nineteenth-century mathematician Arthur Cayley called it "in fact like Euclid's theory of ratios an absolutely perfect one." [1894, Preface].) If the double-entry bookkeeping system is in fact absolutely perfect, it is understandable why there has been no change in the basic scheme of double-entry since Pacioli's work. The duality involved in double-entry seems to be unique and absolute. Nevertheless it is not possible to say that we have exploited the mathematical, philosophical, and behavioral foundations of the double-entry bookkeeping system completely. For example, it is not clear whether we have realized 1) that there are two distinct types of double-entry which may be called *classificational double-entry* and *causal double-entry*, 2) that classificational double-entry can be logically extended to multiple-entry by incorporating more than two classifications; 3) that the causality between an increment and a decrement in assets is what makes the double-entry system double; and 4) that the real significance of the double-entry system lies not in the beauty of the system itself but rather in its impact upon our thinking because it forces us to search for the causal links among the changes in assets.[1] Here, we attempt to discuss these points so that the double-entry bookkeeping system can be assessed from a new viewpoint.

Let us consider a journal entry

(5.1)   (Dr.) Account A $100:   (Cr.) Account B $100

There are two entirely different reasons why the amount of the debit entry should be equal to the amount of the credit entry. One is that Accounts A and B are both descriptions of the same objects looked at from two different angles; the other is that the two accounts are descriptions of two different objects looked at from the same angle but tied together by means of the causal relationship between them. We shall call the system based on the first reason classificational double-entry and that based on the second causal double-entry.

The classificational double-entry system classifies the same set of objects or their total value twice. For example, the $100 (million) total value of the assets of a firm may be classified first by the physical character-

[1] Pacioli's discussions in *Summa* are all technical and do not reveal how far he had comprehended the logic behind double-entry. However, it is rather clear that he had no distinction in mind between classificational double-entry and causal double-entry. For example, his definition of capital, "Capital means the entire amount of what you now possess" [1494, Chapter 12], is classificational, whereas his entry "Debit Palermo Sugar, credit Cash" [1494, Chapter 18] is clearly causal. Of course, such a mixture of classificational and causal double-entry seems to be common in most of the accounting literature on the system. Even Arthur Cayley [1894] apparently did not realize that classificational double-entry could be extended to multiple-entry and, therefore, his appraisal of double-entry as being absolutely perfect cannot be justified from this angle because the system is not unique.

istics of the assets and second by the claims on them as follows:

	(Dr.)		(Cr.)	
	Cash	$10	Payables	$20
	Receivables	20	Accruals	10
(5.2)	Inventories	20	Loans	40
	Buildings	40	Capital	30
	Equipment	10		
		$100		$100

The classification on the left is called the asset classification and that on the right, the equity classification.

Suppose that the total value of the assets is increased (or decreased) by $10 (million). Such an increment (or decrement) is also classified from the two viewpoints. If by such an increment (or decrement) only inventories are affected in the asset classification and only payables are affected in the equity classification, we have

(5.3)   (Dr.) Inventories $10:   (Cr.) Payables $10

in the case of an increment, and

(5.4)   (Dr.) Inventories −$10:   (Cr.) Payables −$10

in the case of a decrement. Since only two classifications are involved, we adopt a convention of transposing accounts in the case of decrements to avoid the use of negative numbers. Thus (5.4) is replaced by

(5.5)   (Dr.) Payables $10:   (Cr.) Inventories $10

with the understanding that if accounts in the asset classification appear on the credit side or if accounts in the equity classification appear on the debit side, they indicate decrements. Notice here that in classificational double-entry the total value of the assets and its changes are always recorded under two different classifications.[2]

---

[2] The two classifications may have the relationship of details versus summary. For example, the debit side may consist of detailed accounts and the credit side summary accounts.

The causal double-entry system, on the other hand, involves only one classification. Here an increment is tied to a decrement. For example, take two accounts, inventories and cash, in the asset classification. If we recognize a cause-and-effect relationship between an increment, $10 in inventories, and a decrement, $10 in cash, we express this relationship by a double-entry

(5.6)   (Dr.) Inventories $10:   (Cr.) Cash $10

using the convention of putting decrements in assets on the credit side.

The meanings of the entries in (5.3) and (5.5) and the entry in (5.6) are entirely different. The entries in (5.3) and (5.5) express an increment (or a decrement) in the total value of the assets. We have two accounts, one on the debit side and the other on the credit side, because the increment (or the decrement) is classified from two different viewpoints. The entry in (5.6) is based on only one classification. We have two accounts here, one on the debit side and the other on the credit side, because the entries express the cause-and-effect relationship between an increment and a decrement.

There is a significant difference in the kinds of abilities required to use these two double-entry systems. In classificational double-entry, we need to be able 1) to recognize the total value of the assets as well as their changes, and 2) to classify the total value of the assets as well as their changes in two different ways. However, in causal double-entry, in addition to these[3] we must have the ability 3) to recognize the cause-and-effect relationship between an increment and a decrement.[4]

Thus, in both double-entry systems we must be able to recognize increments and decrements and classify them according to a predetermined scheme or schemes. But under causal double-entry, we must in addition be able to say which increment is causally related to which decrement. In other words, classificational double-entry treats each increment or decrement in the total value of assets independently and the duality comes from subjecting the increment or the decrement to two different classifications. On the other hand, causal double-entry treats increments and decrements as having a cause-and-effect relationship and the duality comes from pairing an increment with a decrement. Figure 5.1 shows the difference between the two types more clearly.

---

[3] Here we need the ability to classify in only one way, not the two ways (by asset and by equity) stated in 2).

[4] These three abilities correspond, respectively, to the axioms of control, quantities, and exchanges discussed in the previous chapter.

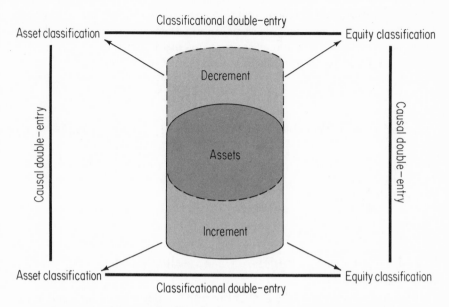

Fig. 5.1.   Classificational Double-Entry and Causal Double-Entry

2. MULTIPLE-ENTRY BOOKKEEPING

Having separated the two types of double-entry that coexist in our current bookkeeping system, we will next show that there is no logical reason why classificational double-entry should be double and no more. Let us, for example, add classifications of assets by their locations and their ages—the number of years the entity has owned them—to the ordinary asset and equity classifications. The example presented in (5.2) may then be modified to

	Asset		Equity		Location		Age	
	Cash	$10	Payables	$20	Head Office	$30	Under 6 mo.	$40
	Receivables	20	Accruals	10	Factory	40	Under 1 yr	10
(5.7)	Inventories	20	Loans	40	Warehouse	30	Under 2 yr	10
	Buildings	40	Capital	30			Over 2 yr	40
	Equipment	10						
		$100		$100		$100		$100

Here, the total value of the assets of the entity ($100 million) is classified four ways. Increments and decrements are then similarly classified. For example, a $10 purchase, on account, of inventories which are to be stored in the warehouse is recorded in the quadruple-entry journal as

(5.8)

Inventories, $10: Payables, $10: Warehouse, $10: Under 6 months, $10

Similarly, if loans of $10 are repayed, assuming that cash is located at the head office and has been held less than six months, we may make the following quadruple-entry:

(5.9)

Cash, $-\$10$: Loans, $-\$10$: Head Office, $-\$10$: Under 6 months, $-\$10$

We may then apply the convention used in deriving (5.5) from (5.4), and eliminate negative entries by recording accounts under a column for a different classification. In the case of double-entry we had only one method of doing this—transposing the two accounts. Here we have a number of ways. However, since this is simply a convention, we may agree upon any one method such as using the column immediately to the right except for accounts in the last column, which are entered in the first column. Then, (5.9) is recorded as

(5.10)   Under 6 months, $10: Cash, $10: Loans, $10: Head Office, $10

There is no ambiguity whatsoever in interpreting the journal entries in (5.10) providing the convention for negative entries has been established. Thus, just as easily as we interpret a cash account on the credit side of double-entry as a decrease in cash, we interpret a loans account in the third column of quadruple-entry as a decrease in loans. The fact that there are different ways of handling negative entries (such as using the column immediately to the left instead of to the right) should not bother us since this is merely a recording convention which does not give any more information than that which we obtain without it.

How are entries such as sales of inventories recorded under classificational multiple-entry? In the classificational systems, an increment and a decrement are recorded separately and independently because the first two abilities discussed earlier are not sufficient for recognizing the causal relationship between a decrease in inventories and an increase in receivables. Therefore, sales of inventories are handled as follows, assuming the inventories cost $20 and are sold for $25.

(5.11)

Under 6 months, $20:Inventories, $20:Capital, $20:Warehouse, $20

(5.12)

Receivables, $25:Capital, $25:Head Office, $25:Under 6 months, $25

Thus, the duality in classificational double-entry is not unique since classificational multiple-entry bookkeeping actually has the same basis in the sense that the underlying abilities required to make the entries are the same.[5]

What about causal double-entry? Can we extend it to causal multiple-entry? To answer this question, let us note the three essential aspects of an entry in the causal double-entry system. 1) It always relates an increment and a decrement in a set of resources controlled by an entity; 2) the increment and the decrement have a cause-and-effect relationship; i.e., the decrement is considered to be the cause of the increment or vice versa; and 3) the amount (or value) of the increment and the amount of the decrement are always set equal.[6] Thus, in causal double-entry one side of the entry must deal with an increment and the other side with a decrement. Moreover, the two must be connected by cause-and-effect relationship. This dichotomy of an increment and a decrement which are combined by a causal relationship makes causal double-entry unique. Therefore, there is no logical extension to causal multiple-entry. We may note here that the three factors described above are an expression of the cost principle, which imputes the value of the increment from the value of the decrement. Therefore, what makes the double-entry system double is not the double classification (Assets = Equity) that is often described in accounting literature but rather the cost principle, which recognizes the causal relationship between an asset acquired and an asset foregone. In this sense, the

---

[5] Obviously, classification need not be limited to the four types discussed above. According to the need for information, many different classifications may be added. Furthermore, by introducing more than one unit of measurement, the double-entry system can be extended to multidimensional, multiple-entry accounting, as discussed in Section 4, to accommodate the increasing variety of information that needs to be processed in business.

[6] If there is a difference in the two values, the difference is accounted for by means of classificational double-entry. See, however, the entry in (5.14) for a causal interpretation of profit and loss.

double-entry system and the historical cost principle, which is elaborated in detail in the previous chapter, have a logical connection since one is a form developed to express the other.[7]

3. CAUSALITY AS THE FOUNDATION OF DOUBLE-ENTRY BOOKKEEPING

Would it be possible to describe the current double-entry bookkeeping system from the viewpoint of causal double-entry only? This could be done if we regard equity accounts as future cash decrements, i.e., future negative assets as discussed in Chapter 3. In relating an increment and a decrement in the assets of an entity, we must consider the fact that in most cases the two do not occur simultaneously. For example, suppose the entity purchases materials from a supplier and pays cash the following month. We recognize the causal relationship between an increment (materials) and a decrement (cash), but the decrement does not occur until the following month. However, since we must make an entry for the increment, we determine, from our past experience, what the decrement will be and make an entry in an account which is to be used until the decrement actually occurs. Liabilities may thus be considered anticipated decrements in cash whose corresponding increments have already occurred. By the same token, capital accounts may be considered as decrements in cash that will occur when dividends are paid or when the entity is liquidated. Therefore, from this standpoint, we make the entry

(5.13)   (Dr.) Cash $100: (Cr.) Capital stock $100

not as a double classification of the same assets but as recognition of the causal relationship between the current increment in cash and the anticipated decrement in cash. Similarly, the entry

(5.14)   (Dr.) Receivables $25: (Cr.) Inventories $20

                                                Profit   5

indicates the causality between the anticipated increment in cash (receivables, $25) and the current decrement in inventories (inventories, $20) plus the anticipated decrement in cash (profit, $5). There is nothing artificial in this way of interpreting capital accounts since owners of the entity actually have the ultimate right to receive any residual resources of the entity.

---

[7] For a network interpretation of double-entry bookkeeping, see Charnes, Cooper, and Ijiri [1963] and Ijiri [1965a].

Thus, current double-entry bookkeeping practices can be completely described from only the causal viewpoint. On the other hand, they cannot be described from only the classificational viewpoint since an entry like (5.6), where an increase in inventories is matched with a decrease in cash, requires a judgment on the causal relationship between an increment and a decrement.

Therefore, the essential element in double-entry accounting is the causal relationship between an increment and a decrement in the present or future resources of an entity. This point needs more emphasis in accounting education. For example, perhaps it is better to teach the double-entry system not as a double-classification mechanism as is currently done (i.e., by means of the equation, Assets = Equity) but rather as a system by which an increment and a decrement in the present or future resources of an entity are tied together by a causal relationship. That is, we should describe the double-entry system not statically but dynamically. Thus, we can teach in elementary accounting courses that a debit entry is always an increment in the present or future resources or a cancellation of a decrement, while a credit entry is always a decrement or a cancellation of an increment, emphasizing the point that the purpose of double-entry is to relate an increment and a decrement by cause and effect.

In this way we can state the fact that the double-entry bookkeeping system forces us not to look at an increment or a decrement in the assets of the entity in isolation but to look at the way they are linked by causal chains. The bookkeeping system is a language, and we see here a significant effect of this language on our behavior. An accountant who has been trained in double-entry bookkeeping does not and cannot look at an increase in inventories itself since he has no means to express such an isolated change in assets. In order to express the change he must search for a credit account (or a debit account) and in doing so he is unconsciously looking for the cause or the effect of the change in inventories. This puts tremendous pressure on his thinking processes, considering the fact that he has to make a judgment on causality every time he records business operations. Eventually, he acquires a habit of always looking at a change in assets in relation to some other change in the past or in the future. He associates coming and going, input and output, past and future.[8] Thus, the real significance

[8] Sombart states, "One can scarcely conceive of capitalism without double-entry book-keeping: they are related as are form and content. It is difficult to decide, however, whether in double-entry book-keeping capitalism provided itself with a tool to make it more effective, or whether capitalism derives from the 'spirit' of double-entry book-keeping." [1928, Vol. II, Part I, p. 118], translated in Yamey [1956, p. 9]. Although it is hard to substantiate historically the truth of this statement (see Yamey [1964]), the more we understand the double-entry system, the more we admire the insight that Sombart has shown in this phrase. See Charnes, Cooper, and Ijiri [1963] for a more detailed discussion on the historical aspect of the double-entry systems.

of the bookkeeping system involving double-entry compared with the one involving single-entry does not lie in its formality—no matter how beautiful and perfect it may be. It lies in the fact that the double-entry bookkeeping system compels us to look into the causal relationships among changes in assets. As is clear from our discussion in Chapters 2 and 3, this is essential for our understanding of the concept of values, which are derived from pain and pleasure by means of a causal network.

4. MULTIDIMENSIONAL BOOKKEEPING

It has been shown, in the previous sections and in Chapter 4, that the essential element in double-entry bookkeeping and in historical cost accounting is recognition of the unity between an increment and a decrement in the present and future resources of an entity, which is derived from the causal relationship between them. From the recording viewpoint, an increment and a decrement are recorded by putting the same amount on a debit side and on a credit side, respectively. From the measurement viewpoint, the amounts are the same because the value of the increment is imputed from the value of the decrement. Recognizing the unity of certain increments and decrements because they are interrelated does not depend on having a single value measure which is applied to all such increments and decrements. The value measure based on historical cost that was elaborated in Chapter 4 is a result of judgments on the relationships between increment and decrements and is not a prerequisite for the judgments.

This gives us the idea that perhaps we can extend double-entry to cases where we have multiple quantity measures and not a single value measure. To begin, we set up asset accounts (present and future, positive and negative) as we do in the ordinary double-entry bookkeeping system, but we keep each account by its own quantity measure. Then, in each journal entry an increment (debit) and a decrement (credit) are united and recorded in their quantity measures. Here, as we shall see below in an example, it is convenient to classify these entries by the activities which caused the changes in the resources, e.g., material-purchase activities, labor-procurement activities, production activities, sales activities. Therefore, we set up *activity accounts*, where these journal entries are classified and aggregated. Activity accounts are similar to profit-and-loss accounts in the ordinary double-entry bookkeeping system in the sense that they are "flow" accounts (compared with asset accounts which are "stock" accounts) but are much broader since they include activities which are not directly related to profit and loss.

For example, suppose that an entity has the assets listed in Table 5.1

TABLE 5.1   Beginning Balance Sheet

POSITIVE ASSETS	UNITS	ASSETS
Cash	Dollar	10,000
Materials	Pounds	5,000
Finished goods	Cases	1,000
Machinery (3 years old)	Units	3
NEGATIVE ASSETS		
Loans	Dollar	15,000

at the beginning of a given period and that the activities of the entity during the period are summarized as follows:

1. Purchased 10,000 pounds of materials for $40,000 cash.

2. Procured 3,000 man-hours of labor and paid $9,000 cash.

3. Produced 4,000 cases of finished goods consuming 12,000 pounds of materials, 2,000 man-hours of labor, and one year's service of three machines.

4. Sold 3,500 cases of finished goods, received $63,000 in cash, and consumed 600 man-hours of labor for selling.

5. Consumed 400-man-hours of labor for administrative work.

6. Paid $5,000 in cash as a partial repayment of the loan.[9]

Then, at the end of the period, the balance sheet of the entity would appear as in Table 5.2. Asset and activity accounts would show the entries in Tables 5.3 and 5.4, respectively.

TABLE 5.2   Ending Balance Sheet

POSITIVE ASSETS	UNITS	AMOUNTS
Cash	Dollars	19,000
Materials	Pounds	3,000
Finished goods	Cases	1,500
Machinery (4 years old)	Units	3
NEGATIVE ASSETS		
Loans	Dollars	10,000

[9] In order to simplify the illustration, interest on the loans is neglected. However, it can be treated in the same way as labor in this example.

TABLE 5.3   Asset Accounts

CASH (IN DOLLARS)

Beginning balance	10,000	Material purchases	40,000
Sales	63,000	Labor procurements	9,000
		Loan repayments	5,000
		Ending balance	19,000
	73,000		73,000

MATERIALS (IN POUNDS)

Beginning balance	5,000	Production	12,000
Material purchases	10,000	Ending balance	3,000
	15,000		15,000

FINISHED GOODS (IN CASES)

Beginning balance	1,000	Sales	3,500
Production	4,000	Ending balance	1,500
	5,000		5,000

MACHINERY—3 YEARS OLD (IN UNITS)

| Beginning balance | 3 | Production | 3 |

MACHINERY—4 YEARS OLD (IN UNITS)

| Production | 3 | Ending balance | 3 |

LABOR (IN MAN-HOURS)

Labor procurements	3,000	Production	2,000
		Sales	600
		Administration	400
	3,000		3,000

LOANS (IN DOLLARS)

Loan repayments	5,000	Beginning balance	15,000
Ending balance	10,000		
	15,000		15,000

TABLE 5.4 Activity Accounts

MATERIAL PURCHASES

Cash (dollars)	40,000	Materials (pounds)	10,000

LABOR PROCUREMENTS

Cash (dollars)	9,000	Labor (man-hours)	3,000

PRODUCTION

Materials (pounds)	12,000	Finished goods (cases)	4,000
Labor (man-hours)	2,000	Machinery—4 years	
Machinery—3 years		old (units)	3
old (units)	3		

SALES

Finished goods (cases)	3,500	Cash (dollars)	63,000
Labor (man-hours)	600		

ADMINISTRATION

Labor (man-hours)	400		

LOAN REPAYMENTS

Cash (dollars)	5,000	Loans (dollars)	5,000

It will be noted that entries in each asset account are homogeneous (additive), but entries in each activity account are not. Also, every entry in each asset account, except entries for beginning and ending balances, is made through activity accounts. Since every number is entered twice, once on the debit side and once on the credit side, the flash total of entries on the debit side of all accounts is equal to the flash total on the credit side. Furthermore, if a set of prices is applied to the entries in physical units, the ordinary entries in the monetary unit are obtained. Therefore, the ordinary double-entry bookkeeping system is a special case of a more general double-entry bookkeeping system based on multiple physical units.

The above assets and their changes during the period as reflected in the set of activity accounts can be summarized in an Asset-Activity Statement. (See Table 5.5.) Note that the statement includes the whole relationship between the assets and the activities and provides all necessary information for the valuation of assets and income. If, for example, we want to introduce responsibility accounting, the activities may be classified

TABLE 5.5 Asset-Activity Statement

| | POSITIVE ASSETS | | | | | | NEGATIVE ASSETS |
	CASH (DOLLARS)	MATERIALS (POUNDS)	FINISHED GOODS (CASES)	MACHINERY, 3 YEARS OLD (UNITS)	MACHINERY, 4 YEARS OLD (UNITS)	LABOR (MAN-HOURS)	LOANS (DOLLARS)
BEGINNING BALANCE	10,000	5,000	1,000	3	—	—	15,000
ACTIVITIES DURING THE PERIOD							
1. Material purchases	−40,000	10,000	—	—	—	—	—
2. Labor procurements	−9,000	—	—	—	—	3,000	—
3. Production	—	−12,000	4,000	−3	3	−2,000	—
4. Sales	63,000	—	−3,500	—	—	−600	—
5. Administration	—	—	—	—	—	−400	—
6. Loan repayments	−5,000	—	—	—	—	—	−5,000
Total activities (income)	9,000	−2,000	500	−3	3	—	−5,000
ENDING BALANCE	19,000	3,000	1,500	—	3	—	10,000

according to the responsibility centers (e.g., division, departments) instead of by the types of activities as in Table 5.5.

Of course, there are many problems that need to be solved in order to implement multidimensional accounting. First, since it is practically impossible to list all assets and activities individually, we must aggregate them into a relatively small number of classes based upon the use and the conversions of economic resources. Then, we must develop an appropriate measure for each class that will best indicate the characteristics of the resources in it. For example, dollars may be used as a measure of monetary assets, units of a standard product may be used as a measure of inventory, or a measure of productivity may be used for fixed assets.

Furthermore, we must develop a way in which current resources and future resources may be aggregated. For example, all receivables and payables involve cash to be received or paid in the future. Should we aggregate them with cash on hand and if so, how?[10] We must also consider the way in which economic resources that are under different degrees of control by an entity may be aggregated. For example, if we have two machines of an identical type, one owned by the entity and one rented, should we aggregate them together and if so, how?

These problems are not easy to solve. However, they at least make us reconsider whether the use of a single value measure, which we have been acquainted with for centuries, is necessary or even appropriate. There is nothing inherent in double-entry bookkeeping that makes using only a single value measure to record changes in assets necessary. Actually, recording based on multiple measures presents more flexible information since the measures can then be aggregated in various ways (by applying different sets of prices) and the way most suitable for a particular use of the information can be chosen.

This leads to the topic in the next chapter, valuation as a linear aggregation, i.e., a weighted sum where the weights are the prices, of quantity measures. We shall study the mathematical relationship between quantity measures and a value measure and develop an indicator which shows how suitable a particular aggregation method is for a given use of the data.

---

[10] The use of an interest rate for discounting future cash should also be considered as a possible way of aggregating current and future cash, e.g., the discounted future cash flow method.

CHAPTER SIX

The Linear Aggregation Coefficient and the Identifiability of Accounting Valuation

In the remaining three chapters of this book, our discussion will center on the relationship between accountants and the users of accounting information. In particular, we shall analyze in this chapter a mathematical relationship between two valuation methods, one that an accountant uses and the other that a user of accounting information wants to be used, by introducing a new concept—the linear aggregation coefficient.

1. VALUATION AS A LINEAR AGGREGATION OF QUANTITIES

The most important and the most basic characteristic of the accounting valuation methods that currently exist is that they are a linear aggregation of quantities—a weighted sum of quantities where the weights are prices. For example, the net assets in Table 5.2 are aggregated as

$$(6.1) \quad \$19,000 + \$4 \times 3,000 + \$15 \times 1,500 + \$2,000 \times 3$$

$$- \$10,000 = \$49,500$$

if we evaluate materials at \$4 per pound, finished goods at \$15 per case, and machinery (four years old) at \$2,000 a unit. These prices may represent the historical costs as derived in Chapter 4 or their market values. If we evaluate the assets at the beginning at \$4 per pound for materials, \$15 per case for finished goods, and \$4,000 per unit for machinery (three years old), then the beginning assets (Table 5.1) are aggregated as

(6.2) $10,000 + \$4 \times 5,000 + \$15 \times 1,000 + \$4,000 \times 3$

$$- \$15,000 = \$42,000$$

Hence, the income for the period is valued at \$7,500 (= \$49,500 − \$42,000). This amount for income can also be obtained by applying the same prices to the figures in the total activity row in Table 5.5, i.e.

(6.3) $9,000 - \$4 \times 2,000 + \$15 \times 500 - \$4,000 \times 3$

$$+ \$2,000 \times 3 + \$5,000 = \$7,500$$

In general, we can describe an accounting valuation method in the following manner. Let us represent by $(q_1, q_2, \cdots, q_n)$ the assets A of a given entity at the beginning of a given period, where q_i's are the quantities of assets in different classes, and by $(q'_1, q'_2, \cdots, q'_n)$ the assets A' of the entity at the end of the period. In addition, let $p_1, p_2, \cdots, p_n$ be the unit prices at the beginning of the period of the assets in each class, and let $p'_1, p'_2, \cdots, p'_n$ be the unit prices at the end of the period. Then the values of A and A' denoted by $v(A)$ and $v(A')$,[1] respectively, are

$$(6.4) \qquad v(A) = p_1 q_1 + p_2 q_2 + \cdots + p_n q_n = \sum_{i=1}^{n} p_i q_i$$

$$(6.5) \qquad v(A') = p'_1 q'_1 + p'_2 q'_2 + \cdots + p'_n q'_n = \sum_{i=1}^{n} p'_i q'_i$$

Thus, accounting valuation is always a weighted sum of quantities (weights being prices) or alternatively it is a *linear aggregation of quantities* q_i's. Different valuation methods, such as the cash basis, the historical cost basis, the market value basis, the deflated dollar value basis—all

---

[1] As discussed in Chapter 2, the value of assets A, $v(A)$, is a dual concept and must be expressed by a pair—a sacrifice value $s(A)$ and a benefit value $b(A)$. However, here we shall follow the practices in conventional accounting and consider only one, either a sacrifice value or a benefit value, as the value of assets A.

result in different sets of weights, but they are essentially all linear aggregations of quantities.[2]

Since the income I of the entity in the period is $A' - A$ and the values of A' and A are linear aggregations of quantities, the value of the income is also derived as a linear aggregation of quantities, i.e.

$$(6.6) \qquad v(I) = v(A') - v(A) = \sum_{i=1}^{n} (p_i' q_i' - p_i q_i)$$

where $v(I)$ is the value of income.[3] Notice that because of the linearity of the valuation methods in accounting, a change in any class of assets adds to or subtracts from the value of the income independently of the effects of assets in other classes.[4] Moreover, whether a change in assets in Class i increases or decreases the value of the income for the period depends entirely upon the relationship between $p_i' q_i'$ and $p_i q_i$. The value $p_i' q_i' - p_i q_i$, which is the amount added to (or subtracted from, if negative) the income because of a change in assets in the ith class, can be further decomposed to

$$(6.7) \quad p_i' q_i' - p_i q_i = p_i(q_i' - q_i) + q_i(p_i' - p_i) + (p_i' - p_i)(q_i' - q_i)$$

We may call the first element in the right-hand side of the equation, $p_i(q_i' - q_i)$, the *activity gain* (or loss) since this is the effect activities have upon income. Similarly, we may call the second term, $q_i(p_i' - p_i)$, the *valuation gain* (or loss)[5] since this is entirely due to the change in the weight used in the valuation. Finally, the third term, $(p_i' - p_i)(q_i' - q_i)$, represents the joint effect of the activity gain and the valuation gain.

We thus clearly see that the valuation of income results from activity gains and valuation gains along with their "interactions." One advantage

---

[2] We use linear aggregations in accounting valuation perhaps because of our desire to have the value of a whole equal to the sum of the value of all its parts. Of course, it is possible to start with the valuation of an entity as a whole based on, for example, the discounted future cash flow of the entity as a whole, and then "disaggregate" the total value into a collection of classes of assets. However, conventional accounting valuation methods have always been "grass-roots" methods and not "top-down" methods. On the valuation of the firm as a whole, see Bierman [1965, Chapter 9], Jaedicke and Sprouse [1965], Paton [1965], etc. See also Paton [1922, Chapter 13], Devine [1962, Chapter 22], etc. on goodwill and related valuation problems for the cases where the value of a whole is not equal to the sum of the values of all its parts.

[3] Of course, it is possible to define $v(I)$ as being equal to $v(A'-A)$ instead of $v(A')-v(A)$. In this case, $v(I)$ is a linear aggregation of $(q_i'-q_i)$, $(i=1, 2, \ldots, n)$.

[4] They are ultimately related to each other through activities. But as far as valuation is concerned, assets in each class have effects on the value of income that are independent of the effects of assets in other classes.

[5] This should be distinguished from *value gains and losses*, which were discussed in Chapter 4. They constitute the entire income of a firm aggregated for a whole period, and therefore include both activity gains or losses and valuation gains or losses.

of the multidimensional accounting approach discussed in the previous chapter now becomes apparent. As in standard costing, we have here a separation of the sources of income, which are confounded at the start in ordinary accounting. In multidimensional accounting, only activity gains are recorded, so valuation gains can be derived in a wholly flexible way by reference to different weights that the users of the financial statements may want to apply.

A question naturally arises now as to which set of weights is "best" or whether one set of weights (e.g., based on market values) is "better" than another set (e.g., based on historical costs). Here, it should be noted that any aggregation generally involves a loss of information in that the resulting total "value" may be composed of many—possibly infinitely many—different underlying components. Hence, an entirely unambiguous answer to this all-purpose question is not possible. Before we can even attempt to compare two sets of weights, we must have a clear notion of how the quantities should be aggregated. This is the problem of defining unambiguously the principal for which the accounting valuation is to serve as a surrogate. Furthermore, in order to say that one set of weights is better than another set, we must know which of society's goals we want to attain by using accounting valuation. And even this does not settle the matter. We must then consider how individuals will behave[6] in response to the values of assets or income that are based on the given set of weights and decide whether or not such reactions are desirable from the viewpoint of the goals of the society and of the individuals to be served. If people are likely to behave in a more "desirable" manner in response to the values of assets and income prepared under one set of weights than to those prepared under another set, then and only then can we say that one set is better than another.

Of course, it is a very difficult task to estimate the reactions of individuals and to evaluate how the reactions relate to given goals. The problem is compounded when there are many different goals and a variety of persons and entities to be served. Indeed, this is the problem that one faces when he makes any assertion that one accounting valuation is better than another. We shall take up this problem again in Chapter 8 from the viewpoint of how the choice of an accounting measurement may influence decision makers.

2. THE LINEAR AGGREGATION COEFFICIENT

With this in mind we can retreat to a more limited consideration of the usefulness of accounting valuation and study the problem of identifi-

---

[6] See Stedry [1960] for experimental evidence on the behavioral consequences of different accounting standards (or targets). See also our discussion in Chapter 8.

cation of the principal when accounting valuation is the surrogate. For
accounting valuation to be of use, there must be a particular method of
aggregating quantities which is most suitable for a given application since
aggregating quantities without reference to the way in which the aggregation will be used does not make sense. In other words, for every case
there must be a particular relation between a set of quantities and an
aggregate. In terms of the discussions in Chapter 1, this is the *principal
relation* that we want to represent by means of a *surrogated relation* among
accounting values. How do we recognize the principal relation? This is a
purely empirical question, which becomes a problem in finance, marketing,
production, economics, etc., where empirical phenomena are the objects of
study. As we emphasized in Chapter 1, however, the determination of the
principal relation is not a problem in measurement per se.

The problem in measurement is how to represent quantitatively the
principal relation by a surrogated relation. Or, when dealing with aggregations, how to represent a principal aggregation of quantities specified
for a particular use by a surrogated aggregation. If we let f and g represent
the functions of quantities that are a principal and a surrogate, respectively, i.e.

$$(6.8) \qquad\qquad y = f(q_1, q_2, \cdots, q_n)$$

$$(6.9) \qquad\qquad w = g(q_1, q_2, \cdots, q_n)$$

then we want to make it possible to identify the value of y from the value
of w without checking the details, i.e., the q_i's. In other words, we want to
select g for a given f so that there is a functional relation between w and y
which may be represented by

$$(6.10) \qquad\qquad y = h(w)$$

If the principal aggregation is linear, as in

$$(6.11) \qquad\qquad y = r_1q_1 + r_2q_2 + \cdots + r_nq_n$$

then it may be represented by a surrogated linear aggregation[7]

$$(6.12) \qquad\qquad w = p_1q_1 + p_2q_2 + \cdots + p_nq_n$$

This sounds like a trivial problem since we can always set the function
g precisely equal to the function f or set the p_i's precisely equal to the r_i's.

---

[7] If the principal aggregation is not linear then a surrogated linear aggregation
is at best an approximation and the precise identification of the value of y from the value
of w is usually not possible.

However, there is an important practical problem. The users of data provided by an accounting valuation method have perhaps numerous different applications in mind, which have different principal aggregations most suitable for them. Nevertheless it is practically impossible to develop different accounting aggregations for such principal aggregations. For example, the users of financial statements may have diversified applications for the information in them, but accountants can provide only a few varieties of such statements.

In order to attack this problem of coordination between a principal aggregation and a surrogated aggregation, let us first define a *perfect aggregation*. A surrogated aggregation $w = g(q_1, q_2, \cdots, q_n)$ is said to be perfect with respect to a given principal aggregation $y = f(q_1, q_2, \cdots, q_n)$ if the value of y is uniquely determined from only the value of w for all values of $q_1, q_2, \cdots, q_n$; otherwise it is said to be *imperfect* with respect to the principal aggregation.

In the case of linear aggregations, it is easy to see that a surrogated aggregation $w = p_1q_1 + p_2q_2 + \cdots + p_nq_n$ is perfect with respect to a given principal aggregation $y = r_1q_1 + r_2q_2 + \cdots + r_nq_n$ if and only if

$$p_1 = \alpha r_1$$

(6.13)
$$p_2 = \alpha r_2$$

$$p_n = \alpha r_n$$

where α is a number not equal to zero. For example, if the principal aggregation is

(6.14)
$$y = 5q_1 + 3q_2$$

then the coefficients of a perfect surrogated aggregation must be in the form of $p_1 = 5\alpha$ and $p_2 = 3\alpha$; for example, $w = 5q_1 + 3q_2$, $w = 10q_1 + 6q_2$, $w = 15q_1 + 9q_2$, $w = -\frac{5}{7}q_1 - \frac{3}{7}q_2$ are all perfect aggregations with respect to (6.14). In these cases, we have

(6.15)
$$y = w/\alpha$$

which is true whatever the value of the q_i's may be.

Unfortunately, it is rare that an accounting aggregation is perfect with respect to a given principal aggregation for a particular use. In many cases, as mentioned earlier, there are a number of uses of an accounting aggregate and it is impossible for it to be perfect with respect to all such principal aggregations. If Person A wants to have q_1 and q_2 aggregated as

$$(6.16) \qquad\qquad y_A = 5q_1 + 3q_2$$

and Person B wants to have them aggregated as

$$(6.17) \qquad\qquad y_B = 2q_1 + 2q_2$$

it is obvious that there is no single accounting aggregation

$$(6.18) \qquad\qquad w = p_1q_1 + p_2q_2$$

which is perfect with respect to both principal aggregations.[8]

This gives rise to another problem. If accounting aggregations are imperfect most of the time, are there any ways of ordering imperfect aggregation in terms of their closeness to being perfect? Intuitively, if the principal aggregation is

$$(6.19) \qquad\qquad y = 5q_1 + 3q_2$$

an aggregation

$$(6.20) \qquad\qquad w_1 = 5q_1 + 2q_2$$

seems closer to being perfect than an aggregation

$$(6.21) \qquad\qquad w_2 = 5q_1 + q_2$$

Analytically, w_1 and w_2 are equally poor as surrogates of y since for any given value of w_1 or w_2, the value of y can be anywhere from $-\infty$ to $+\infty$, assuming there is no constraint on q_1 and q_2. This occurs because from (6.19)–(6.21) we have $5q_1 = w_1 - 2q_2 = w_2 - q_2$; hence

$$(6.22) \qquad\qquad y = w_1 + q_2 = w_2 + 2q_2$$

and for any given w_1 and w_2 the value of y can be anything depending upon the value of q_2. (Since there are no constraints on q_1 and q_2, it is assumed that they can take negative values as well.)

However, suppose that the range of the variable q_2 is limited to 1,000–2,000 units; then a significant difference between w_1 and w_2 as

---

[8] If $y_B = 2q_1 + 1.2q_2$, then a single aggregation in the form of $w = 5\alpha q_1 + 3\alpha q_2$ is perfect with respect to both aggregations. But, of course, this is an exceptional case.

surrogates for y is highlighted. For any given value of w_1 the maximum and the minimum values that y can take are derived from (6.22) as

(6.23)
$$\text{Max } y = w_1 + 2{,}000$$
$$\text{Min } y = w_1 + 1{,}000$$

while for any given value of w_2 the corresponding values are

(6.24)
$$\text{Max } y = w_2 + 4{,}000$$
$$\text{Min } y = w_2 + 2{,}000$$

That is, the error range in identifying y is \$1,000 if w_1 is used, whereas it is \$2,000 if w_2 is used, assuming a price aggregation into dollars. This agrees with our intuition that w_1 is closer to being perfect than w_2.

Although a range is one of the indicators of the degree of dispersion of a variable, it is a rather poor indicator since its takes into account only two extreme values of the variable and nothing in between. For example, suppose that we have two bags; a white bag contains five white balls which weigh 1, 3, 4, 5, and 7 ounces, while a black bag contains two black balls which weigh 2 and 8 ounces. Suppose further that each ball has an equal chance of being selected from its respective bag, i.e., the probability of being selected is 0.2 for each white ball and 0.5 for each black ball. A variable such as the weight of a white ball, which can have a value of 1, 3, 4, 5, or 7 depending upon which ball is selected, is called a *random variable* if the probability of selecting each value is defined.[9] Therefore, the weight of a white ball is a random variable and so is the weight of a black ball. Notice that in spite of the fact that the range of the variables is 6 ounces in each case, it is easier to guess the weight of a white ball than that of a black ball. If we guess the weight of a white ball to be 4 ounces, our error is ± 1 ounce three-fifths of the time. This is, of course, not true for black balls.

A better indicator of the degree of dispersion of a random variable is a *variance*. It shows the average degree of the deviation from the mean (arithmetic average), where the deviation is measured as the distance from the mean and then squared. Let us calculate the mean and the variance for the white balls and the black balls, assuming that each ball in the white bag has an equal chance of being selected and that the same is true for balls in the black bag. We calculate the mean of the weights, take the

---

[9] More precisely, if a (probability) distribution function is defined for the variable.

differences between each weight and the mean, square the differences, add
the squared differences, and then divide by the number of balls. Table 6.1

TABLE 6.1   Mean and Variance

WHITE BALLS			BLACK BALLS		
q_1	$q_1 - \bar{q}_1$	$(q_1 - \bar{q}_1)^2$	q_2	$q_2 - \bar{q}_2$	$(q_2 - \bar{q}_2)^2$
1	-3	9	2	-3	9
3	-1	1	8	3	9
4	0	0			
5	1	1			
7	3	9			
5)20	0	5)20	2)10	0	2)18
$\bar{q}_1 = 4$	Variance: $\sigma_1^2 = 4$		$\bar{q}_2 = 5$	Variance: $\sigma_2^2 = 9$	
(mean)	Standard deviation: $\sigma_1 = 2$		(mean)	Standard deviation: $\sigma_2 = 3$	

shows how the variance is calculated for the white balls and for the black
balls. In it, q_1 is the weight of a white ball and q_2 is the weight of a black
ball; the mean of white balls is $\bar{q}_1$ and the mean of black balls is $\bar{q}_2$. The
variance of white balls is denoted by σ_1^2, while the variance of black balls
is denoted by σ_2^2. The square root of a variance is called the *standard deviation* of the variable.

Let us now use this variance in determining how good an aggregation
method is. Suppose that User A of accounting information wants to have
the weights of two balls, one white ball and one black ball selected from
their respective bags independently, to be aggregated as

$$(6.25) \qquad y = 5q_1 + 3q_2$$

Suppose further that Accountant B has already established an accounting
aggregation

$$(6.26) \qquad w = q_1 + 2q_2$$

and that it is not possible for A to obtain any information on q_1 and q_2
other than the value of w calculated by (6.26). How is this information
on w useful to A in identifying the value of y?

Here, we must introduce the concept of errors in an estimate. If y
and $\hat{y}$ denote an actual and an estimated value of $5q_1 + 3q_2$, respectively,

$y - \hat{y}$ is the error of estimate. Since in general we want to avoid over-estimation as well as underestimation, the significance of an error may be indicated by the absolute value of $y - \hat{y}$, denoted by $|y - \hat{y}|$, or the square of $y - \hat{y}$, $(y - \hat{y})^2$, among other possibilities. Let us use the squared error here since it is closely related to the variance of y and provides a convenient basis for analyses. Of course, this quantity depends upon the particular combination of q_1 and q_2 selected. Hence, let us consider an average of all possible combinations of q_1 and q_2. We then try to minimize the average of the squared error in estimating the value of y.

If A does not have information on w, he must simply guess the value of y. It can be shown that if A guesses the value to be the mean of all possible values of y, the average of the squared error from such an estimate is minimized and the minimum value is given by the variance of the variable y, denoted by σ_y^2.[10] On the other hand, if information on w is available, he may estimate the value of y based on the value of w. It can be shown that when he makes the best use of w the average of the squared error is given by the variance of the variable $e = y - \hat{y}$, denoted by σ_e^2.[11] Then the quantity ρ^2 defined by

$$(6.27) \qquad \rho^2 = \frac{\sigma_y^2 - \sigma_e^2}{\sigma_y^2}$$

shows the proportion of the variance of y that is eliminated as a result of estimating y by w. Therefore, this may be used as an indicator of how useful an aggregate is in determining the value of a given function. Let us call ρ^2 defined by (6.27) the *aggregation effectiveness coefficient*. Table 6.2 shows how ρ^2 may be calculated for the above example. The first two columns are various combinations of q_1 and q_2. Since there are five white balls and two black balls, we have ten combinations, each of which is equally likely to occur. Then, in the third column y is calculated by (6.25). The mean of y, denoted by $\bar{y}$, is given at the bottom of the third column. Note that $\bar{y}$ may be calculated by the relationship

$$(6.28) \qquad \bar{y} = 5\bar{q}_1 + 3\bar{q}_2$$

where $\bar{q}_1$ and $\bar{q}_2$ are 4 and 5 as given in Table 6.1. Columns 4 and 5 are for the computation of the variance of y, σ_y^2, which is given as 181 at the bottom of Column 5. Note that this figure is also obtained from the relationship

$$(6.29) \qquad \sigma_y^2 = 5^2\sigma_1^2 + 3^2\sigma_2^2$$

---

[10] See Appendix B, Section 5 for a proof.
[11] See again Appendix B, Section 5 for a proof.

TABLE 6.2   A Computation of the Aggregation Effectiveness Coefficient I

(1)	(2)	(3)	(4)	(5)	(6)	(7)	(8)	(9)
q_1	q_2	y	$y - \bar{y}$	$(y - \bar{y})^2$	w	$\hat{y} = 1.85w + 9.1$	$e = y - \hat{y}$	$(e - \bar{e})^2 = e^2$
1	2	11	-24	576	5	18.35	-7.35	54.0225
3	2	21	-14	196	7	22.05	-1.05	1.1025
4	2	26	-9	81	8	23.90	2.10	4.4100
5	2	31	-4	16	9	25.75	5.25	27.5625
7	2	41	6	36	11	29.45	11.55	133.4025
1	8	29	-6	36	17	40.55	-11.55	133.4025
3	8	39	4	16	19	44.25	-5.25	27.5625
4	8	44	9	81	20	46.10	-2.10	4.4100
5	8	49	14	196	21	47.95	1.05	1.1025
7	8	59	24	576	23	51.65	7.35	54.0225
—	—	10)350	0	10)1810	10)140		10)0	10)441.0000
		$\bar{y} = 35$		$\sigma_y^2 = 181$	$\bar{w} = 14$		$\bar{e} = 0$	$\sigma_e^2 = 44.1000$

where σ_1^2 and σ_2^2 are 4 and 9 as derived in Table 6.1. In general, it can be proved[12] that if

$$(6.30) \qquad z = ax + by + c$$

where x and y are independent random variables and a, b, and c are constants, then the variance of z, σ_z^2, can be calculated from the variances of x and y, σ_x^2 and σ_y^2, as

$$(6.31) \qquad \sigma_z^2 = a^2\sigma_x^2 + b^2\sigma_y^2$$

In Column 6, w is calculated based on (6.26). We then estimate y based on

$$(6.32) \qquad \hat{y} = 1.85w + 9.1$$

We shall show later how these numbers are derived. In any case it can be proved that the variance of the error between an actual and an estimate is minimized if we estimate y as $\hat{y}$ given in (6.32). Column 7 calculates $\hat{y}$ and Column 8 determines the error $e = y - \hat{y}$. Note that the mean of the errors, denoted by $\bar{e}$, is zero. The estimate $\hat{y}$ in (6.32) is derived in such a

[12] See, e.g., Gnedenko [1962, pp. 206–7].

way that this is true. In Columns 8 and 9 the variance of the error e is calculated. It is shown at the bottom of Column 9 as 44.1. Hence, by (6.27) ρ^2 is calculated as

$$(6.33) \qquad \rho^2 = \frac{181 - 44.1}{181} = \frac{136.9}{181} = 0.756$$

That is, by using w approximately three-quarters of the variance of y is eliminated. Therefore, User A can improve his estimate of y substantially by using the data provided by Accountant B even though the data are not perfect for the purpose of identifying the value of y.

Fortunately, it is not necessary to go through all the computations in Table 6.2 in order to calculate ρ^2 and determine a function (6.32). Suppose as before that the principal aggregation is

$$(6.34) \qquad y = r_1q_1 + r_2q_2 + \cdots + r_nq_n$$

and the surrogated aggregation is

$$(6.35) \qquad w = p_1q_1 + p_2q_2 + \cdots + p_nq_n$$

Let $\sigma_1, \sigma_2, \cdots, \sigma_n$ be the standard deviations—the square root of variances—of the variables $q_1, q_2, \cdots, q_n$, respectively, and $\bar{q}_1, \bar{q}_2, \cdots, \bar{q}_n$ be the means of the same variables. Then, we calculate the values of the factors P, Q, and R defined as

$$(6.36) \qquad P = (p_1\sigma_1)^2 + (p_2\sigma_2)^2 + \cdots + (p_n\sigma_n)^2$$

$$(6.37) \qquad Q = (p_1\sigma_1)(r_1\sigma_1) + (p_2\sigma_2)(r_2\sigma_2) + \cdots + (p_n\sigma_n)(r_n\sigma_n)$$

$$(6.38) \qquad R = (r_1\sigma_1)^2 + (r_2\sigma_2)^2 + \cdots + (r_n\sigma_n)^2$$

We shall assume that neither P nor R is zero to avoid a trivial situation. Then ρ^2 and the estimate $\hat{y}$ are

$$(6.39) \qquad \rho^2 = \frac{Q^2}{PR}$$

and

$$(6.40) \qquad \hat{y} = sw + m$$

where

$$(6.41) \qquad\qquad s = Q/P$$

and

$$(6.42) \quad m = (r_1 - sp_1)\bar{q}_1 + (r_2 - sp_2)\bar{q}_2 + \cdots + (r_n - sp_n)\bar{q}_n$$

In the above example, P, Q, and R are calculated as

$$P = (1 \times 2)^2 + (2 \times 3)^2 = 40$$

$$Q = (1 \times 2)(5 \times 2) + (2 \times 3)(3 \times 3) = 74$$

$$R = (5 \times 2)^2 + (3 \times 3)^2 = 181$$

Then, ρ^2, s, and m are

$$\rho^2 = \frac{Q^2}{PR} = \frac{74^2}{40 \times 181} = \frac{5476}{40 \times 181} = \frac{136.9}{181} = 0.756$$

$$s = \frac{74}{40} = 1.85$$

$$m = (5 - 1.85 \times 1) \times 4 + (3 - 1.85 \times 2) \times 5 = 9.1$$

which agree with our previous results.

Before we proceed further, let us give a slightly more complicated example. Suppose that y and w are

$$y = 5q_1 + 26q_2 + 2q_3 - 50q_4 - q_5$$

$$w = 8q_1 - 6q_2 + 10q_3 - 16q_4 + 3q_5$$

and the mean and the standard deviation of each variable are

		q_1	q_2	q_3	q_4	q_5
Mean	$\bar{q}_i$	5	0	-3	10	2
Standard deviation	σ_i	1	2	2	1	3

TABLE 6.3   A Computation of the Aggregation Effectiveness Coefficient II

i	σ_i	p_i	r_i	$p_i\sigma_i$	$r_i\sigma_i$	$(p_i\sigma_i)^2$	$(p_i\sigma_i)(r_i\sigma_i)$	$(r_i\sigma_i)^2$	$\bar{q}_i$	$r_i - sp_i$	$(r_i - sp_i)\bar{q}_i$
1	1	8	5	8	5	64	40	25	5	2.6	13.0
2	2	-6	26	-12	52	144	-624	2704	0	27.8	0.0
3	2	10	2	20	4	400	80	16	-3	-1.0	3.0
4	1	-16	-50	-16	-50	256	800	2500	10	-45.2	-452.0
5	3	3	-1	9	-3	81	-27	9	2	-1.9	-3.8
						945	269	5254			-439.8

$$\rho^2 = \frac{269^2}{945 \times 5254} = \frac{72361}{4965030} \doteq 0.015$$

$$s = \frac{269}{945} \doteq 0.3 \qquad \hat{y} = 0.3w - 439.8$$

Then, ρ^2, s, and m are calculated as in Table 6.3, which shows that w makes only a negligible contribution to reducing the variance of y (reduces by only 1.5 per cent), and thus it is almost useless information for determining the value of y. Actually, it is possible to have $\rho^2 = 0$, in which case w is of no use in identifying the value of y. It can be shown that if $\rho^2 = 0$, $s = 0$ and vice versa. If $s = 0$, y becomes

(6.43) $\hat{y} = m = r_1\bar{q}_1 + r_2\bar{q}_2 + r_3\bar{q}_3 + \cdots + r_n\bar{q}_n = \bar{y}$

and this is precisely what User A would do if he had no information on w.

Let us define ρ to be

(6.44) $$\rho = \frac{Q}{\sqrt{PR}}$$

and call it the *linear aggregation coefficient*. The range of ρ is limited to

(6.45) $-1 \leq \rho \leq 1$

whereas the range of ρ^2 is limited to

(6.46) $0 \leq \rho^2 \leq 1$

Note that $\rho > 0$ if and only if $s > 0$, $\rho = 0$ if and only if $s = 0$, and $\rho < 0$ if and only if $s < 0$ since the numerators of s and ρ are both Q, which can be positive, zero, or negative, while their denominators are always positive. This linear aggregation coefficient is mathematically the same expression as the linear correlation coefficient widely used in statistics. The difference is that the former is defined in a "function space" while the latter is defined in a "data space," the two spaces being the dual of each other. We have avoided mathematical derivation here in the main text. However, in Appendix B, Section 5, we have provided proofs that ρ^2 given by (6.39) actually shows the proportion of the variance of y that is eliminated by the use of w and that $\hat{y}$ given by (6.40) actually minimizes the variance of errors in the estimate. In addition, the mathematical properties of the linear aggregation coefficient are analyzed in a general way, including a discussion on the multiple linear aggregation coefficient, in Appendix B, Sections 1–4. Therefore, interested readers are referred to these appendices for a more rigorous and complete discussion on this topic.

The crucial requirement in applying this linear aggregation coefficient is that each random variable be independent of the rest of the variables, just as each observation must be independent of the rest of observations in applying the linear correlation coefficient. However, if there are interdependences, there may still be a possibility of eliminating them by transforming variables.

3. A MEASURE OF IDENTIFIABILITY

In any case by means of this linear aggregation coefficient, the identifiability of an accounting aggregation is now quantified. Just as the linear correlation coefficient has been playing an important role in quantifying the relationship between two variables, the linear aggregation coefficient will play a vital role in quantifying the degree of identifiability of accounting aggregations. We may set up a standard such as $\rho^2 \geq 0.95$ as a minimum satisfactory level for a given use or for a given user group, and then try to design an accounting aggregation that is satisfactory for a variety of uses.

The above analysis also makes a contribution to the problem of price-level changes. For example, if r_i's represent current market values of assets and p_i's represent historical costs of assets, we may ask how useful the historical cost data are in estimating the market value of assets and what kind of general price-level adjustment is likely to be most useful. The answers are clearly given by the linear aggregation coefficient and the formula for s in (6.41), where s may be considered the most suitable price index for adjusting historical costs to current market values.[13]

It is expected that the linear aggregation coefficient will be used just as much as the linear correlation coefficient in the future, and that there will be many more uses than those stated above. As accountants, who engage in the measurement of economic resources and activities, we must pay attention also to measuring the effectiveness of what we are doing.

---

[13] See Tritschler [1966] for an analysis of index numbers by means of the linear aggregation coefficient.

CHAPTER SEVEN

Objectivity and Reliability
of Accounting Measurement[1]

Having analyzed accounting valuation in the previous chapter in terms of its usefulness in identifying what the user of the information wants to know, we next move on to analyzing accounting measurement in general in terms of objectivity and reliability. Just as we quantified identifiability by the linear aggregation coefficient, we shall try to devise some means of quantifying the degree of objectivity and reliability of accounting measurement by an analogy to the concepts of variance and mean-squared error that have been developed in the area of statistical sampling.

1. THE CONCEPT AND A MEASURE OF OBJECTIVITY

The objectivity (like identifiability) of accounting measurement is usually regarded as an important criterion for choosing among measurement methods. For example, Paton and Littleton [1940, p. 18] states, "Verifiable, objective evidence has therefore become an important element in accounting and a necessary adjunct to the proper execution of the accounting function of supplying dependable information." Similarly, Moonitz [1961, p. 41] writes, "Changes in assets and liabilities, and the related effects (if any) on revenues, expenses, retained earnings, and the like, should not be given

---

[1] This chapter was reproduced from Ijiri and Jaedicke [1966a] with minor modifications. See the preface.

133

formal recognition in the accounts earlier than the point of time at which they can be measured in objective terms." Still another example, Fertig [1966, p. 137] states, "The importance of objectivity (i.e., absence of bias) in accounting measurements is easily established . . . . Accounting statements are useful only to the extent that their objectivity can be demonstrated to the satisfaction of the user."

In spite of fairly common agreement that objectivity is important as a criterion, there is a surprising lack of agreement on just what the concept should mean and how it should be applied. On one hand, Moonitz [1961, p. 41] defines objective evidence as being subject to verification by a competent investigator. Thus the measures have a meaning separate and apart from the measurer. Paton and Littleton's [1940, p. 18] definition of objectivity is similar to Moonitz'. However, Arnett [1961] points out that the recognition that some useful measures are not objective has caused a loosening of the strict definition of objectivity as expressed by Moonitz and by Paton and Littleton. He concludes that ". . . data still needs to be impersonal in order to be objective. However, 'impersonal' is now much more flexible in its application than under the strict construction." [1961, p. 68.] Fertig [1966, p. 142] joins those who want to broaden the definition of objectivity when he states, ". . . we must be able to say that a given measurement method is sufficiently objective for accounting purposes only if it fulfills the accounting objective as indicated by the definition of financial position and earnings." Of course, at the extreme, there are accountants who contend that if the measure is useful, further justification is unnecessary. (See for example, McFarland [1961, p. 29].) This latter viewpoint advocates dropping objectivity as a criterion for at least some accounting measures.

Objectivity as a property of accounting measurement does have appeal. However, it is a difficult concept to define and in some cases leads to confusion and disagreement. In general the term *objective* is understood to mean existing outside of the mind, having a separate or independent existence. In other words, objectivity refers to external reality independent of the persons who perceive it. However, the precise nature of the separate existence of external reality is not clear, especially as it relates to accounting. For example, what is meant by the objective income figure of a given firm for a given period? If the above definition is used, it must be something that exists separately from and independently of the accountants who measure it. Although it may be convenient to assume the existence of such an objective income figure, it is impossible to ascertain what this value is without going through the mental processes of the accountants who made the measure.

Therefore, rather than basing the definition of objectivity on the existence of objective factors that are independent of persons who perceive them, it is far more realistic to define objectivity simply as the *consensus* among a given group of observers or measurers. For example, we can say that the amount of cash in a box can be measured more objectively than the annual income of a firm. That is, if we asked a group of accountants to measure both the cash in the box and the income of the firm we would expect a higher degree of consensus on the former measure than on the latter.[2]

We will elaborate on the precise nature of consensus as applied to accounting by a model of measurement. The three factors involved in measurement are 1) an object whose property is to be measured; 2) a measurement system which consists of a set of rules and instruments; and 3) a measurer. These three factors collectively produce a quantity called a measure. (See Figure 7.1.)[3] If the measurement rules in the system are specified in detail, we expect the results to show little deviation from measurer to measurer. On the other hand, if the measurement rules are vague or poorly stated, then the implementation of the measurement system will require judgment on the part of the measurer; hence the output of the measurement system is more likely to show wider deviation from measurer to measurer. In other words, the measurement system and the measurer's judgment are complementary. The degree of objectivity of the measurement system is thus determined by the degree of consensus in the results (output) or the degree to which the output of the system depends on the measurer.

The degree of consensus depends not only on the measurement system but also on the objects whose properties are to be measured. For example, given two systems for measuring income, the first may result in a greater degree of consensus when the income of service firms is the object of mea-

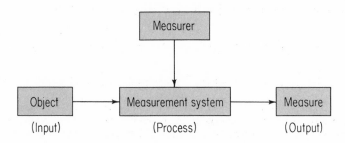

Fig. 7.1.   A Measurement Process

[2] This definition of objectivity agrees with that normally held by accountants' i.e., verifiability by an independent party, if we interpret the independent party to mean a representative of a given group of accountants. See, for example, the above quotations from Moonitz. See also American Accounting Association [1966], which considers verifiability as one of the four accounting standards.

[3] Notice that compared with our analysis in Chapter 1, this analysis emphasizes the behavioral aspect of measurement by introducing a new factor, measurers, into the measurement process.

surement; the second may result in a greater degree of consensus when the income of manufacturing firms is being measured. This could happen because the first measurement system contains vague measurement rules for inventory, which shows up as a lack of objectivity (consensus) when inventory becomes important.

Furthermore, the objectivity of a measurement system depends upon a particular group of measurers. For example, in measuring the income of a firm, a group of experts in accounting will produce a higher degree of consensus than a group of laymen. That is, accounting education tends to homogenize the way in which a group will measure income. In such a case, an income figure which is highly objective from the viewpoint of the experts may be much less objective to the laymen. Therefore, in defining the objectivity of a measurement system, we must specify which group of measurers (which reference group) we are concerned with.

Finally, another important point to be noted here is that objectivity is not a black-or-white issue. There are various degrees of objectivity and we should argue whether one measure is more objective (or less objective) than another and not whether a measure is objective or not. We shall, therefore, elaborate on how the degree of objectivity can be measured. Let us consider a group of n measurers who are asked to measure a given object, such as income of a given firm for a given period, under a specified measurement system. Let x_i be the quantity that the ith measurer $(i = 1, 2, \cdots, n)$ reports by using the specified measurement system. We are now concerned with the degree of unanimity or the degree of variability of x_i's. One commonly used statistical measure of the variability of a set of observations is the variance. We may, therefore, use this as an indicator of the degree of objectivity of the given measurement system in measuring the given object. Namely, objectivity V may be defined to be

$$(7.1) \qquad V = \frac{1}{n}[(x_1 - \bar{x})^2 + (x_2 - \bar{x})^2 + \cdots + (x_n - \bar{x})^2]$$

where $\bar{x}$ is the average of x_i's for all measurers in the reference group.[4]

[4] See Chapter 6 for a computational example of a variance. Obviously, there are many other ways of measuring the variability of observations. For example, we may see the average of $| x_i - \bar{x} |$ instead of $(x_i - \bar{x})^2$. Rel-variance—the variance divided by the square of the mean $V/\bar{x}^2$—is another common measure of variability used in statistics. Its advantage is that it does not depend upon the measurement unit of the x_i's, although difficulty arises as the mean $\bar{x}$ comes closer to zero. Another possibility is the use of the quantity $Pr[| x - \theta | \leq \epsilon]$, i.e., the probability that a measure does not deviate from some preferred or desired value θ by more than a given amount ϵ which is positive. See also the definition of "validation" in Kohler [1952] as well as the use of the Pareto-optimality criterion as a property of accounting measurement, which is discussed in Charnes and Cooper [1966b, p. 10]. Finally, see Churchill's characterization of the objectivity-independence relationship in an auditing context discussed in Churchill [1962] and Churchill and Teitelbaum [1960].

Next, we must note the fact that the above measure of variability depends upon a particular object. We must find a way to state the degree of objectivity of a measurement system independently of a particular object. This may be done by considering a set of all objects that are to be measured under the system and taking an average (weighted, if necessary) of the above measure associated with each object in the set.

One final remark before we move on to the discussion of reliability. If a measure is a highly objective one, it is irrelevant who in the group has actually measured it since most of the people would have produced an identical (or a similar) result. This is the virtue of objectivity. That is, the measure is relatively free of the personal feelings or prejudice of the measurer if it is objective. Therefore, the decision maker can use the measure without being concerned about who the measurer was.[5]

However, this does not mean that objectivity is the same as usefulness. For example, a highly objective measure, such as the cash balance or the number of shares of capital stock, may not be so useful in predicting the future market price of a firm's stock as a highly subjective statement made by the president of the firm giving his forecast of the future stock price. Furthermore, a measure that is very useful for one purpose may not be useful at all for other purposes. Therefore, the usefulness of a measure cannot be determined until a specific use is given, whereas the objectivity of a measure can be determined independently of its use.

2. THE CONCEPT AND A MEASURE OF RELIABILITY

Let us now discuss the reliability of accounting measurement. In general, a system is said to be reliable if it works the way it is supposed to.[6] For example, a barometer is said to be reliable if it reflects accurately the actual barometric pressure since that is what a barometer is supposed to do. Similarly, a reliable man is one who will do what he is supposed to do or, in other words, one who can be "counted on."

However, there is another aspect of reliability which is especially important in accounting measurement. Consider the following question about the barometer: "Is the barometer a reliable indicator of tomorrow's weather?" In this case, the question is not whether the barometer indicates the actual barometric air pressure but whether the barometer reading can be used for predicting tomorrow's weather. This question is more user-

---

[5] See Devine [1962, Chapter 11] for a further analysis of objectivity in accounting in relation to objectivity in other fields of science, as well as the legal approach to evidence.

[6] Reliability is also not a black-or-white issue as we shall see later, but here we are using the term loosely.

oriented. It is the type of question which is of importance in evaluating the reliability of accounting measures.

How can the degree of reliability be determined and measured when the barometer is used for forecasting the weather? Consider a case where the forecaster is simply interested in forecasting whether it is going to rain or not, i.e., the prediction contains two categories, fair and rain. Similarly, suppose the barometer has only two readings, one for fair and the other for rain, instead of a more detailed calibration. If the barometer points to Fair, the forecaster expects the weather tomorrow to be fair, and if the barometer points to Rain, he expects rain.

On the other hand, the relationship can be reversed. That is, if it is fair today the expectation is that the barometer reading yesterday was Fair; if it rains today, the expectation is that the barometer reading yesterday was Rain. If, on the contrary, yesterday's reading was Rain and today is fair, or if the reading yesterday was Fair and today is rainy, the barometer gave the wrong indication. If this occurs many times, the barometer is considered unreliable for predicting the weather.

The degree of reliability of the barometer when used for predicting the weather may, therefore, be measured by the proportion of the total readings which were "right." Likewise the degree of unreliability can be measured by the proportion of readings which were "wrong." This relationship is shown in diagram form in Table 7.1 and Figure 7.2.

TABLE 7.1   Barometer Reading and Actual Weather

		ACTUAL WEATHER TODAY	
		Fair	Rain
BAROMETER READING YESTERDAY	Fair	Right	Wrong
	Rain	Wrong	Right

If the above concept of reliability is to be used in accounting, the simple "right-or-wrong" classifications must be replaced by a detailed classification by introducing a finer calibration (or measurement). This can be done in the barometer example by using a method similar to the one used in dealing with objectivity. That is, reliability can be thought of as the degree of closeness to being right. However, there is one difference: the degree of closeness to "being right" depends primarily upon the way the person uses the indicator (barometer reading).[7] This is something that

---

[7] We had the same problem in defining the degree of closeness to being perfect when dealing with accounting valuation in the previous chapter. The degree of closeness to being perfect depends upon both the user's principal aggregations and the accountant's surrogated aggregation.

was not observed in the discussion of objectivity. In fact, the point was made that the degree of objectivity can be measured independently of the manner in which the measure was to be used.

The relation between the reliability of the measure and the manner in which the person uses the measure can be seen by further examination of the barometer example. Assume, for example, that a forecaster wants to use the barometer reading for predicting the amount of rain for the following day. In doing so he creates in his own mind (perhaps from past experiences) a relationship between today's barometer reading and the amount of rain tomorrow. However, this relationship may not coincide exactly with the actual relationship between today's barometer reading

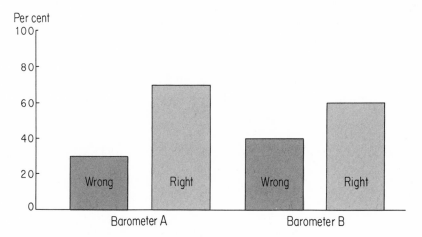

Fig. 7.2.   The Degree of Reliability of Barometers: Barometer A is more reliable than Barometer B

and tomorrow's rainfall. For example, assume that the actual and the forecaster's relationships are as given in Figure 7.3. If the barometer reading is b, the forecaster would predict the amount of rainfall to be r. If the barometer reading is b' then r' amount of rain would be predicted. However, the actual relationship between the barometer reading and the rainfall is given by the line A. That is, if the reading is b the actual amount of rainfall is r'', and if the reading is b' the actual amount of rainfall is r.

In spite of the actual relationship, if the actual amount of rainfall is r, a right barometer reading from the forecaster's viewpoint is b and not b'. That is, if the actual amount of today's rainfall is r, the forecaster alleges that yesterday's barometer reading should have been b and not b'. Let b (in this example) be called the *alleged value* since it depends on the manner in which the forecaster uses the barometer reading for predicting rainfall.

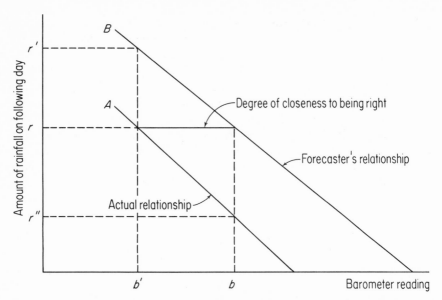

Fig. 7.3. Actual and Forecaster's Relationships Between Today's Barometer Reading and Tomorrow's Rainfall

In the above example, the set of alleged values for various values of r (the rainfall) is represented by the line B. The degree of closeness to being right is then represented by the difference between b and b'. As we did in deriving the objectivity measure, we may use this difference as a basis for the reliability measure, and by taking a suitable "representative" value of such differences at various levels of rainfall we can define the reliability measure of the barometer.

Let us now consider the problem of reliability in terms of accounting measurement. For a user of accounting data, the accounting measure is only a means to an end (i.e., a surrogate). In other words, a user is only interested that the measure gives data which are helpful in his decision process. To make the argument more concrete, let the variable y be a factor which the decision maker wants to determine or predict based on the accounting measure. For example, the variable y may be the price of the firm's stock at a certain point in the future; or, y may be the dividend that the firm will pay at the end of the year; or, y may represent the annual income of the firm during the next five years. Of course, it is also possible for y to represent an event which has occurred in the past, such as the amount of income tax paid in the previous period, the amount of total sales during the last two years.

Now, let x be the output of the accounting measurement which results from the application of a particular set of measurement rules. A decision maker uses x only if he thinks he can determine the value of the variable y from it. In deriving the value of y from the value of x, the user develops a formula (or a function) by which he can associate the two variables. This is done through his experience or by education. That is, he may learn the relationship between the variables x and y by observing the values for a number of past periods, or he may be taught the relationship between the two. In any event, y and x are related by some function such as $y = f(x)$.

To illustrate, assume that a decision maker is interested in the amount of future dividend per share of stock. He has discovered that the dividend in time period $t + 1$ is usually about one-half the per-share income reported in time period t. Thus, he uses the relationship

$$y = 0.5x$$

where y is the expected per-share dividend in time $t + 1$ and x is the per-share income reported in time period t, calculated by using a certain specified set of accounting measurement rules. If income reported in time period t is \$10, the decision maker, using his relationship $y = 0.5x$, would estimate the per-share dividend in time period $t + 1$ to be \$5. Once a user of accounting data develops his own function f, he expects (and hopes) that the relationship between x and y will be stable during future periods.

If, in the above example, the dividend for time period $t + 1$ actually turns out to be \$4 when reported income for time period t is \$10, this event decreases the degree of his reliance upon the reported per-share income in estimating the future dividend. If the dividend turns out to be \$4, the decision maker may say that the reported per-share income should have been \$8. In other words, he alleges that the reported per-share profit should have been \$8 now that the dividend on the stock is \$4. This is the alleged value given his decision function and given that the actual dividend was \$4. We may use this difference between the actual value (\$10) and the alleged value (\$8) as a basis for a reliability measure in the following manner.

We introduce the fact that the actual value (\$10) depends upon the measurers. Under a given set of measurement rules one accountant may derive \$12 as the income figure and another accountant may give \$8. Therefore, we must average the differences between the actual value and alleged value over all measurers in the reference group in the same manner as in the case of the objectivity measure. Since we used the average of the square of the difference between the value derived by the measurer (x_i) and the mean of the values derived by all measurers $(\bar{x})$ in defining the objectivity measure, we shall use the average of the square of the difference between the value derived by the measurer (x_i) and the alleged value (x^*)

in defining the reliability measure R.[8] Namely

$$(7.2) \qquad R = \frac{1}{n}[(x_1 - x^*)^2 + (x_2 - x^*)^2 + \cdots + (x_n - x^*)^2]$$

This formula is exactly the same as the one for mean-squared error,[9] another measure commonly used in statistics.[10]

Since the above reliability measure depends upon a particular object to be measured, we must apply the same averaging method as the one explained in connection with the objectivity measure in order to derive an expression for the reliability of a measurement system.[11]

3. THE RELATIONSHIP BETWEEN OBJECTIVITY AND RELIABILITY

Now notice the similarity and the difference between the measure of reliability (7.2) and the measure of objectivity (7.1). The degree of reliability of an accounting measurement system depends upon how close the actual measures (x_i's) are to the alleged value (x^*), whereas the degree of objectivity depends upon how close the actual measures (x_i's) are to the mean value ($\bar{x}$). A comparison of (7.1) and (7.2) shows this essential difference.

Let us take the difference between R and V as given by (7.2) and (7.1), respectively. We then have

$$(7.3) \qquad R - V = \frac{1}{n}[d_1 + d_2 + \cdots + d_n]$$

[8] This definition of reliability is not the same as the one often used in measurement in psychology. See, e.g., Ghiselli [1964], where reliability is defined by means of parallel tests and the reliability coefficient is discussed. See also Nunnally [1959].

[9] See our analysis in Chapter 6. See also the distinction between precision and accuracy made in Cochran and Cox [1957, p. 16]. Our objectivity notion corresponds to precision and our reliability notion corresponds to accuracy. There, accuracy is measured by means of the deviation from a "true value."

[10] Both the objectivity measure V given by (7.1) and the reliability measure R given by (7.2) actually indicate the degree of "subjectivity" and the degree of "unreliability." That is, the degree of objectivity (or reliability) of the measurement system becomes greater as V (or R) becomes smaller. Conversely, larger values for V (or R) are associated with lower degrees of objectivity (or reliability). The measurement system is perfectly objective if $V = 0$ and is perfectly reliable if $R = 0$.

[11] We may also consider a distribution of x^* based on various uses of the measure or various users of the measure and apply the same averaging method to derive a reliability for a given set of uses or users.

where

$$(7.4) \qquad d_i = (x_i - x^*)^2 - (x_i - \bar{x})^2 \qquad \text{for } i = 1, 2, \cdots, n$$

This expression for d_i may be simplified to

$$(7.5) \quad d_i = x_i^2 - 2x_i x^* + x^{*2} - x_i^2 + 2x_i\bar{x} - \bar{x}^2 = 2x_i(\bar{x} - x^*) - (\bar{x}^2 - x^{*2})$$

Hence if we calculate d_i by (7.5) for $i = 1, 2, \cdots, n$ and add them together, we obtain

$$(7.6) \quad d_1 + d_2 + \cdots + d_n$$

$$= 2(x_1 + x_2 + \cdots + x_n)(\bar{x} - x^*) - n(\bar{x}^2 - x^{*2})$$

$$= 2n\bar{x}(\bar{x} - x^*) - n(\bar{x}^2 - x^{*2}) = 2n\bar{x}^2 - 2n\bar{x}x^* - n\bar{x}^2 + nx^{*2}$$

$$= n\bar{x}^2 - 2n\bar{x}x^* + nx^{*2} = n(\bar{x} - x^*)^2$$

Therefore, we have $R - V = (\bar{x} - x^*)^2$ or if we define $B = (\bar{x} - x^*)^2$

$$(7.7) \qquad\qquad\qquad R = V + B$$

Thus, the degree of reliability is the degree of objectivity plus a term B, which may be called a *reliance bias* or simply a *bias*. This means that R is always greater than or equal to V. R is equal to V if and only if the alleged value is equal to the mean of all measured values. Although several parts of the method would have to be more precisely specified to make it practically operational (such as how to choose the set of accounting measurers), (7.7) is an interesting and highly useful way to conceptualize the essential relationship between objectivity and reliability. These relationships are discussed below in detail.[12]

The concept of reliability is not independent of the concept objectivity as (7.7) shows. If the bias factor B can be held constant, the degree of reliability can be improved by improving the degree of objectivity. This is

---

[12] In the above discussion, it is assumed that the alleged value is unique for each object that is measured. If it is not unique, we may define the bias factor B to be the smallest value of $(x - x^*)^2$ among all alleged values x^*'s of a given object, or we may take into account the probability distribution of x^*'s. See Footnote 11 for this chapter.

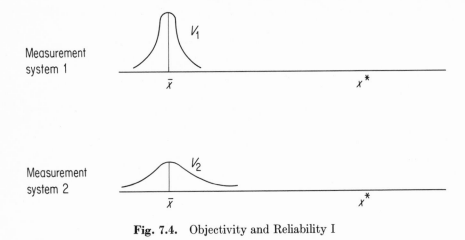

Fig. 7.4. Objectivity and Reliability I

shown in Figure 7.4. Measurement System 1 is more reliable than System 2 since the bias $B = (\bar{x} - x^*)^2$ is the same for both methods but the variance for System 1, V_1, is larger than the variance for System 2, V_2.

On the other hand, (7.7) shows that the most objective measure is not necessarily the most reliable. This is so because the measurement system with the higher degree of objectivity (smaller V) may have a mean $\bar{x}$ which is quite far from the alleged value. Therefore, $V + B$ may be greater for a system with a small V than for a system where V is large but $(\bar{x} - x^*)^2$ is very small. This is shown in Figure 7.5. System 4 is more

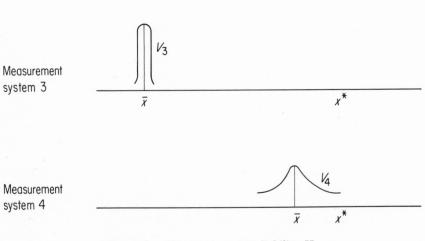

Fig. 7.5. Objectivity and Reliability II

reliable than System 3 despite the fact that $V_4 > V_3$, i.e., System 4 is less objective than System 3.[13]

If there is any misunderstanding on the part of the accountant as to what the user of the accounting data needs and wants, the mean of the reported values $(\bar{x})$ may be quite far from the alleged value (x^*). Even though the degree of objectivity of a measurement method can be determined independently of the use of the measure, it does not make sense to think of the degree of reliability of an accounting measure without studying how the measure will be used, how well the user understands the accounting process by which the measure is made, and (above all) how, in reality, the variable x (the reported value) is related to the variable y, which is of primary interest to the user of the data.

4. HOW TO IMPROVE THE RELIABILITY OF ACCOUNTING MEASUREMENT

In summary, the reliability of accounting measurement was defined as the degree of objectivity plus a bias factor. This relationship shows that the degree of objectivity can be measured without regard for the use of the measure but reliability cannot because the bias depends on the alleged value, which in turn is related to the particular use of the measure.

This conceptual relationship, which depends on the variance of measurement observations from their mean and the distance of this mean from the alleged value, gives valuable insights into some of the possible steps which can be taken by the members of the accounting profession to improve the reliability of accounting measurement. Accountants ought to cooperate to the fullest possible extent with the users of accounting data to search for and define those factors or quantities which will be useful in decision processes. Accountants must then undertake to develop accounting measures that will give good predictions of these decision variables. Furthermore, accountants should attempt to educate users of accounting data as well as to be educated in the manner described above. If users of accounting data can be more effectively educated, they might change their function for relating x and y, and this change could result in decreasing the bias and

---

[13] For years, the advocates of, for example, market values have been urging a trade-off between usefulness and objectivity in favor of usefulness. In fact, it is usually agreed that the key problem in the selection of accounting methods is to achieve the proper balance between objectivity and usefulness. (See, for example, Sprouse, [1964, p. 65].) To the extent that reliability constitutes an important part of usefulness (materiality and timeliness of the data are also important), (7.7) is an effective way to characterize this trade-off using the statistical concept of variance and mean-squared error.

improving reliability. Hence, reliability is definitely a two-way street. The reliability of a measure might be improved by changing the measurement system; on the other hand, reliability may be improved by changing the manner in which the output from the system is used. The attempts by the 1964 Concepts and Standards Committees to include holding gains and losses in financial reports may be considered an attempt to improve the reliability of an accounting measure by reducing the bias factor, even though the new measure may also worsen the degree of objectivity (hopefully, to a lesser extent).[14]

On the other hand, the degree of reliability can be improved by operating on the degree of objectivity. Hence, accountants should constantly try to improve the degree of objectivity if the bias does not increase at a faster rate than the improvement in objectivity. Once the accounting profession finds which alleged values are to be measured, the degree of objectivity might be improved by establishing and more fully specifying a set of accounting measurement principles and procedures. These principles and procedures would, hopefully, produce measures which are less dependent on the measurer than they are in the situation we now have.

We must note that objectivity per se should not be the sole criterion for selecting accounting measurement systems. On the other hand, it is nearsighted to say that objectivity should be discarded altogether in favor of a vague and poorly defined notion of "usefulness." The degree of reliability (which encompasses objectivity) is the important criterion and it will ultimately determine the extent to which the decision-making public will accept and use accounting measures.

[14] See American Accounting Association, Committee on Concepts and Standards—Long-Lived Assets [1964, pp. 693–99] and American Accounting Association, 1964 Concepts and Standards Research Study Committee [1965, pp. 312–22].

CHAPTER EIGHT

A Behavioral Analysis of Accounting Measurement and Decision Making[1]

In the previous two chapters we have considered a decision-making process as given (e.g., the principal aggregation as given in Chapter 6 or the alleged value as given in Chapter 7) and considered accounting measurement with respect to this given decision process. This is a passive aspect of accounting measurement in relation to decision making since the former is simply subordinate to the latter. In this present chapter, however, we will investigate an active aspect of accounting measurement in relation to decision making and see how accounting measurement can influence decision making rather than vice versa. The relationship between measurement and uses of measures is a dual process as discussed in Chapter 1, hence the relationship between accounting measurement and decision making must be analyzed from both angles, active and passive.

1. PREVIOUS STUDIES

Accountants have become increasingly interested in understanding accounting in relation to the entire business decision process. They have

[1] A portion of this chapter was reproduced from part of Ijiri, Jaedicke, and Knight [1966] with some modifications. See the preface.

questioned such factors as the role of accounting in the complex process of decision making in business and what effects, if any, different accounting methods[2] have on this decision process. Research has been aimed at finding out whether decisions made in an organization can be influenced by changing its accounting system.

Until recently, discussions of alternative accounting methods have been directed primarily toward how outputs from accounting systems differ when different accounting methods are used. We know that in many cases, FIFO and LIFO result in different inventory values and hence produce different profit figures even though the firms operate in an identical business environment. But a more important question is whether these different profit figures affect managers' decisions and, if so, under what conditions. Unless we can show that the different figures (or, more precisely, different patterns of figures) lead to different decisions under a given set of conditions, there is no point in arguing the merits or demerits of alternative accounting methods.

Some recent studies have been directed toward understanding how differences in the data affect the behavior of the users. Bonini [1963] has simulated business activity based on some assumptions about how business managers behave and has found that a firm with the LIFO inventory method tends to generate more profit under given conditions than a firm with the average cost method of inventory valuation. The reasoning behind this finding is that the LIFO inventory method increases the variability of profits from period to period more than does the average cost inventory method, and hence it stimulates more attention and pressures by managers toward better profit.

On the other hand, the experimental study by Bruns [1962] leads to contradictory conclusions. He found that there is no apparent relationship between inventory valuation methods and managers' decisions on selling price, promotion, production volume, etc. An even more recent experiment by Dyckman [1964] also led to the same conclusions.

Although these studies raise significant questions about the behavioral problem in accounting, it is difficult to derive general statements from the results. We cannot conclude from Bonini's study that the LIFO method should be preferred to the average cost method of inventory valuation because the former tends to generate higher levels of profits; nor can we conclude from Bruns's study or Dyckman's study that inventory valuation methods have no effect on business decisions. Accounting variations may have significant effects under some conditions and may have no effect

---

[2] More specifically, different accounting measurement methods since we are primarily interested in the measurement aspects of accounting. However, we shall use the term different or alternative accounting methods for simplicity and so that the following analysis may be applied to nonmeasurement aspects of accounting, namely, to accounting language in general.

under other conditions. The basic problem with these studies is that we cannot generalize from a single case.

Therefore, an even more important question than whether different accounting methods have any effect upon decisions is: Under what conditions do variations in accounting methods produce different decisions? In order to answer these questions, we need, in addition to empirical studies, a theoretical clarification of the mechanism by which an accounting process and a decision process are related. This chapter develops a theoretical analysis of the relationship between the two and then uses it to study the effect of accounting alternatives on management decisions.

2. THREE VARIABLES IN A DECISION PROCESS

A decision process in general involves essentially three basic variables: 1) an environmental variable, 2) a decision variable, and 3) a payoff variable. A decision maker has no control over an environmental variable, at least at the time of his decision. He takes it as given. A decision variable is his decision, which he determines based on his own choice. A payoff variable is his reward—the objective he wants to attain or optimize.

For example, in a pricing decision by a gasoline station operator, the price that his competitors will charge is his environmental variable, the price he charges is his decision variable, and his profit is his payoff variable. In an investment decision, the expected cash flow to and from the project is the environmental variable, the investor's decision (invest or not invest) is the decision variable, and the profit from the project is the payoff variable. In a production decision, the expected demand is the environmental variable, the production volume is the decision variable, and the unit production cost is the payoff variable.

If we let x be an environmental variable, y be a decision variable, and z be a payoff variable, they are related to each other, or more precisely, the decision maker thinks they are related to each other, in a certain manner. Among all possible combinations of values of x, y and z, the decision maker thinks only a subset of such a set of combinations is actually feasible.

For example, in the pricing decision of a gasoline station operator, suppose his profit is determined as shown in Table 8.1 depending upon his

TABLE 8.1   A Payoff Matrix

HIS COMPETITOR'S PRICE (x)

		30c	35c
HIS PRICE (y)	30c	$100	$200
	35c	$ 50	$300

HIS DAILY PROFIT (z)

price and his competitor's price. If he charges 35¢ a gallon for gasoline and his competitor charges 35¢ a gallon, his daily profit is $300. However, if his competitor charges 30¢ when his price is 35¢, his competitor takes most of the business and his profit is reduced to $50. On the other hand, if he charges 30¢ when his competitor's price is 35¢, he takes most of the business but his profit amounts to only $200 because of the lower margin. Finally, if both charge 30¢, his profit is $100 a day. This is summarized in Table 8.1, which is called a payoff matrix.[3] Stating the matter differently, he considers the following set of triplets feasible combinations of values of the three variables, assuming that prices must be set either at 30¢ or at 35¢.

$$(8.1) \quad P = (\, \langle 30, 30, 100 \rangle, \; \langle 35, 30, 200 \rangle, \; \langle 30, 35, 50 \rangle, \; \langle 35, 35, 300 \rangle)$$

In these triplets, the first elements represent his competitor's prices in cents per gallon of gasoline, the second elements represent his prices in cents, and the third elements represent his daily profit in dollars. He does not consider such combinations as $\langle 30, 30, 200 \rangle$, $\langle 35, 30, 50 \rangle$ feasible from his pricing decision standpoint. We shall refer to a set of triplets such as that in (8.1) as a *feasible relation*.[4] Such a feasible relation provides a basis for a rational decision. Of course, in an actual situation, such a feasible relation may not be written down for a decision maker, but he will still have some idea of what it is.

The three variables in a feasible relation may be characterized in several ways. First, the payoff variable represents a factor the decision maker wants to influence by changing his decision variable. In other words, the decision variable is a means while the payoff variable is an end in this decision process, and the decision maker assumes they are related to each other in a certain manner, represented by the environmental variable. (See Figure 8.1.) In this case, the feasible relation in (8.1) may be stated as

$$(8.2) \quad \begin{aligned} P &= (\, \langle 30, 100 \rangle, \; \langle 35, 50 \rangle) && \text{if } x = 30 \\[2mm] P &= (\, \langle 30, 200 \rangle, \; \langle 35, 300 \rangle) && \text{if } x = 35 \end{aligned}$$

where the first element in the pair of numbers represents the price (the

---

[3] See, e.g., Luce and Raiffa [1957] on payoff matrices and other related topics in game theory. See also Jeffrey [1965], Chernoff and Moses [1959], etc. for the decision theory and the use of Baysian strategies.

[4] See Chapter 1 and Appendix A for more detailed discussions on relations.

decision variable) and the second element represents the profit (the payoff variable).

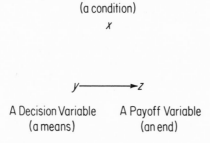

An Environmental Variable
(a condition)

x

y ——→ z

A Decision Variable   A Payoff Variable
(a means)   (an end)

Fig. 8.1.   A Means-Ends Relationship

Another way of looking at the relationship among the three variables is to consider the environmental variable and the payoff variable as being related by causal relationship and to regard the decision variable as a way of influencing this relationship. (See Figure 8.2.) In this case, the

A Decision Variable
(a choice)

y

x ——→ z

An Environmental Variable   A Payoff Variable
(a cause)   (an effect)

Fig. 8.2.   A Causal Relationship

feasible relation in (8.1) may be stated as

(8.3)
$$P = (\,\langle 30, 100 \rangle, \langle 35, 200 \rangle\,) \qquad \text{if } y = 30$$

$$P = (\,\langle 30, 50 \rangle, \langle 35, 300 \rangle\,) \qquad \text{if } y = 35$$

where the first element is the value of x and the second element is the value of z. Since the cause-and-effect notion is a relative matter, a payoff variable in one decision may be an environmental variable in another decision and vice versa. For example, production volume may be an environmental variable in a sales decision, but it may be a payoff variable in a production decision. Actually, the three variables in a decision represent only a segment of a complicated causal network (such as discussed in Chapter 2) which may be written

$$(8.4) \qquad \begin{matrix} y_1 & y_2 & y_3 & & y_{n-1} \\ \downarrow & \downarrow & \downarrow & & \downarrow \\ x_1 \rightarrow & x_2 \rightarrow & x_3 \rightarrow & \cdots & \rightarrow x_n \end{matrix}$$

Here, the causal network is represented by a causal chain to simplify our illustration. The variable x_n represents the decision maker's ultimate goal. Then in any segment

$$\begin{matrix} y_i \\ \downarrow \\ x_i \rightarrow x_{i+1} \end{matrix}$$

x_i represents the cause of an effect x_{i+1}, where the relationship between the two is affected by the choice of a value of y_i. (In some segments, there may be no decisions involved.) Note that x_i's, which represent both environmental variables and payoff variables, are something that the decision maker has no direct control over. He can influence them only by the choice of values of y_i's.

Finally, there is a third way of looking at a feasible relation P—by selecting a combination of an environmental variable x and a decision variable y so that the payoff variable is optimized. In the above example

$$(8.5) \qquad P = (\langle 30, 30 \rangle, \langle 35, 35 \rangle) \text{ under optimum } z$$

which states that the gasoline station operator should charge 30¢ when his competitor charges 30¢ and should charge 35¢ when his competitor charges 35¢. This viewpoint may be represented by Figure 8.3.

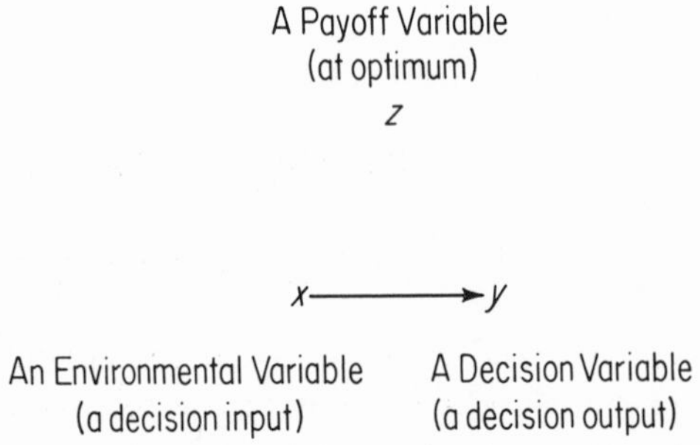

A Payoff Variable
(at optimum)
z

$x \longrightarrow y$

An Environmental Variable   A Decision Variable
(a decision input)   (a decision output)

Fig. 8.3. A Decision Input-Output Relationship

3. THE RELATIONSHIP BETWEEN AN ACCOUNTING PROCESS AND A DECISION PROCESS

Having analyzed the factors involved in a decision process, we now move on to an accounting process. Suppose that Decision Maker A is placed in a room isolated from his environment with three telephone lines connecting the room to the environment. The first line is used to inform A of the current value of the environmental variable x. The second line is used for A to report the value of his decision variable y to his environment. Finally, the third line is used to inform A of the resulting value of the payoff variable z. Let us denote by x', y', and z' representations of x, y, and z, respectively. As we discussed in Chapter 1, x, y, and z are principals in the sense that these are what A is concerned with in making the decision. However, as we shall see later, for some reason he is unable to operate with principals; therefore, he relies upon surrogates x', y', and z', which represent these principals. Thus, A is concerned not with the sounds of telephone conversations per se but rather with what is represented by these sounds.

Using these principals and surrogates, we depict the decision process involving surrogates in Figure 8.4. The inner triangle represents what is going on inside the room and the outer triangle represents what is going on outside the room. The dashed lines represent causal links that exist in the environment. In other words, z is actually produced as a result of x and y jointly. However, for Decision Maker A, the causal links are replaced by the solid lines since what he observes is 1) receive x', 2) transmit y', 3) and receive z'. The dotted lines indicate informational causal links which relate principals to surrogates. An accounting process then is the process represented by dotted lines in the diagram.[5] It converts principals into surrogates under a given set of rules. (See our discussion in Chapter 7 on the measurement process.)

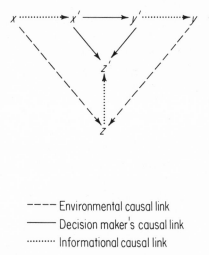

$----$ Environmental causal link

$———$ Decision maker's causal link

$\cdots\cdots$ Informational causal link

Fig. 8.4.   A Decision Process with Surrogates

[5] From the viewpoint of information and communication theory, there are many other important issues that are not discussed here, dealing with coding-decoding, noise, etc. See Wiener [1961], Shannon [1949], etc.

A situation such as this, where surrogates are used in a decision process, is a quite common phenomenon. For example, in the case of the gasoline station operator, he may have to choose his price based on information (a surrogate) on his competitor's price rather than on his competitor's price per se (a principal). In an investment decision, a decision maker would want to rely upon the real cash flow from the project (a principal) if he could do so, but he is forced to rely upon someone's estimate of what the cash flow from the project will be (a surrogate) or, rather on information on the estimate (a surrogate of a surrogate). Also, the gasoline station operator may not be able to identify his real profit, however it may be defined, and may be forced to rely upon a profit reported by an accounting system. Similarly, if it is the objective of a sales manager to increase his sales volume, information on the sales volume is a surrogate of the sales volume per se.

Why does a decision maker use surrogates rather than principals? In Chapter 1 we noted that a surrogate is in general easier to record and communicate to other persons than a principal. Let us explore this point further from the viewpoint of decision making. The situations where a decision maker wants or is forced to use a surrogate rather than a principal may be classified in the following two categories.

Case 1. Difficulty in Obtaining Principals. In many decision-making situation, principals are simply unavailable to decision makers. Business decisions involve many factors which are scattered in time and in space, and it is impossible (literally or practically) for a decision maker to observe everything by himself. In addition, even if a decision maker could obtain principals by himself, it may not be economical (in cost or in time) to do so. For example, a bank manager may be willing to make his lending decision based upon financial statements certified by a C.P.A. even if he is capable of performing an independent investigation of the financial situation of the borrower.

Case 2. Difficulty in Using Principals. A decision maker may be unable to use principals because of lack of technical knowledge or the fact that the principals are too numerous. It is a well-known fact that a human being can use effectively only a limited number of factors in making a decision.[6] If the decision environment is too complicated, the decision maker is likely to prefer to consider simpler factors although he realizes they are only surrogates of what he wants to consider ultimately in his decision process. In addition, even if he is capable of taking into account all principals which are readily available to him, it may not be economical (in cost or in time) to do so. For example, a president of a firm may be able to obtain detailed data on the activities of the firm without too much cost,

---

[6] See, e.g., Simon [1957, pp. 241–260], Garner [1962, pp. 98–137].

but he may want to base his decision upon a summary statement prepared by an accountant because it is not possible for him to use all the details in his firm's operations and environment or it is not worthwhile for him to do so. The use of a representative figure such as mean, median, mode, maximum, minimum, variance of a set of data is an example of the use of a surrogate which reflects the principals in simplified form.

4. DECISION MAKING IN AN ILL-STRUCTURED ENVIRONMENT

We now come to the central issue: What is the effect of an accounting process, represented by the dotted lines in Figure 8.4, upon the behavior of a decision maker who makes decisions based on the accounting data? In discussing the work of a famous Swiss psychologist, Jean Piaget, Carroll [1964, p. 79] states, "The unifying theme in the work of Piaget is the gradual unfolding of the individual's ability to construct an internal 'model' of the universe around him and to perform manipulations on that model so as to draw conclusions about the probable past history of his environment or the probable results of possible actions that could be taken upon that environment. The ability to do this is the essence of all 'thinking' in the nontrivial meanings of the term." In this sense, the causal relationship by means of surrogates x', y', and z', which is represented by the inner triangle in Figure 8.4, provides the decision maker with a model of the actual causal relationship among x, y, and z in the outer triangle in the same figure.

Although there has not been enough convincing evidence in accounting literature that an accounting system does affect the behavior of decision makers, it is a well-accepted fact in linguistics and psychology that language has a material effect upon a man's thinking and even cognition.[7] In this sense, an accounting system provides a means by which a decision maker organizes his experiences and thoughts. Those factors that are recorded and reported in an accounting system tend to get more attention than those that are not recorded in the system. This influence comes essentially from the fact that our environment is complicated and "ill-structured."

Authors who write about the management-decision environment point out the ill-structured nature of the problems that confront business managers. That is, managers face problems for which there is great uncertainty about which alternatives are available and what constitutes an acceptable solution. Leavitt [1964, pp. 352–54] explains that in most managerial situations the decision makers do not have a criterion that enables them to know exactly when they have made the correct decision. One reason for

---

[7] See, for example, Whorf [1956], Carroll [1964], Hall [1959].

the ambiguity is that there is usually a long delay between a decision and the recorded outcome. Also, many other events occur simultaneously in the organization which makes it almost impossible to determine the results of one particular decision. Therefore, as the manager views his world, he is always faced with the question—would another action have worked better? He cannot unambiguously determine the decision rule that he should use.

Recent research describing how people behave in ill-structured or uncertain situations has shed some light on how people probably use accounting data in such situations.[8] The results show that it is unlikely that the person will remain in that situation very long. Instead, he will use his previous experience, available data, friends, etc. to define and structure his situation.[9] This problem is closely related to the one presented in Section 3, where we discussed the limits of the human decision-making capacity. We emphasized that the human mind can handle only a limited amount of information, and that humans simplify their problems by using surrogates—aggregates of a number of principals—or by neglecting some of the principals.

Studies that have described a manager's actual decision-making behavior have indicated that he tries to avoid uncertainty and arrange the environment so that it has a predictable future. This is usually done in an organization by creating and following standard operating procedures, under which roles can be performed "safely."[10] Standard operating procedures define the decision maker's environment and thus remove him from the previously ill-structured situation. We will now show how accounting information is sometimes used to determine a decision maker's standard operating procedures, that is, to define his goals and decision procedures.

We often say that the goal of a business firm is to maximize profit. However, the concept of profit is far from being unambiguous. Therefore, even if a division manager knows that he should maximize profit, he does not know operationally what he should aim for. In this case, an accounting profit provides a means for him to simplify his environment by giving him this information.

Another way that an accounting system determines the goals for a manager is by defining an area for him to pay attention to. For example, assume the accountants suddenly report scrap cost for the first time. The manager now creates a new goal that specifies his objectives in regard to the control of scrap cost. Here, the manager's decision rules change to incorporate the new piece of accounting data. Furthermore, the accounting procedure, in addition to specifying goals or ends for a manager, may also

---

[8] See, for example, Knight [1965], Cyert and March [1963].
[9] Refer to Knight [1965] for further elaboration on this topic.
[10] See Cyert and March [1963].

help him define his means. Thus, if the accountant chooses to report a given set of surrogates, it may provide a basis for the manager's decision in terms of both its means and its ends.[11]

Behavioral science literature describes situations where accounting information has been used in the way we have just described and has been found to influence both the goals of the decision maker and the alternatives which he considers in making his decisions. Ridgeway, studying the problem of accounting measures and behavior in American industry, found that "even where performance measures are instituted purely for purposes of information, they are probably interpreted as definitions of the important aspects of that job. . ."[12] The results of Ridgeway's study directly support the theoretical framework that we have presented in this section.

Additional support for our analysis comes from studies of behavior in Russian industrial firms. They show that when specific performance surrogates are provided, they are used by the decision maker to structure his uncertain world. Smolinski reports, "The project of the Novo Lipetsk steel mill . . . comprises 91 volumes totaling 70,000 pages (one is not surprised to learn that the designers are paid by the sheet . . .). 'Literally everything is anticipated in these blueprints, the emplacement of each nail, lamp or washstand. Only one aspect of the project is not considered at all: its economic effectiveness.' "[13] Smolinski shows that because of the measuring and recording of the number of pages in a report, this surrogate has become a factor that defines the decision maker's world. The decision maker then restricts his goals and alternatives to ones other than those which are most useful for the organization.[14]

In a study of the Russian executive, Granick points out several dramatic shortcomings of a system where pressures result in the decision maker receiving a limited number of performance surrogates which he then uses to determine his goals and alternatives. Granick discusses the standard operating practice of "storming," the phenomenon of getting everything possible out at the end of the month because monthly bonuses are determined by the volume produced.[15] He found that the volume of pro-

---

[11] Scott [1931, p. 264] states, "Accounting and statistical methods are serving as vehicles of the current cultural reorganization because of their characteristic limitation of expression to objective terms."

[12] Ridgeway [1960, p. 377].

[13] Smolinski [1964, p. 604].

[14] Note that many of the arguments in support of transfer pricing have been based on arguments about their psychological advantages or disadvantages. See Hirshleifer [1956] and Dean [1955]. See also Ijiri [1965a], where the degree of divergence between the organizational goal and the goals of its subsystem are analyzed by means of a "goal indicator chart" and a "goal indicator divergence coefficient." See also Whinston [1964] for his analysis of transfer pricing.

[15] Granick [1960, pp. 267–70].

duction was used as a surrogate of other principals that should have been considered by the decision maker in determining his overall effectiveness. The result of the limited accounting data available to Russian managers shows how accounting systems greatly influence the behavior of the decision maker in an ill-structured situation. Phenomena similar to those observed in Russia frequently are found in the United States where surrogates such as direct cost as a percentage of total cost, profit, return on investment are used to define the manager's goals and alternatives. In the examples just described, the choice of an accounting method becomes very important in view of the fact that alternative accounting systems will tend to produce different decisions.

5. A CHANGE IN THE ACCOUNTING PROCESS

Once an accounting measurement system, or, more broadly, an accounting language, is accepted by a decision maker as a means of organizing his decision process, his behavior can be influenced by a change in the accounting method. Psychologists have found so-called *functional fixation* in most human behavior, in which a person attaches a meaning to a title or, more generally, a surrogate, and is unable to see alternative meanings or uses. A person intuitively associates a meaning with a surrogate through his past experiences and often does not recognize that what a surrogate represents depends, in fact, upon the particular moment in time and that it may be significantly different from what it was in the past.[16] Therefore, when a person is placed in a new situation, he uses the surrogate as he has previously.[17] If the outputs from different accounting methods have the same names, such as profit, cost, people who do not understand accounting will tend to neglect the fact that alternative methods may have been used to prepare the outputs. In such cases, a change in the accounting process clearly influences the decisions. We shall call this type of functional fixation *endogenous functional fixation* since it occurs within the mind of the decision maker.

There is another aspect to functional fixation. For example, once ac-

---

[16] As mentioned in Chapter 2, the basis of our predictions and decisions lies in the similarity assumption, i.e., the estimate that unknown phenomena will be similar to those that are known to the decision maker. However, an image that has been formed over many years cannot be changed by just a few new incidents, just as adding a few millionaires does not change the per capita income of a country much. In a sense we are protected from disaster by this slowness of adjustment; otherwise we would probably have to adjust ourselves to a new environment almost minute by minute, without taking full advantage of past experiences.

[17] This phenomenon is discussed by Duncker [1945].

counting data are used in determining standard operating procedures, a division manager may use the data in the same way as before even if a significant change has been made in the accounting system. Suppose he himself knows that he should change his decision rule in order to use the new set of accounting data and is fully capable of doing so, but he sticks to the old rule because he is afraid that his supervisor may not be able to understand the change and may devaluate his performance as a result. Then we have a situation which may be classified as *exogenous functional fixation* since it occurs outside of the mind of the decision maker.

Let us illustrate this by means of a simple accounting example. Suppose that in a consulting firm it is a standard operating procedure to charge a client 300 per cent of the cost of the project, where the cost is strictly based on direct costs. Now suppose that the firm's accounting method has been changed in such a way that the cost of a project includes overhead allocated to the project, which amounts to 100 per cent of the direct cost. Then, under the new cost accounting method, the manager should charge to his clients an amount equal to 150 per cent of the cost of the project. However, he may still keep using the old rule of charging 300 per cent of the cost because he is unable to see an alternative meaning of "costs" (endogenous functional fixation) or because he is afraid that his supervisor may be unable to adjust himself to the change in the accounting system and may blame him for not charging the clients enough (exogenous functional fixation).

In addition to these two types of functional fixation, there are two other conditions under which decisions are influenced by a change in an accounting method. In the first case, a decision maker has no feedback on the change in the accounting method. In order to understand the change and to adjust his decision rule so that the net effect is unchanged, he must be informed of the change or must have some indirect feedback about the change. The use of an auditor to check any significant change in the accounting method is one way to discover that the accounting system is performing differently from the way it is supposed to perform. Stockholders who in their investment decisions use profit figures reported in financial statements are protected by auditors, who report any significant changes in the accounting method used in generating profit figures. In addition, a decision maker may have a number of surrogates which will collectively indicate any irregular performance in the accounting method. Or, an unexpected outcome from a decision may cause him to investigate the accounting method in detail.

It seems almost inconceivable to have a situation in business where a decision maker has absolutely no feedback on the performance of the accounting method. Therefore, it is highly unlikely to have a decision change which results solely from a change in an accounting method which has not been fed back to the decision maker. This is especially true if we exclude a possible short-run effect due to the time lag between the change in the accounting process and the indication of the change to the decision maker.

In the second case, applying an old decision rule to new accounting data may not create much difference in payoff. There are always implicit or explicit costs attached to changing a decision rule and unless the decision maker thinks that there is enough difference in his payoff to justify a change in the decision rule, he will not be willing to do so even if he is fully aware of the change in the accounting method and is capable of adjusting himself to the new method.

Thus, we have observed four cases where a change in the accounting method affects decisions: 1) endogenous functional fixation, 2) exogenous functional fixation, 3) lack of feedback, and 4) little difference in payoffs. An interesting analogy may be made to consumers' brand loyalty. We all know that we as consumers heavily rely upon brand names. We often purchase goods merely by checking their brand names rather than by testing the contents. We do so either because we are incapable of testing the contents as in the case of electric appliances or because it is too much trouble to do so as in the case of some grocery items. (Compare this with our points in Section 3 on the reasons for the use of surrogates.) Now suppose a brewery which has been selling its beer in 12-ounce bottles under the name of Brand A has reduced the content of the bottles to 11 ounces. Since the change is so small, we may not notice it at all. Although the label of the bottle may indicate the content to be 11 ounces, it may be in such fine print that most of us would be unable to read without a magnifying lens (lack of feedback). Or even if we realized that the volume had been reduced to 11 ounces and even if we were unable to tell the difference in taste between Brand A beer and any other beer selling in 12-ounce bottles at the same price as Brand A beer, we may still continue to buy Brand A beer because the change is insignificant (little difference) or because we just have a habit of buying Brand A beer (endogenous functional fixation). Or we may buy Brand A beer for a party because it is generally accepted and preferred, although we ourselves know that it is inferior to other beer, both in quality and in quantity, and we would not buy it for our own consumption (exogenous functional fixation).

All these phenomena may be described as our attempts to simplify our environment. If we can rely upon brand names in judging contents, the regularity helps us simplify this segment of our environment substantially. We become very uncomfortable when we find that this expected regularity does not hold any more, for this means an additional effort on our part to reduce uncertainty regarding the contents of goods. Therefore, we try our best to preserve the regularity that has been created in our mind by finding some excuse for devaluating the significance of events that do not follow the expected regularity. Here we may easily be influenced by someone else. Just as the brewery of Brand A may be able to reduce the volume of beer in bottles to 11 ounces without changing the consumer's purchasing pattern, we may, for example, be able to influence the decisions of a manager who has been applying undesirable decision rules stubbornly by changing the accounting data for his decisions without forcing him to change his rules.

However, it is highly unlikely that such effects will last for a relatively long period of time because of the adaptive mechanism of decision makers. How long the effect will last depends upon the degree of manipulation[18] as well as the adaptation speeds of individuals, which may differ from individual to individual. An analogous situation exists in a number-guessing game in which Person A guesses the next number to be equal to the previous number, while Person B guesses the next number to be equal to the average of the preceding ten numbers. In this case, A can adapt to the changing environment quickly—actually so quickly that he is easily affected by minor disturbances. On the other hand, B is little influenced by minor disturbances in the environment, but the slowness of his adjustment can leave him behind a major trend or cycle. Thus, the speed of adaptation is much faster for A than for B.[19] In general we can say that the speed of adaptation is faster for a younger generation than for an older generation, and is faster for those living in an unstable environment than for those living in a stable environment.[20]

In any case, this adaptive mechanism makes it unlikely that we will

---

[18] Consumers will stop buying if the content of beer bottles is reduced to, for example, 6 ounces while the price of beer is held constant.

[19] But this does not mean A will be more successful in guessing numbers than B. For example, if the number generator consists of a disturbance without any major trend or cycle, where the disturbance is a random number with a finite variance, then it can be shown that B is on the average more successful than A in the sense that B's average of squared errors is smaller than A's. See Chapter 6, Section 2, as well as Appendix B, Section 5, for a discussion of the error of an estimate.

[20] The adaptive mechanism discussed here essentially comes from the similarity assumption elaborated in Chapter 2. We all guess that the future will be similar to the past, but we consider that the near future will be more similar to the recent past than to the remote past because based on our experiences we expect changes in our environment to be gradual. Thus we discount remote past events in estimating the near future, and the discount rate (in the above example, the length of preceding numbers from which the average is calculated) determines the speed of adaptation. We shall not argue where this adaptive mechanism comes from other than referring to Darwin [1859, especially Chapter 4] by saying that those who adapt to the environment will have more chance of surviving. See Ijiri and Simon [1964 and 1967] for an exponential weighting of past experience in the growth of a firm. See also Bush and Mosteller [1955] and Suppes and Atkinson [1960] for a learning model using Markov chain analyses.

be affected by appearances rather than contents for any long period of time if we know what we want to achieve (ends) and how to achieve it (means). It is when the environment is too complicated and too ill-structured for us to handle in a straightforward manner, as is often the case in business, that an accounting system has a lasting effect upon our behavior.

6. THE ACCOUNTANT REACCOUNTED

In Chapter 1, we started our inquiry into the foundations of accounting measurement by looking at it as a representation of the economic events of an entity. In contrast to this passive aspect of accounting, we have now seen its active aspect—how it positively affects the real world. Thus, the two worlds, the real world and the informational world, interact. One is not merely a shadow of the other. The importance of accounting in business should be analyzed within this dual framework. In order to highlight this point, we quote from Sapir [1929, pp. 209–10].

"Human beings do not live in the objective world alone, nor alone in the world of social activity as ordinarily understood, but are very much at the mercy of the particular language which has become the medium of expression for their society. It is quite an illusion to imagine that one adjusts to reality essentially without the use of language and that language is merely an incidental means of solving specific problems of communication or reflection. The fact of the matter is that the 'real world' is to a large extent unconsciously built up on the language habits of the group."

In this regard, the mathematical analyses that have been employed in this book should also be regarded as examples of how a language affects our behavior. We use mathematics to express phenomena in the empirical world. From this standpoint, applied mathematics is a language, although mathematics per se is a discipline and a philosophy. The empirical phenomena are there whether we represent them by mathematics or by ordinary language. The results of mathematical operations on a model constructed as a surrogate of empirical phenomena are by no means guaranteed to be applicable to the empirical phenomena.[21] However, mathematical language forces us to look at the empirical phenomena logically and systematically since, otherwise, they cannot be expressed in mathematical language. Any logical inconsistency in the empirical phenomena is likely to be highlighted when they are represented in a mathematical model,

---

[21] They are guaranteed to work empirically if all the assumptions of the model are satisfied. However, the two statements, "all assumptions of the model hold" and "the results derived from the model are empirically applicable" are, operationally, two expressions of the same thing.

whereas it may never be noticed if they are expressed only in our ordinary language. Complicated phenomena which are difficult to express in ordinary language can be expressed easily and compactly, making it possible for us to analyze the phenomena in more depth and with more precision. We become less reluctant to tackle such phenomena because the language has given us the facility to do so.

In addition, a rich vocabulary of mathematical concepts makes it possible for us to discover new elements or new regularities among the elements in empirical phenomena by means of analogies. For example, we ask, "If this empirical operation corresponds to the mathematical operation $\oplus$ in a field, is there an empirical operation which corresponds to another mathematical operation $\odot$ in the field?" Thus, the translation goes not only from empirical phenomena to mathematical expressions, but also from mathematical expressions to empirical phenomena. Of course, we should not lose the substance by grasping the shadow, but often the shadow helps us grasp the substance.

The same thing may be said of the role of accounting in business. Just as culture affects and is affected by language, business affects and is affected by accounting. In fact, capitalism without accounting is simply inconceivable. (See the quotation from Sombart [1928] in Chapter 5, Footnote 8.) In his satirical article on clothes, *Sartor Resartus* (The Tailor Retailored), Thomas Carlyle states, "Society is founded upon Cloth," and ". . . Man's earthly interests, 'are all hooked and buttoned together, and held up, by Clothes.' " [1834, p. 51]. Indeed, is it not true that business is founded upon accounting? Without accounting where can we hook and button our interests together? Nevertheless, the same injustice that has been done to the tailor (Carlyle [1834, pp. 288–89]) seems to have also been done to the accountant. Somehow the dandy and the decision maker attract more attention than the tailor and the accountant do.

Society should reaccount the accountants and recognize the rich, colorful stream of thought working underneath the voluminous rules and data. It should recognize by whom the interests of the members of the society are organized, protected, and cultivated. It is toward this end that our inquiry into the foundations of accounting measurement has been aimed.

APPENDIX A

An Introduction to
Relational Systems

Here we elaborate the concepts of relational systems and their homomorphism and isomorphism, which were discussed in Chapter 1. Since we start with the basic concept of sets, this appendix is self-contained. Various concepts are organized systematically and examples are provided at the end of each definition to make it easier for readers without background in mathematics to follow. The materials are presented here in the most compact manner, and some important concepts in set theory and mathematical logic which are not directly related to the discussion in other parts of this book have been omitted. Therefore, those who want to study the topics covered in this appendix more intensively and extensively should read such books as Suppes [1957], [1960], Kleene [1952], Robinson [1963], and Curry [1963].

1. SETS

1.1. An *element* is an identifiable object that is to be considered in a discussion.

Examples. a; b; c; d; e.

Remarks. In the following discussion, we shall use these five lower-case letters to represent specific elements.

1.2. A *set* is a collection of distinct elements. An element a is an *element of a set A*, or is a *member of A*, or *belongs to A*, or simply is *in A*, denoted by $a \, \epsilon \, A$, if A contains the element.

Examples. (a, b); (a, d, e); (a, b, c, d, e); (a); $(\ )$. The last example is an empty set. (See 1.6.) If A is a set given by (a, b), a is an element of the set A and so is b, but c is not an element of the set A.

Remarks. The order in which elements of a set appear in a description of the set is irrelevant. Therefore, (a, b) and (b, a) are different ways of describing the same set. (See the equality of sets in 1.5.) (a, a) is not allowed to be a description of a set since the two elements are not distinct. (The element a is either in or not in the set and cannot be in the set "twice.") See, however, 2.1. *Elements* and a *collection* are two basic concepts in the set theory. On the other hand, it can also be developed based on the concepts of a *whole* and a *partition*. The latter has some advantages over the former in applications where it is easier to define the whole than the individual elements. (See Ijiri [1964b].) However, here we shall follow the ordinary way of structuring the set theory.

1.3. An element of a set may be a set in itself. In particular, a collection of sets is a *class* and a collection of classes is a *family*.

Examples. Classes: $\{(a, b), (a), (a, b, d), (b, c), (c)\}$; $\{(a, b)\}$; $\{\ \}$. Families: $[\{(a), (a, b)\}, \{(a, b)\}, \{(a), (b)\}]$; $[\{(a)\}]$; $[\ ]$.

Remarks. Various definitions involving sets in the following discussion are, of course, applicable to classes and families since they are also sets; the only difference lies in the interpretation of elements.

1.4. A set A *includes* a set B, or a set B is *included* in a set A, denoted by $A \supseteq B$ or $B \subseteq A$, if every element of B is in A. If A includes B, B is a *subset* of A and A is a *superset* of B. A set A *strictly includes* a set B or a set B is *strictly included in* a set A, denoted by $A \supset B$ or $B \subset A$, if every element of B is in A but not every element of A is in B. If A strictly includes B, B is a *proper subset* of A and A is a *proper superset* of B.

Examples. $(a, b) \subseteq (a, b, c)$; $(a, c, b) \subseteq (a, c, b)$; $(b, d) \subseteq (d, b)$; $(b, d) \supseteq (d, b)$; $(a, b, d) \supseteq (b, d)$; $(a) \supseteq (\ )$; $(\ ) \supseteq (\ )$; $(a, b) \subset (a, b, c)$; $(a, b) \supset (a)$; $(a, b) \supset (\ )$.

1.5. Two sets A and B are *equal*, denoted by $A = B$, if every element of A is an element of B and every element of B is an element of A. Otherwise the two sets are *not equal*, denoted by $A \neq B$.

Examples. $(a, b) = (a, b)$; $(b, c, d) = (d, b, c)$; $(a) = (a)$; $(\ ) = (\ )$. $(a, b) \neq (a, b, c)$; $(a, b, c) \neq (c, a, d)$; $(a) \neq (\ )$.

Remarks. If two sets are equal, they are actually two names for the same thing.

1.6. An *empty set*, denoted by ∅, is a set which contains no elements. A *nonempty* set is a set which contains at least one element.

Examples. ( ) = ∅; (a) ≠ ∅; (a, b, c, d, e) ≠ ∅.

Remarks. An empty set may contain some things which are not considered elements in the discussion. For example. (p) = ∅ if p is not considered an element in the discussion. If only pencils are considered elements, a box which contains no pencils is empty even if it contains pens.

1.7. A *unit set* is a set which contains one and only one element.

Examples. (a); (b); (c); (d); (e).

Remarks. A unit set and the element in the unit set are two different concepts. When we say the element a, a itself is of concern, but when we say the unit set (a), what is of concern is the set that contains only the element a, e.g., a box which contains only a.

1.8. The *union* of n sets, A_1, A_2, $\cdots$, A_n, denoted by

$$A_1 \cup A_2 \cup \cdots \cup A_n \quad \text{or} \quad \bigcup_{i=1}^{n} A_i$$

is a set of all elements that belong to at least one of the n sets.

Examples. (a, b) ∪ (c) = (a, b, c); (a, b) ∪ (a, d) = (a, b, d); (a, b) ∪ (a, b, c) = (a, b, c); (a, c) ∪ ( ) = (a, c); (a) ∪ (a) = (a); ( ) ∪ ( ) = ( ); (a) ∪ (b) ∪ (c) = (a, b, c); (a, b) ∪ (b, c) ∪ (c, d) = (a, b, c, d).

1.9. The *intersection* of n sets, A_1, A_2, $\cdots$, A_n, denoted by

$$A_1 \cap A_2 \cap \cdots \cap A_n \quad \text{or} \quad \bigcap_{i=1}^{n} A_i,$$

is a set of all elements that belong to all of the n sets.

Examples. (a, b) ∩ (c, a) = (a); (a, b) ∩ (a, b, c) = (a, b); (a, b) ∩ (c, d) = ( ); (a, b, c) ∩ ( ) = ( ); (a, b, c) ∩ (a, b) ∩ (b, c) = (b).

1.10. The *difference* between a set A and a set B, denoted by A − B, is a set of all elements in A but not in B.

Examples. (a, b) − (a) = (b); (a, b, c) − (c, d) = (a, b); (a, b, c) − ( ) = (a, b, c); (a, b, c) − (a, b, c, d) = ( ).

Remarks. In general $A - B$ is not the same as $B - A$. $(a, b, d) - (c, d) = (a, b)$, but $(c, d) - (a, b, d) = (c)$. $A - B = B - A$ if and only if $A = B$.

1.11. The *symmetrical difference* of n sets, A_1, A_2, $\cdots$, A_n, denoted by

$$A_1 \triangle A_2 \triangle \cdots \triangle A_n \quad \text{or} \quad \mathop{\triangle}_{i=1}^{n} A_i,$$

is a set of all elements that belong exactly to an odd number of the sets.

Examples. $(a, c) \triangle (c, d) = (a, d)$; $(b, a) \triangle (c, d, a) = (b, c, d)$; $(a, b, c) \triangle (d, a) \triangle (a, b) = (a, c, d)$; $(a) \triangle (b, c) \triangle (d) = (a, b, c, d)$; $(a, b) \triangle (b, c) \triangle (c, a) = (\ )$; $(a, b, c) \triangle (b, c, d) \triangle (c, d, a) \triangle (d, a, b) = (a, b, c, d)$.

Remarks. $A \triangle B$ is always equal to $B \triangle A$. $A \triangle B = \emptyset$ if and only if $A = B$.

1.12. A set A and a set B are *disjoint*, denoted by $A \cap B = \emptyset$, if the intersection of A and B is an empty set. Otherwise, they are *not disjoint*, denoted by $A \cap B \neq \emptyset$. In general, a class of sets A_1, A_2, $\cdots$, A_n is disjoint if $A_i \cap A_j = \emptyset$, where $i \neq j$ for all i and $j = 1, 2, \cdots, n$, and not disjoint otherwise.

Examples. $(a, b) \cap (c) = \emptyset$; $(a, b, c) \cap (d, e) = \emptyset$; $(a, b) \cap (\ ) = \emptyset$; $(a, c) \cap (c) \neq \emptyset$; $(a, b) \cap (a, b) \neq \emptyset$. (a, b), (c, d) and (e) are disjoint. (a, b), (b, c), (c, d), (e), and (b) are not disjoint even though their intersection is empty.

1.13. The *complement* of a set A with respect to its superset B, denoted by $\tilde{A}^B$, is a set $B - A$.

Examples. $(\tilde{c})^{(a, b, c)} = (a, b)$; $(\tilde{\ })^{(a, b)} = (a, b)$; $\widetilde{(a, b)}^{(a, b)} = (\ )$; $(\tilde{\ })^{(\ )} = (\ )$.

Remarks. If it is clear with respect to which set the complement is taken, the complement of a set is denoted simply by $\tilde{A}$. Note that $\tilde{\tilde{A}} = A$, i.e., the complement of a complement is the original set. The complement of A is undefined with respect to a set B if A is not a subset of B.

1.14. A *universal set*, denoted by U, is a set of all elements to be considered in a discussion.

Examples. $U = (a, b, c, d, e)$.

Remarks. If a complement of a set A is taken with respect to the universal set, it is simply called the complement of A, denoted by $\tilde{A}$.

2. BINARY RELATIONS

2.1. An *ordered pair* of elements x and y, denoted by $\langle x, y \rangle$, is a special set of the two elements with the property that $\langle x, y \rangle = \langle y, x \rangle$ if and only if $x = y$. In the ordered pair $\langle x, y \rangle$, x is the *first element* of the ordered pair and y, the *second element*.

Examples. $\langle a, b \rangle$; $\langle b, a \rangle$; $\langle a, a \rangle$; $\langle c, b \rangle$. The first elements in these ordered pairs are a, b, a, and c and the second elements are b, a, a, and b in that order.

Remarks: One way to distinguish between $\langle x, y \rangle$ and $\langle y, x \rangle$ is to take recourse to the distinction between an element and a unit set containing the element as discussed in 1.7. Thus we may define $\langle x, y \rangle$ as $\{x, (y)\}$ where the latter is an (ordinary) set consisting of an element x and a unit set containing an element y. Since $\{x, (y)\} \neq \{(x), y\}$ unless $x = y$, we have $\langle x, y \rangle \neq \langle y, x \rangle$ unless $x = y$. (Note that since x and (x) are distinct $\{x, (x)\}$ meets the definition of a set given in 1.2.)

2.2. A *binary relation*, denoted by R, is a set of ordered pairs.

Examples. $(\langle a, c \rangle, \langle b, c \rangle, \langle a, d \rangle)$; $(\langle a, a \rangle, \langle a, b \rangle, \langle b, c \rangle, \langle a, c \rangle)$.

Remarks. In this section the term *binary* will be omitted since all relations discussed here are binary. This definition of a relation is close to the idea that "the relation *holds* between the ordered pair" than to the ordinary concept of a relationship. If we state R using the ordinary concept, it is defined as "a set of all ordered pairs for which a given relationship holds."

2.3. The *domain* of a relation is the set of all first elements in the relation. The *range* of a relation is the set of all second elements in the relation. The *field* of a relation is the set of all first and second elements.

Examples. If $R = (\langle a, a \rangle, \langle a, b \rangle, \langle b, c \rangle, \langle a, c \rangle)$, the domain of R is (a, b), the range of R, (a, b, c), and the field of R, (a, b, c).

2.4. A relation R is *reflexive* in a set A if $\langle x, x \rangle$ is in R for all x in A; otherwise, it is *not reflexive* in A. A relation R is *irreflexive* in A if $\langle x, x \rangle$ is not in R for all x in A.

Examples. In the set (a, b, c), $(\langle a, a \rangle, \langle a, b \rangle, \langle b, b \rangle, \langle c, c \rangle)$ is reflexive, $(\langle a, b \rangle, \langle b, a \rangle, \langle c, b \rangle)$ is irreflexive (and not reflexive), and $(\langle a, a \rangle, \langle a, b \rangle, \langle b, c \rangle)$ is not reflexive.

Remarks. The relationships "equal to," "greater than or equal to," etc. yield reflexive relations. The relationships "greater than," "less than," etc. yield irreflexive relations. We omit the term "in a set A" and say "R is reflexive" if A is the field of R. This remark applies to all definitions in 2.4.–2.7.

2.5. A relation R is *symmetrical* in A if $\langle y, x \rangle$ is in R whenever $\langle x, y \rangle$ is in R for all x and y in A, otherwise, it is *not symmetrical* in A. A relation R is *asymmetrical* in A if $\langle y, x \rangle$ is not in R whenever $\langle x, y \rangle$ is in R for all x and y in A. A relation R is *antisymmetrical* in A if $x = y$ whenever $\langle x, y \rangle$ and $\langle y, x \rangle$ are both in R for all x and y in A.

Examples. In the set (a, b, c), $(\langle a, a \rangle, \langle a, b \rangle, \langle b, a \rangle)$ is symmetrical, $(\langle a, b \rangle, \langle b, c \rangle, \langle a, c \rangle)$ is asymmetrical (and not symmetrical), $(\langle a, a \rangle, \langle a, b \rangle, \langle b, b \rangle, \langle b, c \rangle, \langle a, c \rangle)$ is antisymmetrical (and not symmetrical), and $(\langle a, b \rangle, \langle b, a \rangle, \langle a, c \rangle, \langle a, a \rangle)$ is not symmetrical.

Remarks. The relationships "equal to," "equivalent to," "in the same class," etc. yield symmetrical relations. The relationships "greater than," "less than," etc. yield asymmetrical relations. The relationships "greater than or equal to," "in the same class or above," etc. yield antisymmetric relations.

2.6. A relation R is *transitive* in A if $\langle x, z \rangle$ is in R whenever $\langle x, y \rangle$ and $\langle y, z \rangle$ are in R for all x, y, and z in A, otherwise it is *not transitive* in A. A relation R is *intransitive* in A if $\langle x, z \rangle$ is not in R whenever $\langle x, y \rangle$ and $\langle y, z \rangle$ are in R for all x, y, and z in A.

Examples. In the set (a, b, c), $(\langle a, b \rangle, \langle b, c \rangle, \langle a, a \rangle, \langle a, c \rangle)$ is transitive, $(\langle a, b \rangle, \langle b, c \rangle, \langle c, d \rangle, \langle c, a \rangle)$ is intransitive (and not transitive), and $(\langle a, b \rangle, \langle b, c \rangle, \langle c, d \rangle, \langle c, a \rangle, \langle b, d \rangle)$ is not transitive.

Remarks. The relationships "greater than," "greater than or equal to," etc. yield transitive relations. The relationships, "in a different class," "is not equal to," etc., yield relations that are not transitive. The relationships, "is a father of," "is twice as large," etc., yield intransitive relations.

2.7. A relation R is *connected* in A if for every pair of distinct elements x and y in A, $\langle x, y \rangle$ or $\langle y, x \rangle$ is in R, otherwise it is *not connected* in A. A relation R is *strongly connected* in A if R is connected in A and reflexive in A.

Examples. In the set (a, b, c), $(\langle a, b \rangle \langle a, c \rangle, \langle b, c \rangle)$ is connected, $(\langle a, b \rangle, \langle b, a \rangle, \langle a, c \rangle, \langle b, c \rangle, \langle a, a \rangle, \langle b, b \rangle, \langle c, c \rangle)$ is strongly connected, and $(\langle a, b \rangle, \langle b, c \rangle)$ is not connected.

2.8. The *identity relation* I on a set A is the set of all pairs $\langle x, x \rangle$ where x is in A.

Examples. $(\langle a, a \rangle, \langle b, b \rangle, \langle c, c \rangle)$ is the identity relation on (a, b, c). It is not the identity relation on (a, b, c, d) nor on (a, b).

2.9. An *equivalence relation* is a relation that is reflexive, symmetrical, and transitive.

Examples. $(\langle a, a \rangle, \langle b, b \rangle, \langle c, c \rangle)$; $(\langle a, a \rangle, \langle b, b \rangle, \langle a, b \rangle, \langle b, a \rangle, \langle c, c \rangle)$; $(\langle a, a \rangle, \langle b, b \rangle, \langle c, c \rangle, \langle d, d \rangle, \langle a, b \rangle, \langle b, c \rangle, \langle a, c \rangle, \langle c, a \rangle, \langle c, b \rangle, \langle b, a \rangle)$.

Remarks. A typical interpretation of an equivalence relation R is "x and y are in the same class if $\langle x, y \rangle$ is in R." The domain, the range, and the field of an equivalence relation are all equal to each other.

2.10. The *R-equivalent set* of an element x, denoted by $[x]_R$, is the set of all elements y for which $\langle x, y \rangle$ (and hence $\langle y, x \rangle$) is in the equivalent relation R.

Examples. If $R = (\langle a, b \rangle, \langle b, a \rangle, \langle a, a \rangle, \langle b, b \rangle, \langle c, c \rangle)$, then $[a]_R = (a, b)$, $[b]_R = (a, b)$, $[c]_R = (c)$.

2.11. A *partition* of a nonempty set A is a disjoint class of nonempty subsets of A whose union is A.

Examples. $\{(a, b), (c), (d, e)\}$; $\{(a), (b, d), (c, e)\}$; $\{(a), (d, e, b, c)\}$; $\{(a, b, c, d, e)\}$ are all partitions of (a, b, c, d, e).

2.12. A partition P_1 of a nonempty set A is *finer* than a partition P_2 of the set A, denoted by $P_1 \sqsubseteq P_2$, if every member of P_1 is included in a member of P_2. P_2 is *coarser* than P_1, denoted by $P_2 \sqsupseteq P_1$ if P_1 is *finer* than P_2. P_1 is *strictly finer* than P_2, denoted by $P_1 \sqsubset P_2$, if $P_1 \sqsubseteq P_2$ but $P_1 \neq P_2$. P_2 is *strictly coarser* than P_1, denoted by $P_2 \sqsupset P_1$, if P_1 is strictly finer than P_2.

Examples. $\{(a,b), (c), (d,e)\} \sqsubseteq \{(a,b,c), (d,e)\}; \{(a), (b), (c), (d,e)\} \sqsubseteq \{(a), (b), (c), (d, e)\}$; $\{(a), (b), (c), (d), (e)\} \sqsubseteq \{$any partitions of $(a, b, c, d, e)\}$; $\{(a, b, c, d, e)\} \sqsupseteq \{$any partitions of $(a, b, c, d, e)\}$; $\{(a, b), (c), (d, e)\} \sqsubseteq \{(a, b, c), (d, e)\}; \{(a, b), (c, d, e)\} \sqsupseteq \{(a), (b), (c, d, e)\}$; $\{(a, b), (c, d, e)\} \sqsupseteq \{(a), (b), (c), (d), (e)\}$.

Remarks. $\{(a, b), (c, d, e)\}, \{(a, b, c), (d, e)\}, \{(a, b, c, d), (e)\}, \{(a, c), (b, d, e)\}$ are not comparable with each other with respect to the fineness of partitions. Two partitions are not comparable if they are not partitions of the same set A.

2.13. The *partition P of the field of R generated by an equivalence relation* R, denoted by $P(R)$, is a class of all distinct R-equivalent sets of all elements in the field of R.

Examples. If $R = (\langle a, b \rangle, \langle b, a \rangle, \langle a, a \rangle, \langle b, b \rangle, \langle c, c \rangle)$, $P(R) = \{(a, b),$ $(c)\}$. If $R = (\langle a, b \rangle, \langle b, a \rangle, \langle a, c \rangle, \langle c, a \rangle, \langle b, c \rangle, \langle c, b \rangle, \langle a, a \rangle, \langle b, b \rangle, \langle c, c \rangle)$, $P(R) = \{(a, b, c)\}$.

Remarks. Since $[x]_R$ includes x, for any x in the field of R, x appears in at least one member of $P(R)$. It cannot appear in more than one member of $P(R)$. For if it appears in any two distinct members, p_1 and p_2, of $P(R)$ then there is at least one element y in the field of R that is in only one of p_1 or p_2. One of them implies that $\langle x, y \rangle$ is in R while the other implies $\langle x, y \rangle$ is not in R, which is a contradiction. Hence, every x in the field of R appears in one and only one member of $P(R)$, i.e., $P(R)$ is a partition of the field of R.

2.14. The *equivalence relation R on a set A generated by a partition P of A*, denoted by $R(P)$, is the set of all ordered pairs $\langle x, y \rangle$ where x and y are in the same member of the partition.

Examples. If $P = \{(a, b), (c)\}$, $R(P) = (\langle a, b \rangle, \langle b, a \rangle, \langle a, a \rangle, \langle b, b \rangle, \langle c, c \rangle)$. If $P = \{(a), (b), (c)\}$, $R(P) = (\langle a, a \rangle, \langle b, b \rangle, \langle c, c \rangle)$.

Remarks. If x and y are in the same member of a partition they are clearly reflexive, symmetrical, and transitive. Hence $R(P)$ is an equivalence relation. The following points can easily be proved: If $P_1 = P(R_1)$ for a given equivalence relation R_1, then $R(P_1) = R_1$. If $R_1 = R(P_1)$ for a given partition P_1, then $P(R_1) = P_1$. $P(R_1) \sqsubseteq P(R_2)$ if and only if $R_1 \subseteq R_2$. $R(P_1) \subseteq R(P_2)$ if and only if $P_1 \sqsubseteq P_2$.

2.15. An *ordering relation* is a transitive and antisymmetrical relation.

Examples. $(\langle a, b \rangle)$; $(\langle a, b \rangle, \langle b, c \rangle, \langle b, b \rangle, \langle c, b \rangle, \langle c, c \rangle, \langle a, c \rangle)$; $(\langle a, b \rangle, \langle b, c \rangle, \langle a, c \rangle, \langle d, e \rangle)$.

Remarks. The essential properties of an ordering relation are transitivity and antisymmetry. There are several ordering relations that have stricter requirements as elaborated below. However, they all possess the above two properties.

2.16. A *partial ordering* of a set A is a relation that is reflexive, antisymmetric, and transitive in A.

Examples. $(\langle a, a \rangle, \langle b, b \rangle, \langle c, c \rangle, \langle d, d \rangle, \langle e, e \rangle, \langle a, b \rangle, \langle b, c \rangle, \langle a, c \rangle, \langle d, e \rangle)$; $(\langle a, a \rangle, \langle b, b \rangle, \langle a, b \rangle)$; $(\langle a, a \rangle, \langle b, b \rangle, \langle c, c \rangle, \langle a, b \rangle, \langle a, c \rangle)$ are partial orderings of (a, b, c, d, e), (a, b), and (a, b, c), respectively.

2.17. A *total ordering* (or *simple* or *linear ordering*) of a set A is a partial ordering that is connected in A.

Examples. $(\langle a, a \rangle, \langle b, b \rangle, \langle c, c \rangle, \langle a, b \rangle, \langle b, c \rangle, \langle a, c \rangle)$; $(\langle a, a \rangle, \langle b, b \rangle, \langle c, c \rangle, \langle d, d \rangle, \langle e, e \rangle, \langle a, b \rangle, \langle a, c \rangle, \langle a, d \rangle, \langle a, e \rangle, \langle b, c \rangle, \langle b, d \rangle, \langle b, e \rangle, \langle c, d \rangle, \langle c, e \rangle, \langle e, d \rangle)$ are total orderings of (a, b, c) and (a, b, c, d, e), respectively.

2.18. A *strict partial ordering* of a set A is a relation that is asymmetric and transitive in A.

Examples. $(\langle a, b \rangle, \langle b, c \rangle, \langle a, c \rangle, \langle d, e \rangle)$; $(\langle a, b \rangle)$; $(\langle a, b \rangle, \langle a, c \rangle)$ are strict partial orderings of (a, b, c, d, e), (a, b), and (a, b, c), respectively.

2.19. A *strict total ordering* of a set A is a strict partial ordering that is connected in A.

Examples. $(\langle a, b \rangle, \langle a, c \rangle, \langle a, d \rangle, \langle a, e \rangle, \langle b, c \rangle, \langle b, d \rangle, \langle b, e \rangle, \langle c, d \rangle, \langle c, e \rangle,$ $\langle e, d \rangle)$; $(\langle a, b \rangle, \langle b, c \rangle, \langle a, c \rangle)$; $(\langle a, b \rangle)$ are strict total orderings of (a, b, c, d, e), (a, b, c), and (a, b), respectively.

3. FUNCTIONS

3.1. A *function* is a relation in which no two distinct ordered pairs have the same first element.

Examples. $(\langle a, b \rangle, \langle b, c \rangle, \langle c, c \rangle)$; $(\langle a, a \rangle, \langle b, b \rangle, \langle c, c \rangle)$; $(\langle a, e \rangle, \langle b, e \rangle,$ $\langle c, e \rangle, \langle d, e \rangle)$; $(\langle a, a \rangle, \langle b, a \rangle, \langle c, b \rangle)$.

Remarks. The term *function* means two things: the rule of association and the resulting pairs. The definition above is based on the latter. The key property of a function is that every element in the domain of the relation appears in only one pair as a first element.

3.2. The *image of an element x under a function f*, denoted by $f(x)$, is the unique element y, if any, where $\langle x, y \rangle$ is in f, and is an empty set otherwise. The function f is said to *assign y to x* if $f(x) = y$. The *inverse image of an element y under a function f*, denoted by $f^{-1}(y)$, is a set of all x, if any, where $\langle x, y \rangle$ is in f, and is an empty set otherwise.

Examples. If $f = (\langle a, b \rangle, \langle b, c \rangle, \langle c, c \rangle)$, then $f(a) = b, f(b) = c, f(d) = \emptyset$. Similarly, for the same function f, $f^{-1}(b) = a, f^{-1}(c) = (b, c), f^{-1}(a) = \emptyset$.

3.3. The *image of a set A under a function f*, denoted by $f(A)$, is the set of all y, if any, where at least one element x in A exists so that $\langle x, y \rangle$ is in f, and is an empty set otherwise. The *inverse image of a set B under the function f*, denoted by $f^{-1}(B)$, is the set of all x, if any, where at least one element y in B exists so that $\langle x, y \rangle$ is in f, and is an empty set otherwise.

Examples. If $f = (\langle a, b \rangle, \langle b, c \rangle, \langle c, c \rangle)$, then $f((a, b)) = (b, c), f((a, b, c))$ $= (b, c), f((b, c)) = (c), f((a, d)) = (b), f((d, e)) = \emptyset, f^{-1}((b, c)) =$ $(a, b, c), f^{-1}((c, d)) = (b, c); f^{-1}((a, e)) = \emptyset$.

3.4. The *f-equivalent set of an element* $\hat{x}$, denoted by $[\hat{x}]_f$, is the set of all x, if any, where $\langle x, f(\hat{x}) \rangle$ is in f, and is an empty set otherwise. In other words, $[\hat{x}]_f = f^{-1}(f(\hat{x}))$.

Examples. If $f = (\langle a, b \rangle, \langle b, b \rangle, \langle c, d \rangle, \langle d, c \rangle)$, $[a]_f = (a, b)$, $[b]_f = (a, b)$, $[c]_f = (c)$, $[d]_f = (d)$, $[e]_f = \emptyset$.

Remarks. For any function f the class of all f-equivalent sets is a partition of the domain of the function f since every element in the domain of f belongs to one and only one member of the partition by means of its unique image.

3.5. A function f is *finer* or *stronger* than a function g, denoted by $f \sqsubseteq g$, if f and g have the same domain and the partition generated by the class of all distinct f-equivalent sets, denoted by P_f, is finer than the partition generated by the class of all distinct g-equivalent sets, denoted by P_g. A function g is *coarser* or *weaker* than a function f, denoted by $g \sqsupseteq f$, if f is finer than g.

Examples. $(\langle a, b \rangle, \langle b, b \rangle, \langle c, c \rangle) \sqsubseteq (\langle a, d \rangle, \langle b, d \rangle, \langle c, d \rangle)$ $(\langle a, b \rangle, \langle b, b \rangle, \langle c, c \rangle) \sqsubseteq (\langle a, e \rangle, \langle b, e \rangle, \langle c, a \rangle)$; $(\langle a, b \rangle, \langle b, d \rangle, \langle c, d \rangle) \sqsupseteq (\langle a, b \rangle, \langle b, d \rangle, \langle c, e \rangle)$; $(\langle a, b \rangle, \langle b, b \rangle, \langle c, b \rangle) \sqsupseteq (\langle a, d \rangle, \langle b, d \rangle, \langle c, d \rangle)$.

Remarks. $(\langle a, b \rangle, \langle b, c \rangle, \langle c, c \rangle, \langle d, e \rangle)$ and $(\langle a, d \rangle, \langle b, d \rangle, \langle c, e \rangle, \langle d, d \rangle)$ are not comparable with respect to the fineness of functions. Neither are $(\langle a, b \rangle, \langle b, c \rangle, \langle c, d \rangle)$ and $(\langle a, b \rangle, \langle b, c \rangle, \langle c, d \rangle, \langle d, e \rangle)$.

3.6. A function f is *strictly finer* than a function g, denoted by $f \sqsubset g$, if $P_f \sqsubset P_g$. A function g is *strictly coarser* than a function f, denoted by $g \sqsupset f$, if f is strictly finer than g.

Examples. $(\langle a, a \rangle, \langle b, b \rangle, \langle c, d \rangle) \sqsubset (\langle a, d \rangle, \langle b, d \rangle, \langle c, d \rangle)$; $(\langle a, e \rangle, \langle b, e \rangle, \langle c, e \rangle) \sqsupset (\langle a, d \rangle, \langle b, c \rangle, \langle c, c \rangle)$.

3.7. A function f is *equivalent* to a function g, denoted by $f \cong g$, if $P_f = P_g$.

Examples. $(\langle a, b \rangle, \langle b, b \rangle, \langle c, d \rangle) \cong (\langle a, d \rangle, \langle b, d \rangle, \langle c, a \rangle)$; $(\langle a, e \rangle, \langle b, e \rangle, \langle c, e \rangle) \cong (\langle a, d \rangle, \langle b, d \rangle, \langle c, d \rangle)$; $(\langle a, e \rangle, \langle b, d \rangle, \langle c, c \rangle) \cong (\langle a, b \rangle, \langle b, c \rangle, \langle c, d \rangle)$; $(\langle a, a \rangle, \langle b, a \rangle, \langle c, d \rangle) \cong (\langle a, a \rangle, \langle b, a \rangle, \langle c, d \rangle)$.

Remarks. In the last example, the two functions are *equal*. (See the definition of the equality of sets in 1.5.) If two function are equal, they are always equivalent, but the converse is not true.

3.8. A function f *maps a set* X *into a set* Y, denoted by $f : X \to Y$ or $X \xrightarrow{f} Y$, if X is the domain of f and Y is a superset of the range of f.

Examples. ($\langle a, b \rangle$, $\langle b, c \rangle$, $\langle c, d \rangle$), ($\langle a, d \rangle$, $\langle b, d \rangle$, $\langle c, d \rangle$), and ($\langle a, c \rangle$, $\langle b, d \rangle$, $\langle c, d \rangle$) all map (a, b, c) into (b, c, d).

3.9. A function f maps its domain X *onto* Y or f is onto, denoted by $f : X \xrightarrow{\text{onto}} Y$, if Y is the range of f.

Examples. ($\langle a, b \rangle$, $\langle b, b \rangle$, $\langle c, a \rangle$) maps (a, b, c) onto (b, a) but into (a, b, c, d). ($\langle a, b \rangle$, $\langle b, b \rangle$, $\langle c, b \rangle$) maps (a, b, c) onto (b) but into (a, b, c).

3.10. A function f is *one-to-one* if no two distinct ordered pairs have the same second element, otherwise it is *many-to-one*.

Examples. ($\langle a, b \rangle$, $\langle b, c \rangle$, $\langle c, a \rangle$); ($\langle a, a \rangle$, $\langle b, b \rangle$, $\langle c, c \rangle$); ($\langle a, c \rangle$, $\langle b, d \rangle$, $\langle c, e \rangle$) are examples of one-to-one functions. ($\langle a, b \rangle$, $\langle b, b \rangle$); ($\langle a, c \rangle$, $\langle b, d \rangle$, $\langle c, c \rangle$) are examples of many-to-one functions.

3.11. The *inverse function* of a one-to-one function f, denoted by f^{-1}, is a function generated by interchanging the first element and the second element of every pair in f.

Examples. ($\langle a, b \rangle$, $\langle b, c \rangle$, $\langle c, d \rangle$) is the inverse function of ($\langle b, a \rangle$, $\langle c, b \rangle$, $\langle d, c \rangle$). ($\langle a, a \rangle$, $\langle b, b \rangle$, $\langle c, c \rangle$) is the inverse function of ($\langle a, a \rangle$, $\langle b, b \rangle$, $\langle c, c \rangle$).

Remarks. The inverse function of a given one-to-one function is always unique. The inverse function does not exist for a many-to-one function. The inverse function of an inverse function is the original function.

3.12. The *identity function* on a set A is a function which consists of all ordered pairs $\langle x, x \rangle$ where x is in A and does not contain any other ordered pairs.

Examples. ($\langle a, a \rangle$); ($\langle a, a \rangle$, $\langle b, b \rangle$); ($\langle a, a \rangle$, $\langle b, b \rangle$, $\langle c, c \rangle$) are identity functions on (a), (a, b), and (a, b, c), respectively.

Remarks. If the domain of an identity function, i.e., the set A, is immaterial, the function may be simply called an identity function. Note that $f = f^{-1}$ if and only if f is an identity function.

3.13. A *constant function* is a function whose range consists of only one element.

Examples. ($\langle a, a \rangle$, $\langle b, a \rangle$, $\langle c, a \rangle$); ($\langle a, d \rangle$, $\langle b, d \rangle$, $\langle c, d \rangle$).

3.14. The *composite function* h of a function $f : X \rightarrow Y$ and a function $g : Y' \rightarrow Z$ where Y' contains the range of f, denoted by $h = gf$, is the function which maps X into Z so that $h(x) = g(f(x))$ for every x in X.

Examples. If $f = (\langle a, b \rangle, \langle b, b \rangle, \langle c, c \rangle)$ and $g = (\langle b, d \rangle, \langle c, e \rangle, \langle a, b \rangle)$, then $gf = (\langle a, d \rangle, \langle b, d \rangle, \langle c, e \rangle)$. If $f = (\langle a, b \rangle, \langle b, b \rangle, \langle c, a \rangle)$ and $g = (\langle b, a \rangle, \langle a, a \rangle, \langle c, d \rangle)$, then $gf = (\langle a, a \rangle, \langle b, a \rangle, \langle c, a \rangle)$.

Remarks. A composite function is not defined unless the range of the function f is included in the domain of the function g.

3.15. A nonempty set A is *numerically equivalent* to a nonempty set B, denoted by $\nu(A) = \nu(B)$, if a one-to-one function exists which maps A onto B.

Examples. $\nu(a, b, c) = \nu(d, e, a)$; $\nu(a, c) = \nu(b, d)$.

Remarks. The numerical equivalence is reflexive, symmetrical, and transitive.

3.16. A set A is a *finite set* if it is empty or if a natural number N exists so that a set of all natural numbers from 1 to N is numerically equivalent to the set A; otherwise it is an *infinite set*.

Examples. Finite sets: (a, b); (a); (a, b, c, d, e); $(\ )$. Infinite sets: (all integers); (all real numbers).

3.17. A set A *is countable* (or *denumerable*) if it is finite or is numerically equivalent to the set of all natural numbers; otherwise it is *uncountable*.

Examples. Countable sets: (a, b, c); $(\ )$; (all rational numbers); (all even integers); (all integers). Uncountable sets: (all real numbers); (all real numbers from 0 to 1 inclusive).

3.18. The *cardinality* of a nonempty finite set A is the natural number N such that A is numerically equivalent to the set of all natural numbers from 1 to N. The cardinality of an empty set is defined to be zero. The cardinality of a countable and infinite set, i.e., a countably infinite set is defined to be $\aleph_0$ (aleph zero). The cardinality of a set which is numerically equivalent to the set of all real numbers is defined to be c (the cardinal number of the continuum).

4. RELATIONAL SYSTEMS

4.1. An *ordered n-tuple of elements* $x_1, x_2, \cdots, x_n$, denoted by $\langle x_1, x_2, \cdots, x_n \rangle$, is a special set of the n elements with the property that for every $i, j = 1, 2, \cdots, n$

$$\langle x_1, x_2, \cdots, x_{i-1}, x_i, x_{i+1}, \cdots, x_{j-1}, x_j, x_{j+1}, \cdots, x_n \rangle$$

$$= \langle x_1, x_2, \cdots, x_{i-1}, x_j, x_{i+1}, \cdots, x_{j-1}, x_i, x_{j+1}, \cdots, x_n \rangle$$

if and only if $x_i = x_j$. In the ordered n-tuple $\langle x_1, x_2, \cdots, x_n \rangle$, x_i ($i = 1, 2,$ $\cdots, n$) is the ith element or ith coordinate of the ordered n-tuple.

Examples. $\langle a, b \rangle$; $\langle a, a, c \rangle$; $\langle a, b, c, d, e \rangle$; $\langle c, b, e, d, d, d, a \rangle$; $\langle d \rangle$. The third element or the third coordinate of $\langle a, a, c \rangle$ is c, and the same of $\langle c, b, e, d, d, d, a \rangle$ is e.

Remarks. As in 2.1., where an ordered pair is defined, we may define an ordered n-tuple by means of an element x_1, a unit set containing x_2, a unit class which contains a unit set containing x_3, and so on. That is,

$$\langle x_1, x_2, \cdots, x_n \rangle = \{x_1, (x_2), ((x_3)), \cdots, ((\cdots(x_n)\cdots))\}$$

4.2. The *product set* or the *Cartesian product* of ordered n sets, $A_1, A_2, \cdots, A_n$, denoted by

$$A_1 \times A_2 \times \cdots \times A_n \quad \text{or} \quad \prod_{i=1}^{n} A_i$$

where $A_1, A_2, \cdots, A_n$ are all nonempty and are not necessarily distinct, is the set of all ordered n-tuples $\langle a_1, a_2, \cdots, a_n \rangle$, where a_i is an element of A_i for $i = 1, 2, \cdots, n$.

Examples. $(a, b) \times (c, d) = (\langle a, c \rangle, \langle a, d \rangle, \langle b, c \rangle, \langle b, d \rangle)$; $(a, b) \times (a, b) = (\langle a, a \rangle, \langle a, b \rangle, \langle b, a \rangle, \langle b, b \rangle)$; $(a, b) \times (c) \times (b, d) = (\langle a, c, b \rangle, \langle a, c, d \rangle, \langle b, c, b \rangle, \langle b, c, d \rangle)$.

Remarks. A product set is not defined if one or more of the n sets are empty. If $n = 1$, the product set is equal to an ordinary set. The product set $A \times B$ is not equal to the product set $B \times A$ unless $A = B$.

4.3. A *relation* is a set of ordered n-tuples, or equivalently, a subset of a product set.

Examples. $(\langle a, c \rangle, \langle a, d \rangle, \langle b, c \rangle)$; $(\langle a, a \rangle, \langle a, b \rangle, \langle b, a \rangle, \langle b, b \rangle)$; $(\langle a, c, b \rangle, \langle b, c, d \rangle)$; $(\langle a \rangle, \langle b \rangle, \langle c \rangle)$; $(\langle a, a, b, e, c \rangle)$; $(\langle a, a, a, a, a, a \rangle, \langle b, b, b, b, b, b \rangle)$; ( ).

Remarks. Compare the first three examples above with the product sets in 4.2, of which they are subsets. A relation may be defined by describing a rule which determines whether or not a given relationship holds for the elements in the n-tuples or by enumerating all ordered n-tuples for which the given relationship holds. The latter is used in the above definition of a relation. Each ordered n-tuple in a product set may be classified by using a relation R of the product set into two categories depending upon whether the n-tuple is in R (the relationship holds) or not in R (the relationship does not hold).

4.4. A relation is *n-ary*, or the relation is of *order n*, if it is a subset of a product set of ordered n sets. In particular, if $n = 1, 2$, or 3, the relation is *unary*, *binary*, or *ternary*, respectively. A relation is *empty* if it does not contain any element. A relation is *universal with respect to a product set* if it is equal to the product set.

Examples. In the examples in 4.3., the first two relations are binary, the third is ternary, and the fourth is unary. The order of the first five relations above is 2, 2, 3, 1, 5, 6, in that sequence. The order of the last one, which is an empty relation, depends upon which product set is used in defining the relation. The second relation is universal with respect to the product set $(a, b) \times (a, b)$.

Remarks. The binary relation discussed in Section 2 is a special case of the relations defined above.

4.5. A *complement* of a relation R with respect to a product set Π, where $R \subseteq \Pi$, denoted by $\tilde{R}^\pi$, is a relation $\Pi - R$.

Examples. Complements of the first three relations in 4.3 with respect to their respective product sets given in 4.2 are $(\langle b, d \rangle)$; $(\ )$; $(\langle a, c, d \rangle, \langle b, c, b \rangle)$.

Remarks. If it is clear with respect to which product set the complement is taken, the complement of a relation R is denoted simply by $\tilde{R}$. Note that $\tilde{\tilde{R}} = R$, i.e., the complement of the complement of a relation is the original relation. The complement of R is undefined with respect to a product set Π if R is not a subset of Π.

4.6. A *relation defined on a set* X is a subset of a product set $X \times X \times \cdots \times X$.

Examples. $(\langle a, a \rangle, \langle a, b \rangle)$; $(\langle a, a \rangle, \langle a, b \rangle, \langle b, a \rangle, \langle b, b \rangle)$; $(\langle a, b, a \rangle, \langle b, b, b \rangle)$; $(\langle a, b, a, a \rangle)$; $(\ )$; are all relations defined on (a, b).

4.7. A *relational system* $\langle X, \Re \rangle$ is a mathematical structure which consists of a nonempty set X and a nonempty set $\Re$ of relations defined on X.

Examples. $\langle (a,b), \{(\langle a, a \rangle, \langle b, b \rangle)\} \rangle$; $\langle (a,b), \{(\langle a, b \rangle, \langle b, a \rangle), (\langle a, a \rangle)\} \rangle$; $\langle (a, b, c), \{(\langle a, b \rangle), (\langle a, b, c \rangle, \langle a, a, b \rangle), (\langle a \rangle, \langle b \rangle)\} \rangle$; $\langle (a), \{(\langle a \rangle), (\langle a, a \rangle), (\langle a, a, a \rangle), (\langle a, a, a, a \rangle)\} \rangle$.

Remarks. Each of these four examples of relational systems has 1, 2, 3, and 4 relations in that order.

4.8. A relational system $\langle X, \Re \rangle$ is *homomorphic* to a relational system $\langle Y, \mathcal{S} \rangle$ *under a function* f, denoted by $\langle X, \Re \rangle \subseteq_f \langle Y, \mathcal{S} \rangle$, if f maps X into

Y and $\mathcal{R}_i$ into $\mathcal{S}_i$ for each $i = 1, 2, \cdots$ (where $\mathcal{R}_i$ and $\mathcal{S}_i$ are sets of all relations of order i in $\mathcal{R}$ and $\mathcal{S}$, respectively), so that for every $x_1, x_2, \cdots, x_i$ in X and for every relation R of order i ($i = 1, 2, \cdots$) in $\mathcal{R}$, $\langle x_1, x_2, \cdots, x_i \rangle$ is in R implies $\langle f(x_1), f(x_2), \cdots, f(x_i) \rangle$ is in $f(R)$. Otherwise $\langle X, \mathcal{R} \rangle$ is *not homomorphic to* $\langle Y, \mathcal{S} \rangle$ *under the function f*, denoted by $\langle X, \mathcal{R} \rangle \not\subseteq_f \langle Y, \mathcal{S} \rangle$.

A relational system $\langle X, \mathcal{R} \rangle$ is *homomorphic* to a relational system $\langle Y, \mathcal{S} \rangle$, denoted by $\langle X, \mathcal{R} \rangle \subseteq \langle Y, \mathcal{S} \rangle$, if there is a function f where $\langle X, \mathcal{R} \rangle \subseteq_f \langle Y, \mathcal{S} \rangle$. Otherwise $\langle X, \mathcal{R} \rangle$ is *not homomorphic to* $\langle Y, \mathcal{S} \rangle$, denoted by $\langle X, \mathcal{R} \rangle \not\subseteq \langle Y, \mathcal{S} \rangle$.

Examples. 1. $\langle X, \mathcal{R} \rangle \subseteq_f \langle Y, \mathcal{S} \rangle$ if $X = (a, b, c)$, $\mathcal{R}$ consists of $R = (\langle a, a \rangle, \langle a, b \rangle, \langle b, a \rangle, \langle b, b \rangle, \langle c, c \rangle)$ only, $Y = (a, b)$, $\mathcal{S}$ consists of $S = (\langle a, a \rangle, \langle b, b \rangle)$ only, and $f = (\langle a, a \rangle, \langle b, a \rangle, \langle c, b \rangle, \langle R, S \rangle)$. $\langle X, \mathcal{R} \rangle \not\subseteq_g \langle Y, \mathcal{S} \rangle$ if $X, \mathcal{R}, Y$, and $\mathcal{S}$ are as above and $g = (\langle a, b \rangle, \langle b, a \rangle, \langle c, b \rangle, \langle R, S \rangle)$.

2. $\langle X, \mathcal{R} \rangle \subseteq_f \langle Y, \mathcal{S} \rangle$ if $X = (a, b)$; $\mathcal{R}$ consists of $R_1 = (\langle a, a \rangle, \langle b, b \rangle)$, $R_2 = (\langle a, b \rangle)$, and $R_3 = (\langle a, a, b \rangle)$; $Y = (c, d, e)$; $\mathcal{S}$ consists of $S_1 = (\langle c, c \rangle, \langle d, d \rangle, \langle e, e \rangle)$, $S_2 = (\langle c, d \rangle, \langle c, e \rangle, \langle d, e \rangle)$, $S_3 = (\langle c, c, d \rangle, \langle c, d, e \rangle)$, and $S_4 = (\langle e, d, d, c \rangle)$; and $f = (\langle a, c \rangle, \langle b, d \rangle, \langle R_1, S_1 \rangle, \langle R_2, S_2 \rangle, \langle R_3, S_3 \rangle)$. $\langle X, \mathcal{R} \rangle \not\subseteq_g \langle Y, \mathcal{S} \rangle$ if $X, \mathcal{R}, Y$, and $\mathcal{S}$ are as above and $g = (\langle a, d \rangle, \langle b, c \rangle, \langle R_1, S_1 \rangle, \langle R_2, S_2 \rangle, \langle R_3, S_3 \rangle)$ or $g = (\langle a, c \rangle, \langle b, d \rangle, \langle R_1, S_2 \rangle, \langle R_2, S_1 \rangle, \langle R_3, S_3 \rangle)$.

3. $\langle X, \mathcal{R} \rangle \subseteq_f \langle Y, \mathcal{S} \rangle$ if $X = (a, b)$, $\mathcal{R}$ consists of $R = (\langle a, b \rangle)$ only, $Y = (b, c)$, $\mathcal{S}$ consists of $S = (\langle c, b \rangle)$ only, and $f = (\langle a, c \rangle, \langle b, b \rangle, \langle R, S \rangle)$. $\langle X, \mathcal{R} \rangle \not\subseteq_g \langle Y, \mathcal{S} \rangle$ if $X, \mathcal{R}, Y$, and $\mathcal{S}$ are as above and $g = (\langle a, b \rangle, \langle b, c \rangle, \langle R, S \rangle)$ or $g = (\langle a, b \rangle, \langle b, b \rangle, \langle R, S \rangle)$.

4. $\langle X, \mathcal{R} \rangle \subseteq_f \langle Y, \mathcal{S} \rangle$ if $X = (a, b, c)$; $\mathcal{R}$ consists of $R_1 = (\langle a, b \rangle, \langle a, c \rangle, \langle b, c \rangle)$, $R_2 = (\langle a, a \rangle, \langle b, b \rangle, \langle c, c \rangle)$, $R_3 = (\langle a \rangle, \langle b \rangle)$, and $R_4 = (\langle c, c, b, b \rangle)$; $Y = (d)$; $\mathcal{S}$ consists of $S_1 = (\langle d \rangle)$, $S_2 = (\langle d, d \rangle)$, $S_3 = (\langle d, d, d \rangle)$, $S_4 = (\langle d, d, d, d \rangle)$, and $S_5 = (\langle d, d, d, d, d \rangle)$; and $f = (\langle a, d \rangle, \langle b, d \rangle, \langle c, d \rangle, \langle R_1, S_2 \rangle, \langle R_2, S_2 \rangle, \langle R_3, S_1 \rangle, \langle R_4, S_4 \rangle)$. $\langle X, \mathcal{R} \rangle \not\subseteq_g \langle Y, \mathcal{S} \rangle$ if $X, \mathcal{R}, Y$, and $\mathcal{S}$ are as above and $g = (\langle a, d \rangle, \langle b, d \rangle, \langle c, d \rangle, \langle R_1, S_1 \rangle, \langle R_2, S_2 \rangle, \langle R_3, S_1 \rangle, \langle R_4, S_4 \rangle)$ since R_1 and $g(R_1) = S_1$ are not of the same order.

5. $\langle X, \mathcal{R} \rangle \subseteq \langle Y, \mathcal{S} \rangle$ for each of the four examples above since there exists at least one function f such that $\langle X, \mathcal{R} \rangle \subseteq_f \langle Y, \mathcal{S} \rangle$.

6. $\langle X, \mathcal{R} \rangle \not\subseteq \langle Y, \mathcal{S} \rangle$ if $X = (a, b)$; $\mathcal{R}$ consists of $R = (\langle a, b, b \rangle)$ only; $Y = (c, d, e)$; and $\mathcal{S}$ consists of $S_1 = (\langle c, c \rangle, \langle d, d \rangle, \langle e, e \rangle)$ and $S_2 = (\langle c, d, e \rangle)$ since there is no function f such that $\langle X, \mathcal{R} \rangle \subseteq_f \langle Y, \mathcal{S} \rangle$.

Remarks. In Example 1, R and S are both equivalent relations by which X and Y are partitioned into $(a, b \mid c)$ and $(a \mid b)$, respectively, and $f(a) = f(b) = a$ and $f(c) = b$. Thus for every x and y in X, if $\langle x, y \rangle$ is in R, which means x and y are in the same equivalent set in X, then $\langle f(x), f(y) \rangle$ is in S, which means that $f(x)$ and $f(y)$ are in the same equivalent set Y. Hence,

$\langle X, \mathcal{R} \rangle \subsetneqq_f \langle Y, \mathcal{S} \rangle$. However, this is clearly not true under the function g. In Example 2, the elements c, d, and e in Y may be interpreted as the numbers 1, 2, and 3, respectively. The relations in $\mathcal{R}$ and $\mathcal{S}$ may also be interpreted as: R_1, equality in weight; R_2, lighter than; R_3, the first element plus the second equals the third in weight; S_1, equality in numbers; S_2, less than; S_3, the first element plus the second equals the third; and S_4, the first element minus the second equals the third minus the fourth.

4.9. A relational system $\langle X, \mathcal{R} \rangle$ is *strongly homomorphic to* a relational system $\langle Y, \mathcal{S} \rangle$ *under a function* f, denoted by $\langle X, \mathcal{R} \rangle \subsetneqq_f \langle Y, \mathcal{S} \rangle$, if (1) $\langle X, \mathcal{R} \rangle \subsetneqq_f \langle Y, \mathcal{S} \rangle$, (2) for every R in $\mathcal{R}$, R is in $\mathcal{R}$ implies that its complement with respect to the product set $X \times X \times \cdots \times X$, denoted by $\tilde{R}$, is in $\mathcal{R}$ and for every S in $\mathcal{S}$, S is in $\mathcal{S}$ implies that its complement with respect to the product set $Y \times Y \times \cdots \times Y$, denoted by $\tilde{S}$, is in $\mathcal{S}$ and (3) $f(R) = S$ implies $f(\tilde{R}) = \tilde{S}$ for every R in $\mathcal{R}$. Otherwise $\langle X, \mathcal{R} \rangle$ is *not strongly homomorphic to* $\langle Y, \mathcal{S} \rangle$ *under the function* f, denoted by $\langle X, \mathcal{R} \rangle \not\subsetneqq_f \langle Y, \mathcal{S} \rangle$.

A relational system $\langle X, \mathcal{R} \rangle$ is *strongly homomorphic* to a relational system $\langle Y, \mathcal{S} \rangle$, denoted by $\langle X, \mathcal{R} \rangle \subsetneqq \langle Y, \mathcal{S} \rangle$, if there is a function f where $\langle X, \mathcal{R} \rangle \subsetneqq_f \langle Y, \mathcal{S} \rangle$. Otherwise $\langle X, \mathcal{R} \rangle$ is *not strongly homomorphic* to $\langle Y, \mathcal{S} \rangle$, denoted by $\langle X, R \rangle \not\subsetneqq \langle Y, \mathcal{S} \rangle$.

Examples. 1. $\langle X, \mathcal{R} \rangle \subsetneqq_f \langle Y, \mathcal{S} \rangle$ if $X = (a, b, c)$; $\mathcal{R}$ consists of $R_1 = (\langle a, a \rangle, \langle a, b \rangle, \langle b, a \rangle, \langle b, b \rangle, \langle c, c \rangle)$, $R_2 = \tilde{R}_1 = (\langle a, c \rangle, \langle c, a \rangle, \langle b, c \rangle, \langle c, b \rangle)$, $R_3 = (\langle a, c \rangle, \langle b, c \rangle)$, and $R_4 = \tilde{R}_3 = (\langle a, a \rangle, \langle a, b \rangle, \langle b, a \rangle, \langle b, b \rangle, \langle c, a \rangle, \langle c, b \rangle, \langle c, c \rangle)$; $Y = (d, e)$; $\mathcal{S}$ consists of $S_1 = (\langle d, d \rangle, \langle e, e \rangle)$, $S_2 = \tilde{S}_1 = (\langle d, e \rangle, \langle e, d \rangle)$, $S_3 = (\langle d, e \rangle)$, $S_4 = \tilde{S}_3 = (\langle d, d \rangle, \langle e, d \rangle, \langle e, e \rangle)$, $S_5 = (\langle e, d \rangle)$, and $S_6 = \tilde{S}_5 = (\langle d, d \rangle, \langle d, e \rangle, \langle e, e \rangle)$; and $f = (\langle a, d \rangle, \langle b, d \rangle, \langle c, e \rangle, \langle R_1, S_1 \rangle, \langle R_2, S_2 \rangle, \langle R_3, S_3 \rangle, \langle R_4, S_4 \rangle)$ or $f = (\langle a, e \rangle, \langle b, e \rangle, \langle c, d \rangle, \langle R_1, S_1 \rangle, \langle R_2, S_2 \rangle, \langle R_3, S_5 \rangle, \langle R_4, S_6 \rangle)$. $\langle X, \mathcal{R} \rangle \not\subsetneqq_g \langle Y, \mathcal{S} \rangle$ if X, $\mathcal{R}$, Y, and $\mathcal{S}$ are as above and g is any function other than those given above.

2. In the above example, $\langle X, \mathcal{R} \rangle \subsetneqq \langle Y, \mathcal{S} \rangle$ since there exists at least one function f such that $\langle X, \mathcal{R} \rangle \subsetneqq_f \langle Y, \mathcal{S} \rangle$.

3. Examples 1, 2, 3, and 4 in 4.8 are not strongly homomorphic but the first three examples can be made strongly homomorphic by adding the complement of every relation in $\mathcal{R}$ to $\mathcal{R}$ and the complement of every relation in $\mathcal{S}$ to $\mathcal{S}$; such an adjustment cannot be made for the last example. Example 6 in 4.8 is not homomorphic, hence it is not strongly homomorphic.

Remarks. The elements d and e in Y in Example 1 above may be interpreted as the numbers 1 and 2, respectively. Also the relations in $\mathcal{R}$ and $\mathcal{S}$ may be interpreted as: R_1, equality in length,; R_2, nonequality in length; R_3, shorter than; R_4, not shorter than; S_1, equality in numbers; S_2, nonequality in numbers; S_3, less than; S_4, not less than; S_5, greater than; S_6, not greater than. If $\langle X, \mathcal{R} \rangle \subsetneqq \langle Y, \mathcal{S} \rangle$, then for any relation R in $\mathcal{R}$ of order i and for any elements x_1, x_2, $\cdots$, x_i in X, $\langle x_1, x_2, \cdots, x_i \rangle$ is in R implies that $\langle f(x_1), f(x_2), \cdots, f(x_i) \rangle$ is in $f(R)$ and $\langle x_1, x_2, \cdots, x_i \rangle$ is not in R implies that $\langle f(x_1), f(x_2), \cdots, f(x_i) \rangle$ is not in $f(R)$. Therefore, whether or not a given relation R in $\mathfrak{R}$ holds for a given set of elements x_1, x_2, $\cdots$, x_i in X can be determined from whether or not the corresponding relation $S = f(R)$ in $\mathfrak{S}$ holds for the set of corresponding elements $f(x_1), f(x_2), \cdots, f(x_i)$ in Y. This is the property of a perfect measurement discussed in Chapter 1. Here, X, $\mathfrak{R}$, Y, and $\mathfrak{S}$ may be interpreted as: X, a set of objects; $\mathfrak{R}$, a set of relations among objects; Y, a set of numbers; $\mathfrak{S}$, a set of relations among numbers.

4.10. A relational system $\langle X, \mathfrak{R} \rangle$ is *isomorphic to* a relational system $\langle Y, \mathfrak{S} \rangle$ *under a function* f, denoted by $\langle X, \mathfrak{R} \rangle \approx_f \langle Y, \mathfrak{S} \rangle$, if (1) f is one-to-one and onto, and (2) $\langle X, \mathfrak{R} \rangle \subseteq_f \langle Y, \mathfrak{S} \rangle$ and $\langle Y, \mathfrak{S} \rangle \subseteq_{f^{-1}} \langle X, \mathfrak{R} \rangle$. Otherwise $\langle X, \mathfrak{R} \rangle$ is *not isomorphic to* $\langle Y, \mathfrak{S} \rangle$ *under* f, denoted by $\langle X, \mathfrak{R} \rangle \not\approx_f \langle Y, \mathfrak{S} \rangle$. $\langle X, \mathfrak{R} \rangle$ is *isomorphic* to $\langle Y, \mathfrak{S} \rangle$, denoted by $\langle X, \mathfrak{R} \rangle \approx \langle Y, \mathfrak{S} \rangle$, if there is a function f where $\langle X, \mathfrak{R} \rangle \approx_f \langle Y, \mathfrak{S} \rangle$. Otherwise $\langle X, \mathfrak{R} \rangle$ is *not isomorphic* to $\langle Y, \mathfrak{S} \rangle$, denoted by $\langle X, \mathfrak{R} \rangle \not\approx \langle Y, \mathfrak{S} \rangle$.

Examples. 1. $\langle X, \mathfrak{R} \rangle \approx_f \langle Y, \mathfrak{S} \rangle$ if $X = (a, b)$; $\mathfrak{R}$ consists of $R_1 = (\langle a, b \rangle)$ and $R_2 = (\langle b, a \rangle)$; $Y = (c, d)$; $\mathfrak{S}$ consists of $S_1 = (\langle c, d \rangle)$ and $S_2 = (\langle d, c \rangle)$; and $f = (\langle a, c \rangle, \langle b, d \rangle, \langle R_1, S_1 \rangle, \langle R_2, S_2 \rangle)$ or $f = (\langle a, d \rangle, \langle b, c \rangle, \langle R_1, S_2 \rangle, \langle R_2, S_1 \rangle)$. $\langle X, \mathfrak{R} \rangle \not\approx_g \langle Y, \mathfrak{S} \rangle$ if X, $\mathfrak{R}$, Y, and $\mathfrak{S}$ are as above and $g = (\langle a, c \rangle, \langle b, d \rangle, \langle R_1, S_2 \rangle, \langle R_2, S_1 \rangle)$ or $g = (\langle a, d \rangle, \langle b, c \rangle, \langle R_1, S_1 \rangle, \langle R_2, S_2 \rangle)$.

2. $\langle X, \mathfrak{R} \rangle \approx_f \langle Y, \mathfrak{S} \rangle$ if $X = (a, b, c)$; $\mathfrak{R}$ consists of $R_1 = (\langle a \rangle, \langle b \rangle)$ and $R_2 = (\langle a, b \rangle, \langle a, c \rangle, \langle b, c \rangle)$; $Y = (c, d, e)$; $\mathfrak{S}$ consists of $S_1 = (\langle d, e \rangle, \langle c, e \rangle, \langle d, c \rangle)$ and $S_2 = (\langle c \rangle, \langle d \rangle)$; and $f = (\langle a, d \rangle, \langle b, c \rangle, \langle c, e \rangle, \langle R_1, S_2 \rangle, \langle R_2, S_1 \rangle)$. $\langle X, \mathfrak{R} \rangle \not\approx_g \langle Y, \mathfrak{S} \rangle$ if X, $\mathfrak{R}$, Y, and $\mathfrak{S}$ are as above and $g = (\langle a, c \rangle, \langle b, d \rangle, \langle c, e \rangle, \langle R_1, S_2 \rangle, \langle R_2, S_1 \rangle)$ or $g = (\langle a, d \rangle, \langle b, c \rangle, \langle c, e \rangle, \langle R_1, S_1 \rangle, \langle R_2, S_2 \rangle)$.

3. In the above examples, $\langle X, \mathfrak{R} \rangle \approx \langle Y, \mathfrak{S} \rangle$ since there is at least one function f such that $\langle X, \mathfrak{R} \rangle \approx_f \langle Y, \mathfrak{S} \rangle$. Example 3 in 4.8 is also isomorphic.

4. $\langle X, \mathfrak{R} \rangle \not\approx \langle Y, \mathfrak{S} \rangle$ if $X = (a, b, c)$; $\mathfrak{R}$ consists of $R_1 = (\langle a, b \rangle, \langle b, a \rangle, \langle a, a \rangle, \langle b, b \rangle)$ and $R_2 = (\langle a, c \rangle, \langle b, c \rangle)$; $Y = (c, d, e)$; $\mathfrak{S}$ consists of $S_1 = (\langle c, d \rangle, \langle d, c \rangle, \langle c, c \rangle, \langle d, d \rangle)$ and $S_2 = (\langle c, e \rangle, \langle e, d \rangle)$.

5. $\langle X, \mathfrak{R} \rangle \not\approx \langle Y, \mathfrak{S} \rangle$ (1) if the cardinalities of X and Y are not the same, (2) if the cardinalities of $\mathfrak{R}_i$ and $\mathfrak{S}_i (i = 1, 2, \cdots)$ are not the same for any i, or (3) if the cardinalities of R and $f(R)$ are not the same for any R in $\mathfrak{R}$.

Remarks. If $\langle X, \mathfrak{R} \rangle \approx \langle Y, \mathfrak{S} \rangle$, then $\langle X, \mathfrak{R} \rangle \subseteq \langle Y, \mathfrak{S} \rangle$ and furthermore by adding the complement of every relation in $\mathfrak{R}$ to $\mathfrak{R}$ and the complement of every relation in $\mathfrak{S}$ to $\mathfrak{S}$, $\langle X, \mathfrak{R} \rangle$ can be made strongly homomorphic to $\langle Y, \mathfrak{S} \rangle$. Isomorphism is a sufficient condition for a perfect measurement discussed in Chapter 1 but not a necessary condition, while strong homomorphism is a necessary and sufficient condition for a perfect measurement.

APPENDIX B

Functional Analysis of Aggregations

In this appendix, the problem of aggregations is analyzed from the viewpoint of abstract functional relationships. An aggregation process is represented by a function, called an aggregation function g, defined on a set X of objects or events whose properties are represented by another function, called a property function f. The function g is said to be *perfect with respect to* f if, for any x in X, $f(x)$ can be identified uniquely from $g(x)$ without knowing what x actually is. A perfect aggregation is then discussed in terms of the partition of the set X generated by the aggregation function being finer than the partition of the set generated by a given property function. This abstract discussion of perfect aggregations is next applied to linear aggregations, and the form of any linear aggregation function that is perfect with respect to a linear property function is made explicit by means of the so-called *generalized inverses of matrices*.

Unfortunately, the requirement for a perfect aggregation is so strong that perfect aggregations in economics and elsewhere are rarely observed. Therefore, in Section 3, imperfect aggregations are studied, and the concepts of a "satisfactory" and a "reasonable" aggregation are introduced in connection with a decision function and an outcome function. Finally, partial orderings of imperfect aggregations defined in the same domain are introduced, and *the linear aggregation coefficient* is developed as an indicator of the degree of perfectness of a linear aggregation function with respect to a linear property function.

1. PRELIMINARIES[1]

1.1. A *set* is a collection of identifiable objects called *elements* of the set. If x is an element of X, it is denoted by $x \in X$. A set is *empty* if it contains no elements and *nonempty* otherwise. A set X is *included* or *contained* in another set Y or is a *subset* of Y, denoted by $X \subseteq Y$ or $Y \supseteq X$, if every element in X is also an element in Y. A set X is said to be *equal* to a set Y, denoted by $X = Y$, if X is included in Y and Y is included in X.

1.2. A *function f* is a nonempty set of ordered pairs, $\langle x, y \rangle$, of elements which satisfies the condition that no two distinct ordered pairs in f have the same first element x. The set of all first elements x's of the ordered pairs in f is called the *domain* of the function, and the set of all second elements y's of the ordered pairs in f is called the *range* of the function.

The second element y of an ordered pair $\langle x, y \rangle$ in a function f is called the *image* of x under the function f and is denoted by $f(x)$. If A is a set of elements and X is the domain of a function f, $f(A)$ denotes the set of images of all elements that are in A and simultaneously in X. In particular, $f(X)$ denotes the range of f.

1.3. A function f is said to *map a set X into a set Y*, denoted by $f : X \to Y$ or $X \xrightarrow{f} Y$, if the set X is the domain of f and the set Y contains the range of f. In particular, if the set Y is equal to the range of f, the function f is said to map the set X *onto* the set Y, denoted by

$$f : X \xrightarrow{\text{onto}} Y$$

A function f is one-to-one if no two distinct ordered pairs in f have the same second element y.

1.4. A *composite function gf* of functions $f : X \to Y$ and $g : Y' \to Z$, where Y' includes the range of f is a function $h : X \to Z$ such that $g(f(x)) = h(x)$ for all x in X.

1.5. Let $\hat{x}$ be an element in the domain X of a function f. Then the set of all elements x in X such that $f(x) = f(\hat{x})$ is called the *f-equivalent set of $\hat{x}$*, denoted by $[\hat{x}]_f$.

---

[1] Some basic concepts discussed in Appendix A have been reproduced here. For a more extensive explanation with examples, see Appendix A.

1.6. Let f and g be two functions which have the same domain X. The function g is said to be *finer* than the function f, or equivalently the function f is said to be *coarser* than the function g, if $[x]_g$ is contained in $[x]_f$ for all x in X.

1.7. *Theorem 1: Theorem of Composite Functions.* Given two functions $f: X \to Y$ and $g: X \to W$, there exists uniquely a function $h: g(X) \xrightarrow{\text{onto}} f(X)$ such that

(B.1) $h(g(x)) = f(x)$ for all x in X

if and only if g is finer than f.

Proof. Assume that g is finer than f. Then, for any x_1 and x_2 in X, $g(x_1) = g(x_2)$ implies $f(x_1) = f(x_2)$. Therefore, there exists a function $h: g(X) \to f(X)$ satisfying (B.1). Clearly h is onto since for any y in $f(X)$ there exists at least one x in X so that $f(x) = y$ and hence at least one w in $g(X)$ so that $h(w) = y$. Furthermore, h is unique since by definition $f(x)$ and $g(x)$ are both unique for all x in X.

Suppose that there exists uniquely a function $h: g(X) \xrightarrow{\text{onto}} f(X)$ so that (B.1) is satisfied but g is not finer than f. Then, for some x in X, $f([x]_g)$ contains more than one element. Let y_1 and y_2 be two distinct elements in $f([x]_g)$ and x_1 and x_2 be elements such that $f(x_1) = y_1$ and $f(x_2) = y_2$, respectively. Then, $h(g(x_1)) = h(g(x_2))$, but $f(x_1) \neq f(x_2)$. Hence, either $h(g(x_1)) \neq f(x_1)$ or $h(g(x_2)) \neq f(x_2)$ must hold. This is a contradiction. Hence, g is finer than f.   Q.E.D.

We shall now apply the theorem to linear functions after some preliminary review of linear functions.

1.8. Let X^n and X^m be vector spaces of n dimension and m dimension, respectively. Then, when a basis for X^n and a basis for X^m are both fixed, a linear function $f: X^n \to X^m$ can be uniquely represented by an $m \times n$ matrix A so that

$$f(x) = Ax \qquad \text{for all } x \text{ in } X^n$$

where Ax represents the multiplication of a (column) vector x in X^n by the matrix A. We shall alternatively call the function f that is uniquely represented by a matrix A the function A.[2]

1.9. The *generalized inverse* of a matrix A is the unique matrix $A^\dagger$

[2] See, for example, Halmos [1958], Kemeny, Mirkil, Snell, and Thompson [1959] for the definitions of such concepts as vectors, linear (or vector) spaces, basis, dimensions, linear functions, and matrix operations as well as for the uniqueness of the matrix representation of a linear function.

which satisfies the following set of equations:

(B.2a) $$AA^\dagger A = A$$

(B.2b) $$A^\dagger AA^\dagger = A^\dagger$$

(B.2c) $$(A^\dagger A)^* = A^\dagger A$$

(B.2d) $$(AA^\dagger)^* = AA^\dagger$$

where * represents the transpose of a matrix.[3]

1.10. *Lemma 1.* The null space of a matrix A (i.e., the set of all vectors x such that Ax is the null vector 0), denoted by $N(A)$, is the set of all vectors given by $(I - A^\dagger A)z$ where I is the n-dimensional identity matrix, $A^\dagger$ is the generalized inverse of A, and z is an arbitrary vector in X^n, i.e.

$$N(A) = \{(I - A^\dagger A)z : z \in X^n\}$$

Proof. (1) For any z in X^n

$$A(I - A^\dagger A)z = (A - AA^\dagger A)z = 0$$

by (B.2a), hence $(I - A^\dagger A)z$ is in $N(A)$. (2) For any x^0 in $N(A)$ there is at least one z such that $(I - A^\dagger A)z = x^0$ since by setting $z = x^0$, we have $(I - A^\dagger A)x^0 = x^0$.

1.11. *Lemma 2.* Let $[\hat{x}]_A$ be the A-equivalent set of $\hat{x}$ and $\hat{x} + N(A)$ be the set of all vectors given by $\hat{x} + x^0$ where x^0 is in $N(A)$. Then

$$[\hat{x}]_A = \hat{x} + N(A) \qquad \text{for all } \hat{x} \text{ in } X$$

Proof. (1) For any x^0 in $N(A)$

$$A(\hat{x} + x^0) = A\hat{x} + Ax^0 = A\hat{x}$$

hence $\hat{x} + x^0$ is in $[\hat{x}]_A$. (2) For any x in $[\hat{x}]_A$

$$A(x - \hat{x}) = Ax - A\hat{x} = A\hat{x} - A\hat{x} = 0$$

hence $x^0 = x - \hat{x}$ is in $N(A)$, i.e., x is in $\hat{x} + N(A)$.

[3] Moore [1920] and Penrose [1955] proved that for any matrix A, regardless of whether it is singular or nonsingular, square or rectangular, zero or nonzero, the generalized inverse $A^\dagger$ exists uniquely. See Ijiri [1965a, Appendix A] for more detailed introductory discussions on the generalized inverse of a matrix. For computations of $A^\dagger$, see Ben-Israel and Wersan [1963], Ben-Israel and Ijiri [1963], etc.

1.12. *Theorem 2.* Let A and B be an $m \times n$ matrix as well as the functions represented by the matrices A and B, respectively. Then, the following statements are equivalent:

(B.3) $\qquad\qquad\qquad B$ is finer than A

(B.4) $\qquad\qquad\qquad N(B) \subseteq N(A)$

(B.5) $\qquad\qquad\qquad AB^\dagger B = A$

Proof. B is finer than A. $\Leftrightarrow$ For every x in X, there is one and only one element in $A([x]_B)$, hence in $A(x + N(B))$, hence in $A(N(B))$. $\Leftrightarrow A(N(B)) = 0$ since $N(B)$ includes the null vector for which $A(0) = 0$. $\Leftrightarrow N(B) \subseteq N(A)$. Thus, (B.3) is equivalent to (B.4).

$N(B) \subseteq N(A)$. $\Leftrightarrow A(I - B^\dagger B)z = 0$ for all z in X^n by Lemma 1. $\Leftrightarrow A(I - B^\dagger B) = \bar{0}$ where $\bar{0}$ is the $m \times n$ matrix of zeros. $\Leftrightarrow AB^\dagger B = A$. Thus, (B.4) is equivalent to (B.5); hence all the three statements are equivalent.

1.13. *Theorem 3.* Let $f: X^n \to X^m$ and $g: X^n \to X^k$ be linear functions where g is finer than f and let A and B be the unique matrices which represent the functions f and g, respectively, assuming that bases have been fixed for X^n, X^m, and X^k. Then, a matrix C represents the function $h: g(X) \xrightarrow{\text{onto}} f(X)$ satisfying

(B.6) $\qquad\qquad h(g(x)) = f(x) \qquad$ for all x in X^n

if and only if C is in the form of

(B.7) $\qquad\qquad\qquad C = AB^\dagger + D(I - BB^\dagger)$

where D is an arbitrary $m \times k$ matrix.

Proof. (1) Since g is finer than f, $AB^\dagger B = A$ by Theorem 2. Also $(I - BB^\dagger)B = 0$ by (B.2a). Hence if C is given by (B.7), we have

(B.8) $\qquad\qquad CB = AB^\dagger B + D(I - BB^\dagger)B = A$

Therefore, (B.6) is satisfied; hence C represents the function g.

(2) Let G be a matrix which represents the function h. Then, we have

$$GBx = Ax \qquad \text{for all } x \text{ in } X^n$$

or

(B.9) $\qquad\qquad\qquad GB = A$

Let $\bar{D}$ be any given $m \times k$ matrix and let

$$\bar{C} = AB^\dagger + \bar{D}(I - BB^\dagger)$$

Then, we have from (B.8) and (B.9)

$$\bar{C}B = A = GB$$

or
$$(G - \bar{C})B = \bar{0}$$

where $\bar{0}$ is the $m \times n$ matrix of zeros. Hence

$$AB^\dagger + (\bar{D} + G - \bar{C})(I - BB^\dagger)$$

$$= AB^\dagger + \bar{D}(I - BB^\dagger) + (G - \bar{C}) - (G - \bar{C})BB^\dagger$$

$$= \bar{C} + G - \bar{C} = G$$

and G is in the form of (B.7) in which D is set equal to $\bar{D} + G - \bar{C}$.   Q.E.D.

Note that a function $f : X^n \to X^m$ can be uniquely represented by a matrix if bases are fixed for X^n and X^m. However, if the domain of a function is constrained, as in the case of the function h, the same function may be represented by different matrices. For example, the function h is defined only on the range of g, i.e., the set of all vectors in the form of Bx, $x \in X^n$; hence h may be represented by any matrix in the form of $AB^\dagger + D(I - BB^\dagger)$ since the second term always disappears when multiplied by a vector Bx.

2. PERFECT AGGREGATIONS

2.1. We are now ready to apply the theorems developed in the previous section to aggregation problems. To begin we will discuss the aggregation problem in terms of economic examples.

2.2. Consider a set of n elements. The elements may be individuals, firms, etc. Suppose that the behavior of the ith element is represented by a function $\varphi_i : X_i \to V_i$. Such a function may be the consumption function of the ith individual, the production function of the ith firm, etc. We shall call a function which shows the behavior of an individual element in the set an *elementary microfunction*.

2.3. The set of n such functions may be represented by a single function $\varphi:X \rightarrow V$ where X and V are the Cartesian products of X_i's and V_i's, respectively, with the property that for all x in X the ith coordinate of $\varphi(x)$ is equal to $\varphi_i(x_i)$ where x_i is the ith coordinate of x.[4] We shall call such a function φ a *combined microfunction* or simply a *microfunction*.

For example, the consumption function of the ith individual may be written as

$$(B.10) \qquad v_i = a_i x_i + b_i$$

where x_i is a variable representing the amount of income, v_i is a variable representing the amount of consumption, and a_i and b_i are scalars.[5] Then, a set of n linear equations given in (B.10) may be represented by a single function

$$(B.11) \qquad v = Ax + b$$

where x and v are n-dimensional column vectors of variables, A is an $n \times n$ diagonal matrix whose ith diagonal element is a_i, and b is an n-dimensional column vector whose ith element is b_i.

However, in the following discussions the dimensionalities of x's and v's are unimportant, hence we shall represent a combined microfunction simply by an arbitrary function $\varphi:X \rightarrow V$.

2.4. Next, assume aggregation of the variables x_1, x_2, $\cdots$, x_n into a variable w and the variables v_1, v_2, $\cdots$, v_n into a variable y. Such aggregations may be represented by functions $g:X \rightarrow W$ and $\psi:V \rightarrow Y$. We shall call g an *aggregation function of independent variables* or an *active aggregation function* and ψ an *aggregation function of dependent variables* or a *passive aggregation function*. Then, we have four variables x, v, w and y whose values are given by elements of the sets X, V, W and Y, respectively, and three functions, the microfunction, the active aggregation function, and the passive aggregation function, which relate the four variables. We shall call the variable x the *independent microvariable*, the variable v the *dependent microvariable*, the variable w the *independent macrovariable*, and the variable y the *dependent macrovariable*. The following are simple ex-

---

[4] The *Cartesian product* of n sets, X_1, X_2, ..., X_n, is the set of all ordered n-tuples $\langle x_1, x_2, \ldots, x_n \rangle$ where x_i is an element of X_i for each subscript i. The Cartesian product of X_1, X_2, ..., X_n is denoted by $X_1 \times X_2 \times \ldots \times X_n$. The ith *coordinate* of an element $x = \langle x_1, x_2, \ldots, x_n \rangle$ in $X_1 \times X_2 \times \ldots \times X_n$ is the ith element in the n-tuple $\langle x_1, x_2, \ldots, x_n \rangle$. See Appendix A, Sections 4.1–4.2.

[5] In this case, the φ function is a function of only one variable. However, it will be seen that our discussion does not put any constraints on the number of variables involved. That is, X_i may be the Cartesian product of X_{i1}, X_{i2}, ..., X_{im}, and so may V_i.

amples of an active and a passive aggregation function of income and consumption.

$$g: \quad w = \sum_i x_i$$

$$\psi: \quad y = \sum_i v_i$$

where x_i and v_i are the ith elements of x and v, respectively.

2.5. Ordinarily, the domain of an aggregation function has a larger dimension than that of the range of the function. For example, if x is a variable whose values are elements in n-dimensional vector space, an aggregation function transforms x into w, whose values are elements in a vector space with a smaller dimension and in many cases in a one-dimensional vector space. However, since dimensions are irrelevant in most of our following discussions, we shall consider aggregation functions to be simply arbitrary functions which transform microvariables into macrovariables.

2.6. We now come to the central issue of the aggregation problem. That is, under what conditions can we identify the value of the dependent macrovariable y from the independent macrovariable w?[6] In other words, under what conditions can we have a function h so that for each element x in X, $h(g(x)) = \psi(\varphi(x))$?

For example, in the income-consumption relationship, we want to know how much the aggregated consumption is but we do not know the income of individuals, x_i's, nor the consumption of individuals, v_i's. If we know x_i's or v_i's, it is simple to calculate the aggregated consumption y by $\psi(\varphi(x))$ or by $\psi(v)$. However, we know what the three functions φ, ψ, and g are, and also, by some method, we can determine the amount of aggregated income w. The question then is: Is this knowledge of the amount of aggregated income sufficient to identify the amount of aggregated consumption and, if so, under what conditions?

As clearly shown in Figure B.1, the existence of such a function h depends upon the characteristics of the two aggregation functions, g and ψ, assuming that the microfunction φ is fixed. As we shall see later, the coarser the passive aggregation function ψ is, the coarser the active aggregation function g can be without making it impossible to identify the variable y.

---

[6] The aggregation problem is also viewed from other angles. For example, the question raised by Klein [1946b] is "whether or not a particular characteristic of the microfunction is carried over to a macrofunction under an aggregation method." (See also May [1946] and Pu [1946].) However, here we shall limit our attention to the existence of a macrofunction by which the dependent macrovariable is consistently identified using the independent macrovariable. For further analyses of economic aggregation problems, see, for example, Amemiya [1964], Green [1964], Hurwitz [1952], Kemeny, Morgenstern, and Thompson [1956], Klein [1946a], Rosenblatt [1965], Simon and Ando [1961], Theil [1954], [1957], and [1959].

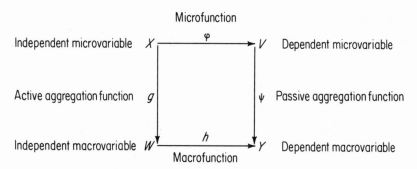

Fig. B.1. Variables and Functions in an Aggregation Problem

If the passive aggregation function is the coarsest, i.e., a constant function, any active aggregation function can be used to identify the value of y.

2.7. To fix the analysis and make more precise statements about aggregation functions, let us assume that the passive aggregation function is given and continue the analysis in relation to the given microfunction φ and the passive aggregation function ψ.[7] Let us call the composite function f of the functions φ and ψ the *property function* since it represents a property of elements in X in real-world problems, and the active aggregation function g simply the *aggregation function* since this is the only aggregation function that we are interested in. Then, the relationships among the variables x, w, and y are given in Figure B.2.

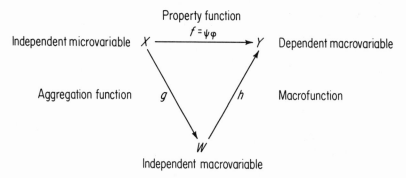

Fig. B.2. Variables and Functions in a Simplified Aggregation Problem

---

[7] Instead of assuming that the three functions $W \xrightarrow{g} X \xrightarrow{\varphi} V \xrightarrow{\psi} Y$ are given, we can start our analysis by assuming that the three functions $V \xleftarrow{\varphi} X \xrightarrow{g} W \xrightarrow{h} Y$ are given and discuss the existence and the uniqueness of the function $\psi : \varphi(X) \xrightarrow{\text{onto}} h(g(X))$ or the function $\bar{\psi} : h(g(X)) \xrightarrow{\text{onto}} \varphi(X)$. Also, we can analyze the case where the three functions $X \xrightarrow{\varphi} V \xrightarrow{\psi} Y \xrightarrow{h} W$ are given or where the three functions $X \xrightarrow{g} W \xrightarrow{h} Y \xrightarrow{\psi} V$ are given, although the latter two cases are somewhat trivial since the condition for the existence and the uniqueness of the fourth function depends only on whether or not the functions are one-to-one and on a relative inclusion condition of their ranges.

We shall say that the aggregation function g is *perfect with respect to the given property function f* if there exists a function $h:g(X) \to f(X)$ so that

(B.12) $$h(g(x)) = f(x) \qquad \text{for all } x \text{ in } X$$

i.e., if g is finer than f (Theorem 1). An aggregation function which is not perfect with respect to the given property function is called *imperfect* with respect to the property function. If f and g are both linear and represented by matrices A and B, respectively, then g is perfect with respect to f if and only if (B.5) holds, in which case h is given by (B.7).[8]

2.8. The concepts and theorems that are discussed above can be applied to the aggregation problem of Leontief input-output systems as follows.[9]

Let x and v be vectors of net output and final demand of an original (unaggregated) Leontief system, and let w and y be vectors of net output and final demand, respectively, of an aggregated Leontief system. The four variables x, v, w and y are related to each other by

(B.13) $$v = (I - A)x \qquad \text{(microfunction)}$$

(B.14) $$w = Tx \qquad \text{(active aggregation function)}$$

(B.15) $$y = Tv \qquad \text{(passive aggregation function)}$$

where I is an identity matrix, A is a matrix of the input coefficients, and T is the matrix of both active and passive aggregations and has one and only one positive element in each column.

Then T corresponds to the function g and $T(I - A)$ corresponds to f in Theorem 1. Let $(I - B)$ be the matrix of transformation which corresponds to h. Then (B.12) may be written

(B.16) $$(I - B)Tx = T(I - A)x \qquad \text{for all } x \text{ in } X$$

(Note that (B.16) is exactly the same as Equation (6) in Hatanaka [1952] except for the difference in notations.) By Theorems 1, 2 and 3, this condition is satisfied if and only if $N(T) \subseteq N(T(I - A))$ or if and only if

(B.17) $$T(I - A)T^\dagger T = T(I - A)$$

in which case the matrix $(I - B)$ is in the form of $T(I - A)T^\dagger + D(I - TT^\dagger)$ where D is an arbitrary matrix which has the same dimensions as $T(I - A)T^\dagger$.

---

[8] Essentially the same result was obtained in Theil [1954], although the use of the generalized inverse here simplifies the derivation and the conclusion considerably.

[9] See, for example, Hatanaka [1952], Charnes and Cooper [1961], Rosenblatt [1956], [1957] for the aggregation problem in Leontief systems.

The condition (B.17) is equivalent to

$$T(I - A)(I - T^\dagger T) = 0$$

or to

(B.18) $$\qquad\qquad TA(I - T^\dagger T) = 0$$

by (B.2a). Namely, for any vector t^0 in $N(T)$, $TAt^0 = 0$. The Hatanaka conditions [1952] can also be derived from these results, except that his condition (A) is a consequence of imposing a further condition on A by requiring the diagonal elements of A to be zero.[10]

3. IMPERFECT AGGREGATIONS

3.1. The requirement for a perfect aggregation is in reality often too strong. We can find practically no aggregations that are perfect. Therefore, it is important to consider whether or not imperfect aggregations are "useful" and if so, under what conditions.

3.2. Consider a decision function d whose domain is the set Y and whose range is contained in a set Z. The set Z is the set of all possible decisions that a decision maker can make and the set Y is the set of all possible values that the dependent macrovariable y can have. (See Figure B.3.) For example, the decision function may deal with a tax policy or a policy on government spending, which depends upon the amount of the aggregated consumption. Here, the macrofunction h cannot identify y uniquely for each choice of x unless g is perfect. Hence, if an imperfect aggregation is used, $h(w)$ is a set of elements in Y instead of a single element.

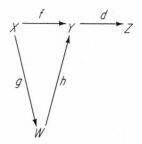   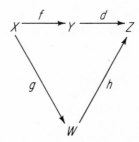

Fig. B.3.   Incorporation of a   **Fig. B.4.**   Incorporation of a
         Decision Function I   Decision Function II

[10] For a further analysis of the aggregation of a Leontief system, see, for example, Charnes and Cooper [1961], Fei [1956], Fisher [1958a], Johansen [1961], Morishima and Seton [1961], and Rosenblatt [1956 and 1965].

However, suppose that for each element y in $h(w)$, $d(y)$ is a unique element, i.e., the decision function calls for the same decision for each element in $h(w)$; then the fact that $h(w)$ consists of more than one element does not matter at all. (See Figure B.4.) In this case, we are actually concerned with the existence of a function h such that

(B.19) $h(g(x)) = d(f(x))$ for all x in X

It is then clear that given f and d there exists uniquely a function $h:g(X) \xrightarrow{\text{onto}} d(f(X))$ so that

(B.20) $h(g(x)) = d(f(x))$ for all x in X

if and only if g is finer than df. Previously, the condition was g finer than f. Now the condition is g finer than df. However, df is always coarser than f whatever the function d may be. (The function df is finer and simultaneously coarser than—i.e., df is equivalent to—f if and only if d is one-to-one.) Therefore, the new condition is weaker than the previous one. We shall call an aggregation function g *satisfactory* if there exists uniquely a function $h:g(X) \xrightarrow{\text{onto}} d(f(X))$ satisfying (B.20).

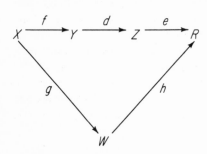

Fig. B.5. Incorporation of an Outcome Function

3.3. We may extend this discussion by incorporating the effect of a decision. Suppose that the outcome of a decision is given by a function $e:Z \to R$ where R is the set of all possible outcomes. Then, if an aggregation is not satisfactory, $h(w)$ does not specify a unique decision but only a set of decisions. However, if for each one of the decisions in $h(w)$ the outcome associated with the decision is the same, then the fact that $h(w)$ consists of more than one element does not matter. In this case, we are concerned with a function $h:g(X) \xrightarrow{\text{onto}} e(d(f(X)))$ where

(B.21) $h(g(x)) = e(d(f(x)))$ for all x in X

(See Figure B.5.) We shall call an aggregation function g *reasonable* if there exists uniquely a function $h:g(X) \xrightarrow{\text{onto}} e(d(f(X)))$ satisfying (B.21).

3.4. In summary, if an aggregation function is one-to-one, it is perfect, satisfactory, and reasonable regardless of the property function, the decision function, and the outcome function. If an aggregation function is perfect, it is satisfactory and reasonable regardless of the decision function and the outcome function. If an aggregation function is satisfactory, it is reasonable regardless of the outcome function.

3.5. In most cases, it is difficult to specify the decision function or the outcome function. However, at least we know that we should not reject imperfect aggregation functions just because they are imperfect since they may be satisfactory or reasonable depending upon the decision function and the outcome function.

3.6. Let us consider an application of this concept of satisfactory aggregations, which is developed in Ijiri [1965a], by introducing constraints on microvariables. For example, in the above income-consumption relationship, unless the marginal propensity to consume is the same for every individual in the population, the aggregated consumption can be any real number regardless of the value of the aggregated income, assuming that the individual income can take any real number. However, in many practical situations in which the aggregation problem arises, the variable x takes only the values in a subset of X^n, i.e., the variable x is constrained by the environmental conditions. In the income-consumption relationship, we can assume that the individual income is nonnegative. This immediately narrows the possible range that the aggregated consumption y can take. Namely, y must be at most equal to the aggregated income times the maximum marginal propensity to consume (i.e., $\text{Max}_i\ a_i$) and at least equal to the aggregated income times the minimum marginal propensity to consume (i.e., $\text{Min}_i\ a_i$). The more constraints we have on x, the narrower the range for y is for a given value of w.

3.7. In general, consider a function $\eta: X^n \to X^2$ where the axes of X^2 are one-dimensional real variables w and y. Suppose that the variable x cannot take all possible points in X^n but can take only points in a set K. Then, $\eta(K)$ gives us the image of K under the function η. The set $\eta(K)$ may be charted on a plane whose axes are w and y as in Figure B.6. This *aggregation chart* indicates the maximum and the minimum values of y (or its supremum and infimum if K is open) at any given value—for example, w_0—of w. It also indicates the maximum and the minimum values

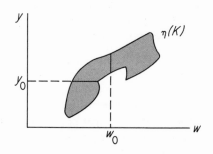

Fig. B.6. An Aggregation Chart

of w (or its supremum or infimum if K is open) at any given value—for example, y_0—of y. If the range for y at any value of w is narrow enough to reach a unique decision, the aggregation function is satisfactory. If the range for y at any value of w is narrow enough to obtain the same outcome, the aggregation function is reasonable.

If the set K is given by a set of linear inequalities, such as the set of all x's which satisfy

$$Ax \leq b$$

where A is an $m \times n$ matrix of constants and b is an n-component column vector of constants, and if the property and aggregation functions are both linear functionals, then the image $\eta(K)$ can be easily derived by the algorithm in Ijiri [1965a, Appendix B], which was developed by making a minor modification in the simplex algorithm.

4. THE LINEAR AGGREGATION COEFFICIENT

4.1. A set of all aggregation functions defined on the same domain can be partially ordered by the relation "finer than." A one-to-one function is the finest and a constant function is the coarsest. Clearly, if an aggregation function g is perfect with respect to a given property function f, any aggregation function that is finer than g is also perfect with respect to f. If an aggregation function g is imperfect with respect to a given property function f, any aggregation function that is coarser than g is also imperfect with respect to f. A one-to-one aggregation function is perfect with respect to any property function, whereas a constant aggregation function is imperfect with respect to any property function except a constant property function. The coarsest perfect aggregation function $g: X \to Y$ is a function g which is equivalent to f, i.e., a function g which is finer and coarser than f.

4.2. A set of aggregation functions can also be partially ordered by the relation "less imperfect than." That is, for a given property function f, an aggregation function g defined on X is said to be less imperfect than another aggregation function $\bar{g}$ defined on the same domain X if

(B.22) $$h([x]_g) \subseteq h([x]_{\bar{g}}) \qquad \text{for all } x \text{ in } X$$

4.3. The above ideas on partial ordering can be developed into the concept of the *linear aggregation coefficient* for the case where the property function and the aggregation function are both linear functions represented by matrices A and B, respectively.

4.4. Notice that the function h given by (B.7) exists uniquely even if B is not perfect with respect to A since C may be calculated for any A and B. What is the significance of the function given by (B.7) in estimating the value of $y (= Ax)$ from the value of $w (= Bx)$ without knowing, of course, what the actual value of x is?

4.5. In order to answer this question, let us assume that the domain X^n of the functions f and g is an n-dimensional Euclidean space,[11] denoted by R^n. We shall denote by $\| A \|$ the Euclidean norm of a matrix A, i.e.

(B.23) $$\| A \|^2 = \tau(A^*A) = \tau(AA^*)$$

where $\tau(\ )$ represents the trace (i.e., the sum of all diagonal elements) of a square matrix inside the parentheses. That is, $\| A \|$ is the square root of the sum of the squares of all elements in A.[12]

Then, the following relationship has been proved by using the properties of the generalized inverses.[13]

(B.24) $\| A - CB \| \leq \| A - ZB \|$ for all $m \times k$ matrices Z

We shall use this property of the matrix C in interpreting the significance of the function h defined by C.

4.6. Note that if x is a vector of mutually independent, n random variables x_j $(j = 1, 2, \cdots, n)$, each of which is normalized, i.e., has a zero mean and a unit variance, then for any $m \times n$ matrix P the sum of variances of the m variables in the vector Px or simply the variance of Px, denoted by $\sigma^2(Px)$, is

(B.25) $$\sigma^2(Px) = \sum_{i=1}^{m} \sigma^2(P_ix) = \sum_{i=1}^{m} \sum_{j=1}^{n} \sigma^2(p_{ij}x_j)^2 = \sum_{i=1}^{m} \sum_{j=1}^{n} p_{ij}^2 = \| P \|^2$$

where P_i is the ith row of P and p_{ij} is the element in the ith row and the jth column of P.[14] Therefore, if the variable $y = Ax$ is estimated from the variable $w = Bx$ as $\hat{y} = Zw$ where Z is an $m \times k$ matrix, the variance of $y - \hat{y}$ is

(B.26) $$\sigma^2(y - \hat{y}) = \sigma^2(Ax - ZBx) = \| A - ZB \|^2$$

Therefore, from (B.24) we can say that if x is a vector of mutually inde-

---

[11] The following analysis is applicable to a unitary space too. However, since complex numbers do not enter our aggregation problem, we shall limit our attention to a Euclidean space.

[12] See, for example, Householder [1964]. Also see Charnes and Cooper [1961] for other types of matrix and vector norms.

[13] See Penrose [1956] and also Ben-Israel and Charnes [1963].

[14] If x_1 and x_2 are mutually independent random variables with variances σ_1^2 and σ_2^2, respectively, a new variable y defined by $y = ax_1 + bx_2 + c$, where a, b, and c are constants, has a variance $a^2\sigma_1^2 + b^2\sigma_2^2$. See Gnedenko [1962, pp. 206–7].

pendent, n normalized variables, then the estimation of y as $\hat{y} = Cw$ produces the minimum variance of the error $y - \hat{y}$. (Note that $\hat{y}$ is an unbiased estimate of y.)

4.7. Since the variance of y is

$$(B.27) \qquad \sigma^2(y) = \sigma^2(Ax) = \| A \|^2$$

which is here assumed to be nonzero,[15] the proportion of the variance of y that is reduced as a result of estimating y by Cw, which we denote by ρ^2, is

$$(B.28) \qquad \rho^2 = \frac{\sigma^2(y) - \sigma^2(y - \hat{y})}{\sigma^2(y)} = \frac{\| A \|^2 - \| A - CB \|^2}{\| A \|^2}$$

However, from (B.7) and (B.2a) we have $CB = AB^\dagger B$, and by the definition of the trace of a matrix

$$\| A - CB \|^2$$

$$(B.29) \qquad = \| A - AB^\dagger B \|^2 = \tau(A - AB^\dagger B)(A - AB^\dagger B)^*$$

$$= \tau[AA^* - AB^\dagger BA^* - A(B^\dagger B)^*A^* + AB^\dagger B(B^\dagger B)^*A^*]$$

Since $(B^\dagger B)^* = B^\dagger B$ and $BB^\dagger B = B$ by (B.2c) and (B.2a), we have

$$\| A - CB \|^2 = \tau(AA^* - 2AB^\dagger BA^* + AB^\dagger BB^\dagger BA^*)$$

$$(B.30)$$

$$= \tau(AA^* - AB^\dagger BA^*) = \| A \|^2 - \tau(AB^\dagger BA^*)$$

However, since

$$\| AB^\dagger B \|^2 = \tau(AB^\dagger B)(AB^\dagger B)^* = \tau(AB^\dagger B(B^\dagger B)^*A^*)$$

$$(B.31)$$

$$= \tau(AB^\dagger BB^\dagger BA^*) = \tau(AB^\dagger BA^*)$$

we can write

$$(B.32) \qquad \| A - CB \|^2 = \| A \|^2 - \| AB^\dagger B \|^2$$

---

[15] Note that $\| A \|^2$ is zero if and only if all elements of A are zero, in which case y is a zero vector regardless of x.

Therefore, ρ^2 is derived simply as

(B.33)
$$\rho^2 = \frac{\| AB^\dagger B \|^2}{\| A \|^2}$$

We shall call this ρ^2 the *aggregation effectiveness coefficient* since it indicates how effective the aggregate w is in estimating the value of y.

4.8. Note that by the definition of ρ^2

(B.34)
$$0 \leq \rho^2 \leq 1$$

and $\rho^2 = 1$ if and only if the aggregation $w = Bx$ is perfect with respect to $y = Ax$ as shown in Theorem 2. Thus, if an aggregation is perfect, the variance of $y - \hat{y}$ is zero since $y = \hat{y} = Cw = CBx$ for all x; hence 100 per cent of the variance of y is eliminated as a result of estimating y by Cw. If on the other hand $\rho^2 = 0$, the estimator $\hat{y} = Bx$ does not help reduce the variance of y since the variance of $y - \hat{y}$ is exactly the same as the variance of y. This means that $AB^\dagger B$ is a zero matrix, in which case

(B.35)
$$\hat{y} = Cw = CBx = AB^\dagger Bx = 0x = 0$$

for all x. This can happen if and only if the range of $B^\dagger$ is included in the null space of A.

4.9. If A is a nonzero row vector a, ρ^2 is reduced to

(B.36)
$$\rho^2 = \frac{\| aB^\dagger B \|^2}{aa^*} = \frac{aB^\dagger B(B^\dagger B)^* a^*}{aa^*} = \frac{aB^\dagger Ba^*}{aa^*}$$

If the ith row of B, denoted by B_i, is a linear combination of the other rows in B, then $B_i x$ is redundant since it does not help us identify the value of y. Therefore, we do not lose anything by eliminating such rows and using only the set of remaining rows, which is linearly independent. If the rows of B are linearly independent, then as in Penrose [1956]

(B.37)
$$B^\dagger = B^*(BB^*)^{-1}$$

(B.38)
$$\rho^2 = \frac{aB^*(BB^*)^{-1}Ba^*}{aa^*}$$

The square root of (B.38) is exactly the same as the expression for the multiple linear correlation coefficient where BB^* corresponds to the co-variance matrix. (See, for example, Anderson [1958], Cramér [1946].)

4.10. If, in addition, B is a nonzero row vector b, then ρ^2 is further reduced to

$$(\text{B.39}) \qquad \rho^2 = \frac{ab^* \cdot ba^*}{aa^* \cdot bb^*} = \frac{\| ab^* \|^2}{\| a \|^2 \cdot \| b \|^2}$$

If we define

$$(\text{B.40}) \qquad \rho = \frac{ab^*}{\| a \| \cdot \| b \|}$$

then the matrix C in (B.7), which is now reduced to a scalar, is

$$(\text{B.41}) \qquad C = ab^\dagger = \frac{ab^*}{bb^*} = \frac{\| a \|}{\| b \|} \rho$$

which implies that $C > 0 \Leftrightarrow \rho > 0$, $C = 0 \Leftrightarrow \rho = 0$, and $C < 0 \Leftrightarrow \rho < 0$. Note that ρ is exactly the same as the simple linear correlation coefficient. The difference between them lies only in the interpretation of the under-lying two spaces, the space R^n and the space for all linear functionals on R^n, which are the dual of each other (see, e.g., Halmos [1958]).

4.11. We shall, therefore, call ρ defined by (B.40) the *simple linear aggregation coefficient*[16] and the square root of ρ^2 defined in (B.38) the *multiple linear aggregation coefficient*. Note that the multiple linear aggregation coefficient is always nonnegative (i.e., $0 \leq \sqrt{\rho^2} \leq 1$) as is the multiple linear correlation coefficient, while the simple linear aggregation coefficient can take negative values (i.e., $-1 \leq \rho \leq 1$) as does the simple linear correlation coefficient. Thus, the linear aggregation coefficient indicates the degree of perfectness of a linear aggregation function B with respect to a linear property function A in the sense that its square (the aggregation effectiveness coefficient) shows the proportion of the variance in $y = Ax$ that is eliminated by using the aggregate $w = Bx$.

4.12. In order to calculate the linear aggregation coefficient or the aggregation effectiveness coefficient in a practical situation, we must make the following adjustment in the matrices A and B before deriving ρ or ρ^2 by means of (B.33) or (B.40). Suppose that the random variable x_j has a mean $\bar{x}_j$ and a variance σ_j^2 $(j = 1, 2, \cdots, n)$. If $\sigma_j^2 = 0$ for some j, we

---

[16] The idea of a linear aggregation coefficient and the analysis of a simple linear aggregation coefficient were originally developed in Ijiri [1965a] in connection with his study on management goals and accounting feedback on goals.

define new matrices $\hat{A}$ and $\hat{B}$ by deleting the jth column of A and B, denoted by A_j and B_j, and a new vector $\hat{x}$ of random variables by deleting the jth element of x. Then we have

$$y = \hat{A}\hat{x} + A_j x_j$$
(B.42)
$$w = \hat{B}\hat{x} + B_j x_j$$

(If there is more than one such variable, we may consider A_j and B_j to be matrices obtained by adjoining the columns of A and B, respectively, which correspond to the variables, and we may consider x_j to be a column vector of the variables.) Since $A_j x_j$ and $B_j x_j$ are constant vectors, we have[17]

$$\sigma^2(y) = \sigma^2(\hat{A}x)$$
(B.43)
$$\sigma^2(y - Cw) = \sigma^2(\hat{A}x - C\hat{B}x)$$

Hence ρ^2 is calculated based on A and B with their jth column deleted. Therefore, in the following discussions, we shall assume that $\sigma_j > 0$ for all $j = 1, 2, \cdots, n$.

Now let $\overset{\ast}{\hat{x}}_j$ be a variable defined as

(B.44)
$$\overset{\ast}{\hat{x}}_j = \frac{x_j - \bar{x}_j}{\sigma_j}$$

and let $\overset{\ast}{\hat{x}}$ and $\bar{x}$ be n-component vectors whose components are $\overset{\ast}{\hat{x}}_j$ and $\bar{x}_j$, respectively $(j = 1, 2, \cdots, n)$. Then, $\overset{\ast}{\hat{x}}_j$ is a normalized variable since it has mean zero and its variance is

(B.45)
$$\sigma^2(\overset{\ast}{\hat{x}}_j) = \sigma^2\left(\frac{x_j - \bar{x}_j}{\sigma_j}\right) = \sigma^2\left(\frac{x_j}{\sigma_j}\right) = \frac{1}{\sigma_j^2}\,\sigma^2(x_j) = 1$$

Since $x_j = \sigma_j \overset{\ast}{\hat{x}}_j + \bar{x}_j$, we have

$$y = Ax = \overset{\ast}{\hat{A}}\overset{\ast}{\hat{x}} + A\bar{x}$$
(B.46)
$$w = Bx = \overset{\ast}{\hat{B}}\overset{\ast}{\hat{x}} + B\bar{x}$$

where $\overset{\ast}{\hat{A}}$ and $\overset{\ast}{\hat{B}}$ are the matrices obtained from A and B by multiplying elements in the jth column by σ_j for $j = 1, 2, \cdots, n$. Here $A\bar{x}$ and $B\bar{x}$ are

---

[17] See Footnote 14 for this appendix.

constant vectors, hence

(B.47)
$$\sigma^2(y) = \sigma^2(\hat{\hat{A}}\hat{\hat{x}}) = \| \hat{\hat{A}} \|^2$$

$$\sigma^2(y - Cw) = \sigma^2(\hat{\hat{A}}\hat{\hat{x}} - C\hat{\hat{B}}\hat{\hat{x}}) = \| \hat{\hat{A}} - C\hat{\hat{B}} \|^2 = \| \hat{\hat{A}}\hat{B}^\dagger\hat{\hat{B}} \|^2$$

and

(B.48)
$$\rho^2 = \frac{\| \hat{\hat{A}}\hat{B}^\dagger\hat{\hat{B}} \|^2}{\| \hat{\hat{A}} \|^2}$$

From (B.46) we have

(B.49)
$$y - A\bar{x} = \hat{\hat{A}}\hat{\hat{x}}$$

$$w - B\bar{x} = \hat{\hat{B}}\hat{\hat{x}}$$

hence by Theorem 3 we estimate $(y - A\bar{x})$ to be $\hat{\hat{A}}\hat{\hat{B}}^\dagger(w - B\bar{x})$ in order to minimize the variance of the error; namely, we estimate y to be

(B.50)
$$\hat{y} = \hat{\hat{A}}\hat{\hat{B}}^\dagger(w - B\bar{x}) + A\bar{x}$$

4.13. Therefore, for any matrices A and B, we multiply each element in the jth columns of A and B by the standard deviation σ_j ($j = 1, 2, \cdots, n$) and calculate ρ^2 based on the new matrices $\hat{A}$ and $\hat{B}$ thus obtained. Actually this rule works for cases where some variables, e.g., x_j, have zero variances. That is, instead of deleting the jth columns of A and B we may multiply them by $\sigma_j = 0$, making all elements in the jth columns equal to zero, and calculate ρ^2 based on the new matrices derived. This is possible for the following reason. If the elements in the jth column of B are all zero and if we let $\hat{B}$ be a matrix obtained from B by striking out the jth *column*, then $B^\dagger$ is identical to $\hat{B}^\dagger$ with a zero row inserted in the jth *row* of $B^\dagger$. (See Ben-Israel and Ijiri [1963].) Hence $B^\dagger B$ is identical to $\hat{B}^\dagger \hat{B}$ with a zero row and a zero column inserted in the jth row and column positions of $B^\dagger B$. Since A also has a zero column in its jth-column position, $AB^\dagger B$ is identical to $\hat{A}\hat{B}^\dagger \hat{B}$ with a zero column inserted in the jth-column position of $\hat{A}\hat{B}^\dagger \hat{B}$ where $\hat{A}$ is a matrix obtained from A by striking out its jth column. Since the Euclidean norm defined in (B.23) is the square root of the sum of the squares of all elements in the matrix, we have $\| AB^\dagger B \| = \| \hat{A}\hat{B}^\dagger \hat{B} \|$ and $\| A \| = \| \hat{A} \|$; hence it is not necessary to eliminate the jth column in calculating ρ^2 insofar as we follow the rule of multiplying each column of A and B by the standard deviation of the corresponding variable.[18]

4.14. The crucial requirement for deriving and using the linear aggregation coefficient and the aggregation effectiveness coefficient is that the variables x_j's be mutually independent, just as in the case of the linear correlation coefficient observations must be mutually independent. (See 4.6.) However, even if they are dependent it is possible in some cases to transform x_j's into another set of variables that are mutually independent and to adjust the matrices A and B accordingly before calculating ρ or ρ^2.

4.15. The linear aggregation coefficient is thus useful for ordering linear aggregation functions according to their effectiveness in identifying the value of a given property function.[19]

5. A SUPPLEMENT

This section is a supplement to the analysis in Chapter 6. We include this material here because it deals with the topic discussed above and also because we want to collect all mathematical derivations in the appendices so that the main text can be read with minimum mathematical background. Here we derive the aggregation effectiveness coefficient in (6.39) and the best estimator of y in (6.40) without using the generalized inverses of matrices as we have done in the above discussions.

Let q_i be a random variable with a mean $\bar{q}_i$ and a variance σ_i ($i = 1, 2, \cdots, n$), and let $q_1, q_2, \cdots, q_n$ be a set of n such random variables which are mutually independent. Let variables y and w be defined as

$$(B.51) \qquad y = \sum_{i=1}^{n} r_i q_i$$

$$(B.52) \qquad w = \sum_{i=1}^{n} p_i q_i$$

where r_i and p_i are constants ($i = 1, 2, \cdots, n$); let $\hat{y}$ be an estimate of y and e be an error of the estimate $y - \hat{y}$. Finally, let $\bar{y}$ and $\bar{e}$ be the means of y and e, respectively, and let σ_y^2 and σ_e^2 be the variances of y and e, respectively. We want to choose an estimator so that $E[e^2]$ is minimized, where E stands for the expected value.

---

[18] Computationally, it is more efficient to strike out zero rows and columns, if any, of a matrix B in calculating $B^\dagger$. See Ben-Israel and Ijiri [1963].

[19] See Chapter 6, Section 2 for simple numerical examples which show the process for computing ρ^2 as well as the estimator for y.

Since $e^2 = e^2 - 2\bar{e}e + \bar{e}^2 + 2\bar{e}e - \bar{e}^2$, we have

$$(\text{B.53}) \quad E[e^2] = E[(e - \bar{e})^2 + 2\bar{e}e - \bar{e}^2] = \sigma_e^2 + 2\bar{e}E[e] - \bar{e}^2 = \sigma_e^2 + \bar{e}^2$$

Note that if $\bar{e}$ is not equal to zero, $E[e^2]$ can be reduced by adjusting the estimate from $\hat{y}$ to $\hat{y} - \bar{e}$ since σ_e^2 is unaffected by adding to e or subtracting from e a constant term and $\bar{e}^2$ is reduced to zero. Therefore, a necessary condition for the minimization of $E[e^2]$ is that

$$(\text{B.54}) \quad E[e] = E[y - \hat{y}] = E[y] - E[\hat{y}] = 0$$

i.e., $\hat{y}$ must be an *unbiased estimate* of y. If $\hat{y}$ is an unbiased estimate of y, $E[e^2]$ is equal to σ_e^2; hence we select $\hat{y}$ so that it is unbiased and at the same time minimizes σ_e^2.

In the absense of any variable that is dependent upon q_i's, $E[e^2]$ is minimized if we set $\hat{y} = \bar{y}$ as is clear from the above comment. The estimate of y by $\hat{y} = \bar{y}$ is an unbiased estimate since $E[y - \bar{y}] = 0$ by the definition of $\bar{y}$, and under this estimate

$$(\text{B.55}) \quad E[e^2] = \sigma_e^2 = \sigma_{(y-\bar{y})}^2 = \sigma_y^2$$

If the value of w is available, we can estimate y by

$$(\text{B.56}) \quad \hat{y} = aw + b$$

where a and b are constants. We can adjust b so that $\hat{y}$ is an unbiased estimate of y, in which case $E[e^2] = \sigma_e^2$. Hence we want to select a so that σ_e^2 is minimized and then determine b so that $\hat{y}$ is an unbiased estimate of y.

Since e is

$$(\text{B.57}) \quad e = y - \hat{y} = \sum_{i=1}^{n} (r_i - ap_i)q_i - b$$

σ_e^2 is

$$(\text{B.58}) \quad \sigma_e^2 = \sum_{i=1}^{n} (r_i - ap_i)^2 \sigma_i^2$$

Then a necessary condition for σ_e^2 to be minimum is obtained by differentiating σ_e^2 with respect to a.

$$(\text{B.59}) \quad \frac{d\sigma_e^2}{da} = \sum_{i=1}^{n} -2p_i(r_i - ap_i)\sigma_i^2 = 0$$

If we denote by s the value of a which minimizes σ_e^2, then s is derived from

(B.59) as follows:

(B.60)
$$s = \frac{\displaystyle\sum_{i=1}^{n} p_i r_i \sigma_i^2}{\displaystyle\sum_{i=1}^{n} p_i^2 \sigma_i^2} = \frac{Q}{P}$$

where P and Q are defined as

$$P = \sum_{i=1}^{n} p_i^2 \sigma_i^2 \quad \text{and} \quad Q = \sum_{i=1}^{n} p_i r_i \sigma_i^2$$

respectively, in order to simplify the notation.

If we denote by m the value of b in (B.56) which makes $\hat{y}$ an unbiased estimate of y given $a = s$, then m is derived by

$$E[e] = E[y - \hat{y}] = E[y] - E[\hat{y}] = \bar{y} - E[sw + m]$$

(B.61)
$$= \bar{y} - sE[w] - m$$

$$= \sum_{i=1}^{n} r_i \bar{q}_i - s \sum_{i=1}^{n} p_i \bar{q}_i - m = 0$$

Hence

(B.62)
$$m = \sum_{i=1}^{n} (r_i - sp_i) \bar{q}_i$$

i.e., we estimate y by

(B.63)
$$\hat{y} = \frac{Q}{P} w + m = \frac{\displaystyle\sum_{i=1}^{n} p_i r_i \sigma_i^2}{\displaystyle\sum_{i=1}^{n} p_i^2 \sigma_i^2} w + \sum_{i=1}^{n} (r_i - sp_i) \bar{q}_i$$

Then, $E[e^2]$, which is equal to σ_e^2 under this estimate, is given by

$$\sigma_e^2 = \sum_{i=1}^{n} (r_i - sp_i)^2 \sigma_i^2 = \sum_{i=1}^{n} r_i^2 \sigma_i^2 - 2s \sum_{i=1}^{n} p_i r_i \sigma_i^2 + s^2 \sum_{i=1}^{n} p_i^2 \sigma_i^2$$

(B.64)

$$= R - 2 \frac{Q}{P} Q + \frac{Q^2}{P^2} P = R - \frac{Q^2}{P}$$

where R stands for $\displaystyle\sum_{i=1}^{n} r_i^2 \sigma_i^2$.

We have obtained in (B.55) the minimum $E[e^2]$ when no variable dependent upon q_i's is available. This minimum is

(B.65)
$$\sigma_y^2 = \sum_{i=1}^{n} r_i^2 \sigma_i^2 = R$$

and we have obtained the minimum $E[e^2]$ when the value of w is available. This minimum is given in (B.64). Hence, the proportion of $E[e^2]$ that is eliminated by using w, denoted by ρ^2, is

(B.66)
$$\rho^2 = \frac{\sigma_y^2 - \sigma_e^2}{\sigma_y^2} = \frac{R - [R - (Q^2/P)]}{R} = \frac{Q^2}{PR}$$

which is (6.39) in Chapter 6.

Bibliography

Adams, E. W. "Survey of Bernoullian Utility Theory," in H. Solomon (editor) *Mathematical Thinking in the Measurement of Behavior*. New York: The Free Press of Glencoe, Inc., 1960, pp. 151–268.

Addison, J. W., L. Henkin, and A. Tarski (editors). *The Theory of Models; Proceedings of the 1963 International Symposium at Berkeley*. Amsterdam: North-Holland Publishing Co., 1965.

Allen, R. G. D. *Mathematical Economics*. 2nd ed. London: Macmillan & Co., Ltd., 1959.

Amemiya, T. *On the Use of Principal Components of Independent Variables in Two-Stage Least Square Estimation*, Technical Report No. 7. Stanford, California: Institute for Mathematical Studies in the Social Sciences, Stanford University, December 14, 1964.

American Accounting Association. "A Tentative Statement of Accounting Principles Affecting Corporate Reports," *The Accounting Review*, XI, 2 (June 1936), pp. 187–91.

―――. "Accounting Principles Underlying Corporate Financial Statements," *The Accounting Review*, XVI, 2 (June 1941), pp. 133–39.

―――. "Accounting Concepts and Standards Underlying Corporate Financial Statements—1948 Revision," *The Accounting Review*, XXIII, 4 (October 1948), pp. 339–44.

———. "Accounting and Reporting Standards for Corporate Financial Statements —1957 Revision," *The Accounting Review*, **XXXII**, 4 (October 1957), pp. 536–46.

———. *A Statement of Basic Accounting Theory*. New York: American Accounting Association, 1966.

American Accounting Association, Committee on Concepts and Standards— Long-Lived Assets. "Accounting for Land, Building, and Equipment," Supplementary Statement No. 1, *The Accounting Review*, **XXXIX**, 3 (July 1964), pp. 693–99.

American Accounting Association, 1964 Concepts and Standards Research Study Committee. "The Realization Concept," *The Accounting Review*, **XL**, 2 (April 1965), pp. 312–22.

American Institute of Certified Public Accountants. *Five Monographs on Business Income*. New York: American Institute of Certified Public Accountants, 1950.

———. *Changing Concepts of Business Income*. New York: The Macmillan Company, 1952.

———. *Reporting the Financial Effects on Price-Level Changes*. New York: American Institute of Certified Public Accountants, 1963.

Anderson, T. W. *An Introduction to Multivariate Statistical Analysis*. New York: John Wiley & Sons, Inc., 1958.

Anton, H. R. "Some Aspects of Measurement and Accounting," *Journal of Accounting Research*, **II**, 1 (Spring 1964), pp. 1–9.

Ara, K. "The Aggregation Problem in Input-Output Analysis," *Econometrica*, **XXVII**, 2 (April 1959), pp. 257–62.

Arnett, H. E. "What Does 'Objectivity' Mean to Accountants?," *Journal of Accountancy*, **CXI**, 5 (May 1961), pp. 63–68.

Bedford, N. M. *Income Determination Theory: An Accounting Framework*. Reading, Massachusetts: Addison-Wesley Publishing Co., Inc., 1965.

Ben-Israel, A. and A. Charnes. "Contributions to the Theory of Generalized Inverses," *Journal of the Society for Industrial and Applied Mathematics*, **XI**, 3 (September 1963), pp. 667–99.

Ben-Israel, A. and Y. Ijiri. *A Report on the Machine Computation of the Generalized Inverse of an Arbitrary Matrix*, Office of Naval Research Memorandum No. 110. Pittsburgh: Carnegie Institute of Technology, March 1963.

Ben-Israel, A. and S. J. Wersan. "An Elimination Method for Computing the Generalized Inverse of an Arbitrary Matrix," *Journal of the Association for Computing Machinery*, **X**, 4 (October 1963), pp. 532–37.

Bentham, J. *An Introduction to the Principles of Morals and Legislation*. Oxford: Clarendon Press, 1879. Originally published in 1789.

Berge, C. *The Theory of Graphs and Its Applications*. Translated by A. Doig. New York: John Wiley & Sons, Inc., 1962. Originally published in 1958.

Bierman, H., Jr. "Measurement and Accounting," *The Accounting Review*, **XXXVIII**, 3 (July 1963), pp. 501–7.

——. *Financial Accounting Theory*. New York: The Macmillan Co., 1965.

Blaug, M. *Economic Theory in Retrospect*. Homewood, Illinois: Richard D. Irwin, Inc., 1962.

Bonini, C. P. *Simulation of Information and Decision System in the Firm*. Englewood Cliffs, New Jersey: Prentice-Hall, Inc., 1963.

Bruns, W. "A Simulation Study of Alternative Methods of Inventory Valuation" Unpublished Ph. D. dissertation, University of California, Berkeley, 1962.

Bunge, M. *Causality*. Cleveland, Ohio: The World Publishing Co., 1963.

Bush, R. R. and F. Mosteller. *Stochastic Models for Learning*. New York: John Wiley & Sons, Inc., 1955.

Canning, J. B. *The Economics of Accountancy*. New York: The Ronald Press Company, 1929.

Carlyle, T. *Sarter Resartus: The Life and Opinions of Herr Teufelsdröckh*. Edited by C. F. Harrold. New York: The Odyssey Press, Inc., 1937. Originally published in 1834.

Carroll, J. B. *Language and Thought*. Englewood Cliffs, New Jersey: Prentice-Hall, Inc., 1964.

Carroll, L. *Through the Looking Glass* in a volume with *Alice's Adventure in Wonderland*. Baltimore: Penguin Books, 1962. Originally published in 1872.

Cayley, A. *The Principles of Bookkeeping by Double Entry*. Cambridge, England: The University Press, 1894.

Chambers, R. J. "Blueprint for a Theory of Accounting," *Accounting Research*, **VI**, 1 (January 1955), pp. 17–25.

——. "Measurement in Accounting," *Journal of Accounting Research*, **III**, 1 (Spring 1965), pp. 32–62.

——. *Accounting, Evaluation and Economic Behavior*. Englewood Cliffs, New Jersey: Prentice-Hall, Inc., 1966.

Charnes, A. and W. W. Cooper. *Management Models and Industrial Applications of Linear Programming*. New York: John Wiley & Sons, Inc., 1961.

——. *Comments on the Use of Accounting in Internal Decision Making*, Management Sciences Research Report No. 75. Pittsburgh: Carnegie Institute of Technology, April 1966. [1966a].

——. *Some Network Characterizations for Mathematical Programming and Accounting Approaches to Planning and Control*, Management Sciences Research Report No. 81. Pittsburgh: Carnegie Institute of Technology, July 1966. [1966b].

Charnes, A., W. W. Cooper, and Y. Ijiri. "Breakeven Budgeting and Programming to Goals," *Journal of Accounting Research*, **I**, 1 (Spring 1963), pp. 16–44.

Charnes, A., W. W. Cooper, and G. L. Thompson. *Chance-Constrained Programming and Related Approaches to Cost Effectiveness*, Management Sciences Research Report No. 39. Pittsburgh: Carnegie Institute of Technology, April 1965.

Chernoff, H. and L. E. Moses. *Elementary Decision Theory*. New York: John Wiley & Sons, Inc., 1959.

Churchill, N. C. "Behavioral Effects of an Audit." Unpublished Ph.D. dissertation, University of Michigan, 1962.

Churchill, N. C. and L. N. Teitelbaum, "The Effects of an Audit: A Statement of the Problem and a Program for Research," a paper prepared for Project NR-047011 (01). Pittsburgh: Carnegie Institute of Technology, 1960.

Churchman, C. W. *Prediction and Optimal Decision*. Englewood Cliffs, New Jersey: Prentice-Hall, Inc., 1961.

Cochran, W. G. and G. M. Cox. *Experimental Designs*. 2nd ed. New York: John Wiley & Sons, Inc., 1957.

Cohen, M. R. and E. Nagel. *An Introduction to Logic and Scientific Method*. New York: Harcourt, Brace & World, Inc., 1934.

Cooper, W. W. "Theory of the Firm: Some Suggestions for Revision," *The American Economic Review*, **XXXIX**, 6 (December 1949), pp. 1204–22.

Cramér, H. *Mathematical Methods of Statistics*. Princeton, New Jersey: Princeton University Press, 1946.

Curry, H. B. *Foundations of Mathematical Logic*. New York: McGraw-Hill Book Company, 1963.

Cyert, R. M. and J. G. March. *A Behavioral Theory of the Firm*. Englewood Cliffs, New Jersey: Prentice-Hall, Inc., 1963.

d'Abro, A. *The Evolution of Scientific Thought*. 2nd ed. New York: Dover Publications, Inc., 1950.

Darwin, C. *The Origin of Species*. New York: Washington Square Press, Inc., 1963. Originally published in 1859.

Davidson, S., D. Green, Jr., C. T. Horngren, and G. H. Sorter. *Income Approach to Accounting Theory*. Englewood Cliffs, New Jersey: Prentice-Hall, Inc., 1964.

Dean, J. "Decentralization and Intracompany Pricing," *Harvard Business Review*, **XXXIII**, 4 (July–August 1955), pp. 65–74.

Devine, C. T. *Essays in Accounting Theory*. (Two volumes.) Berkeley, California: C. T. Devine, 1962.

———. "Some Conceptual Problems in Accounting Measurements," in R. K. Jaedicke, Y. Ijiri, and O. Nielsen (editors), *Research in Accounting Measurement*. New York: American Accounting Association, 1966, pp. 13–27.

Dresch, F. W. "Index Numbers and the General Economic Equilibrium," *Bulletin of the American Mathematical Society*, **XLIV**, 2 (February 1938), pp. 134–41.

Duncker, K. "On Problem-Solving," translated by L. S. Lees, *Psychological Monographs*, **LVIII**, 5 (1945), pp. 1–113.

Dyckman, T. R. "The Effects of Alternative Accounting Techniques on Certain Management Decisions," *Journal of Accounting Research*, **II**, 1 (Spring 1964), pp. 91–107.

Eddington, Sir Arthur Stanley. *Science and the Unseen World*. New York: The Macmillan Co., 1929.

Edwards, E. O. and P. W. Bell. *The Theory and Measurement of Business Income*. Berkeley, California: University of California Press, 1961.

Elmaghraby, S. E. *The Design of Production Systems*. New York: Reinhold Publishing Corp., 1966.

Fei, J. C. H. "A Fundamental Theorem for the Aggregation Problem of Input-Output Analysis," *Econometrica*, **XXIV**, 4 (October 1956), pp. 400–12.

Fertig, P. E. "Current Values and Index Numbers, the Problem of Objectivity," in R. K. Jaedicke, Y. Ijiri, and O. Nielsen (editors), *Research in Accounting Measurement*. New York: American Accounting Association, 1966, pp. 137–49.

Fisher, Irving. *The Nature of Capital and Income*. New York: The Macmillan Company, 1906.

Fisher, W. D. "Criteria for Aggregation in Input-Output Analysis," *The Review of Economics and Statistics*, **XL**, 3 (August 1958), pp. 250–60. [1958a].

———. "On Grouping for Maximum Homogeneity," *Journal of the American Statistical Association*, **LIII**, 284 (December 1958), pp. 789–98. [1958b].

———. "Optimal Aggregation in Multi-Equation Prediction Models," *Econometrica*, **XXX**, 4 (October 1962), pp. 744–69.

Garner, W. R. *Uncertainty and Structure as Psychological Concepts*. New York: John Wiley & Sons, Inc., 1962.

Ghiselli, E. E. *Theory of Psychological Measurement*. New York: McGraw-Hill Book Company, 1964.

Gilman, S. *Accounting Concepts of Profit*. New York: The Ronald Press Company, 1939.

Gnedenko, B. V. *The Theory of Probability*. Translated from the Russian by B. D. Seckler. New York: Chelsea Publishing Co., 1962.

Gorman, W. M. "Separable Utility and Aggregation," *Econometrica*, **XXVII**, 3 (July 1959), pp. 469–81.

Granick, D. *The Red Executive*. Garden City, New York: Doubleday & Company, Inc., 1960.

Green, H. A. J. *Aggregation in Economic Analysis*. Princeton, New Jersey: Princeton University Press, 1964.

Hall, E. T. *The Silent Language*. New York: Doubleday & Co., Inc., 1959.

Halmos, P. R. *Measure Theory*. Princeton, New Jersey: D. Van Nostrand Co., Inc., 1950.

———. *Finite-Dimensional Vector Spaces*. 2nd ed. Princeton, New Jersey: D. Van Nostrand Co., Inc., 1958.

Hatanaka, M. "Note on Consolidation within a Leontief System," *Econometrica*, **XX**, 2 (April 1952), pp. 301–3.

Hayakawa, S. I. *Language in Thought and Action*. 2nd ed. New York: Harcourt, Brace & World, Inc., 1964.

Hegel, G. W. F. *Science of Logic*. 4th ed. Translated by W. H. Johnston and L. G. Struthers. London: George Allen & Unwin, 1929. Originally published in 1812.

Hicks, J. R. *Value and Capital*. 2nd ed. Oxford: The Clarendon Press, 1946.

Hirschleifer, J. "On the Economics of Transfer Pricing," *Journal of Business of the University of Chicago*, **XXIX**, 3 (July 1956), pp. 172–84.

Horngren, C. T. *Accounting for Management Control: An Introduction*. Englewood Cliffs, New Jersey: Prentice-Hall, Inc., 1965.

Householder, A. S. *The Theory of Matrices in Numerical Analysis*. New York: Blaisdell Publishing Co., 1964.

Hume, D. *A Treatise of Human Nature*. Cleveland, Ohio: The World Publishing Company, 1962. Originally published in 1739.

Hurwitz, L. "Aggregation in Macroeconomic Models," *Econometrica*, **XX**, 3 (July 1952), pp. 489–90.

Hutcheson, Francis. *An Essay on the Nature and Conduct of the Passions and Affections*. 3rd ed. London: A. Ward, 1742.

Ijiri, Y. *Functional Analysis of Aggregation*, Working Paper No. 21. Stanford, California: Stanford University Graduate School of Business, August 1964. Presented at the Tenth Annual and First International Meeting of the Western Section of the Operations Research Society of America held on September 14–18, 1964, in Honolulu, Hawaii. [1964a].

———. *On the Methodology of Set-Theoretical Analyses in Business*, a mimeographed report. Stanford, California: Stanford University Graduate School of Business, October 1964. [1964b].

———. *Management Goals and Accounting for Control*. Volume 3 in *The Studies in Mathematical and Managerial Economics*, H. Theil (editor). Amsterdam: North-Holland Publishing Co. and Chicago: Rand McNally & Co., 1965. [1965a].

———. "Axioms and Structures of Conventional Accounting Measurement," (Technical Report No. 128, prepared under Contract Nonr-225(50) at the Institute for Mathematical Studies in Social Sciences, Stanford University, for the Office of Naval Research in April 1964), *The Accounting Review*, **XL**, 1 (January 1965), pp. 36–53. [1965b].

———. "On the Generalized Inverse of an Incidence Matrix," (Technical Report No. 127, prepared under Contract Nonr-225(50) at the Institute for Mathematical Studies in Social Sciences, Stanford University, for the Office of Naval Research in January 1964), *Journal of the Society for Industrial and Applied Mathematics*, **XIII**, 3 (September 1965), pp. 827–36. [1965c].

———. *The Linear Aggregation Coefficient as the Dual of the Linear Correlation Coefficient*, Working Paper No. 82. Stanford, California: Stanford University Graduate School of Business, December 1965. Presented at the 1965 Econometric Society Meeting in New York. [1965d].

———. "Physical Measures and Multi-Dimensional Accounting," in R. K. Jaedicke, Y. Ijiri, and O. Nielsen (editors), *Research in Accounting Measurement*. New York: American Accounting Association, 1966, pp. 150–64. [1966a].

———. *Budget Auditing and Its Implementation*, Working Paper No. 101. Stanford, California: Stanford University Graduate School of Business, April 1966. [1966b].

———. *Causality as the Foundation of the Double-Entry Accounting*, Working Paper No. 73. Stanford, California: Stanford University Graduate School of Business, April 1966. [1966c].

———. *An Application of Input-Output Analysis to Some Problems in Cost Accounting*, Working Paper No. 115. Stanford, California: Stanford University Graduate School of Business, October 1966. [1966d].

———. "On the Convergence of Periodic Reinvestment by an Amount Equal to Depreciation," to be published in *Management Science*, **XIII**, 5 (January 1967). [1967].

Ijiri, Y. and R. K. Jaedicke. "Reliability and Objectivity of Accounting Measurements," *The Accounting Review*, **XLI**, 3 (July 1966), pp. 474–83. [1966a].

———. "Mathematics and Accounting," in M. Backer (editor), *Modern Accounting Theory*. 2nd ed. Englewood Cliffs, New Jersey: Prentice-Hall, Inc., 1966, pp. 535–53. [1966b].

Ijiri, Y., R. K. Jaedicke, and K. E. Knight. "The Effects of Accounting Alternatives on Management Decisions," in R. K. Jaedicke, Y. Ijiri, and O. Nielsen (editors), *Research in Accounting Measurement*. New York: American Accounting Association, 1966, pp. 186–99.

Ijiri, Y., R. K. Jaedicke, and J. L. Livingstone. "The Effect of Inventory Costing Methods on Full and Direct Costing," *Journal of Accounting Research*, **III**, 1 (Spring 1965), pp. 63–74.

Ijiri, Y., F. K. Levy, and R. C. Lyon. "A Linear Programming Model for Budgeting and Financial Planning," *Journal of Accounting Research*, **I**, 2 (Autumn 1963), pp. 198–212.

Ijiri, Y. and A. A. Robichek. *Accounting Measurement and Rates of Return*, Working Paper No. 30. Stanford, California: Stanford University Graduate School of Business, February 1965.

Ijiri, Y. and H. A. Simon. "Business Firm Growth and Size," *The American Economic Review*, **LIV**, 2, Part I (March 1964), pp. 77–89.

———. "A Model of Business Firm Growth," to be published in *Econometrica* in 1967.

Jaedicke, R. K., Y. Ijiri, and O. Nielsen (editors). *Research in Accounting Measurement*. New York: American Accounting Association, 1966.

Jaedicke, R. K. and R. T. Sprouse. *Accounting Flows: Income, Funds, and Cash*. Englewood Cliffs, New Jersey: Prentice-Hall, Inc., 1965.

Jeffrey, R. C. *The Logic of Decision*. New York: McGraw-Hill Book Company, 1965.

Jevons, W. S. *The Theory of Political Economy*. 5th ed. New York: Kelley and Millman, Inc., 1957. Originally published 1871.

———. *The Principles of Economics*. London: Macmillan & Co., Ltd., 1905.

Joad, C. E. M. *Guide to Philosophy*. New York: Dover Publications, Inc., 1936.

Johansen, L. "A Note on 'Aggregation in Leontief Matrices and the Labor Theory of Value,'" *Econometrica*, **XXIX**, 2 (April 1961), pp. 221–22.

Kaulla, R. *Theory of the Just Price*. Translated from German by R. D. Hogg. London: George Allen & Unwin, 1940. Originally published in 1936.

Keller, H. *The Story of My Life*. New York: Grosset & Dunlap, Inc., 1905.

Kemeny, J. G., H. Mirkil, J. L. Snell, and G. L. Thompson. *Finite Mathematical Structures*. Englewood Cliffs, New Jersey: Prentice-Hall, Inc., 1959.

Kemeny, J. G., O. Morgenstern, and G. L. Thompson. "A Generalization of the von Neumann Model of an Expanding Economy," *Econometrica*, **XXIV**, 2 (April 1956), pp. 115–35.

Kleene, S. C. *Introduction to Metamathematics*. Princeton, New Jersey: D. Van Nostrand Co., Inc., 1952.

Klein, L. R. "Macroeconomics and the Theory of Rational Behavior," *Econometrica*, **XIV**, 2 (April 1946), pp. 93–108. [1946a].

———. "Remarks on the Theory of Aggregation," *Econometrica*, **XIV**, 4 (October 1946), pp. 303–12. [1946b].

Knight, F. H. "Notes on Cost and Utility," in F. H. Knight, *The Economic Organization*. New York: Augustus M. Kelley, Publisher, 1951, pp. 122–79.

Knight, K. E. *The Organization as an Ill-Structured Problem Solving System*, Working Paper No. 56. Stanford, California: Stanford University Graduate School of Business, 1965.

Kohler, E. L. *A Dictionary for Accountants*. Englewood Cliffs, New Jersey: Prentice-Hall, Inc., 1952.

Kolmogorov, A. N. *Foundations of the Theory of Probability*. 2nd ed. New York: Chelsea Publishing Co., 1956.

Laird, J. *The Idea of Value*. Cambridge, England: The University Press, 1929.

Lamont, W. D. *The Value Judgement.* Edinburgh: The University Press, 1955.

Leavitt, H. J. *Managerial Psychology.* Revised ed. Chicago: University of Chicago Press, 1964.

Lenzen, V. F. *Procedures of Empirical Science.* Chicago: University of Chicago Press, 1938.

Littleton, A. C. *Structure of Accounting Theory.* New York: American Accounting Association, 1953.

Loéve, M. *Probability Theory.* 3rd ed. Princeton, New Jersey: D. Van Nostrand Co., Inc., 1963.

Luce, R. D. *Individual Choice Behavior.* New York: John Wiley & Sons, Inc., 1959.

Luce, R. D. and H. Raiffa. *Games and Decisions.* New York: John Wiley & Sons, Inc., 1957.

McFarland, W. B. "Concept of Objectivity," *Journal of Accountancy,* **CXII**, 3 (September 1961), pp. 29–32.

Marschak, J. "Problems in Information Economics," in C. P. Bonini, R. K. Jaedicke, and H. M. Wagner (editors), *Management Controls: New Directions in Basic Research.* New York: McGraw-Hill Book Co., 1964, pp. 38–74.

Marshall, A. *Principles of Economics.* 9th (variorum) ed. London: Macmillan & Co., Ltd., 1961.

Marx, K. *Capital.* Translated from the third German edition by S. Moore and E. Aveling. Chicago: Charles H. Kerr & Co., 1906.

Mattessich, R. "Toward a General and Axiomatic Foundation of Accountancy, with an Introduction to the Matrix Formulation of Accounting Systems," *Accounting Research,* **VIII**, 4 (October 1957), pp. 328–55.

————. *Accounting and Analytical Methods.* Homewood, Illinois: Richard D. Irwin, Inc., 1964.

May, K. "The Aggregation Problem for a One-Industry Model," *Econometrica,* **XIV**, 4 (October 1946), pp. 285–98.

Mood, A. M. and F. A. Graybill. *Introduction to the Theory of Statistics.* 2nd ed. New York: McGraw-Hill Book Company, 1963.

Moonitz, M. *The Basic Postulates of Accounting.* New York: American Institute of Certified Public Accountants, 1961.

Moore, E. H. "On the Reciprocal of the General Algebraic Matrix," abstract reported by A. Dresden in "The Fourteenth Western Meeting of the American Mathematical Society," *Bulletin of the American Mathematical Society,* **XXVI**, 9(June 1920), pp. 394–95.

Morgenstern, O. *On the Accuracy of Economic Observations.* 2nd ed. Princeton, New Jersey: Princeton University Press, 1963.

Morishima, M. and F. Seton. "Aggregation in Leontief Matrices and the Labor Theory of Value," *Econometrica,* **XXIX**, 2 (April 1961), pp. 203–20.

Newman, P. *The Theory of Exchange*. Englewood Cliffs, New Jersey: Prentice-Hall, Inc., 1965.

Nunnally, J. C., Jr. *Tests and Measurements*. New York: McGraw-Hill Book Company, 1959.

Pacioli, L. *Summa de Arithmetica, Geometria, Proportioni et Proportionalita: Distintio Nona-Tractatus XI, Particularis de computis et scripturis*. Translated by R. G. Brown and K. S. Johnston in *Paciolo on Accounting*. New York: McGraw-Hill Book Co., 1963. Originally published in Venice, 1494.

Paton, W. A. *Accounting Theory*. Chicago: Accounting Studies Press, Ltd., 1962. Originally published in 1922.

―――. *Corporate Profits*. Homewood, Illinois: Richard D. Irwin, Inc., 1965.

Paton, W. A. and A. C. Littleton. *An Introduction to Corporate Accounting Standards*. New York: American Accounting Association, 1940.

Penrose, R. "A Generalized Inverse for Matrices," *Proceedings of the Cambridge Philosophical Society*, **LI**, 3 (July 1955), pp. 406–13.

―――. "On Best Approximate Solutions of Linear Matrix Equations," *Proceedings of the Cambridge Philosophical Society*, **LII**, 1 (January 1956), pp. 17–19.

Poincaré, H. *Mathematics and Science: Last Essays*. Translated from the French by J. W. Bolduc. New York: Dover Publications, Inc., 1963. Originally published in 1913.

Pu, S. S. "A Note on Macroeconomics," *Econometrica*, **XIV**, 4 (October 1946), pp. 299–302.

Ridgeway, V. F. "Dysfunctional Consequences of Performance Measurements," in A. H. Rubenstein and C. J. Haberstroh (editors), *Some Theories of Organization*. Homewood, Illinois: Richard D. Irwin, Inc., 1960, pp. 371–77.

Robinson, A. *Introduction to Model Theory and to the Metamathematics of Algebra*. Amsterdam: North-Holland Publishing Co., 1963.

Rosenblatt, D. *On Aggregation and Consolidation in Linear Systems*, Technical Report C, prepared under the Office of Naval Research Contract Nonr-1180(00) NR-047-012. Washington: The American University, Department of Statistics, August 1956.

―――. "On Aggregation and Consolidation in Finite Substochastic Systems, I–IV," abstracts published in *The Annals of Mathematical Statistics*, **XXVIII** (1957), pp. 1060–61.

―――. "Aggregation in Matrix Models of Resource Flows," *The American Statistician*, June 1965, pp. 36–39.

Rosenblatt, M. "An Aggregation Problem for Markov Chains," in R. E. Machol (editor), *Information and Decision Processes*. New York: McGraw-Hill Book Co., 1960, pp. 87–92.

Rothenberg, J. "Values and Value Theory in Economics," in S. R. Krupp (editor), *The Structure of Economic Science*. Englewood Cliffs, New Jersey: Prentice-Hall, Inc., 1966, pp. 221–42.

Royden, H. L. *Real Analysis*. New York: The Macmillan Company, 1963.

Sanders, T. H., H. R. Hatfield, and U. Moore. *A Statement of Accounting Principles*. New York: American Institute of Certified Public Accountants, 1938.

Sapir, Edward. "The Status of Linguistics as a Science," *Language*, **V** (1929), pp. 207–14.

Sargan, J. D. "The Estimation of Economic Relationships Using Instrumental Variables," *Econometrica*, **XXVI**, 3 (July 1958), pp. 393–415.

Scott, D. R. *The Cultural Significance of Accounts*. New York: Henry Holt & Co., 1931.

Shannon, C. E. "The Mathematical Theory of Communication," in C. E. Shannon and W. Weaver, *The Mathematical Theory of Communication*. Urbana, Illinois: The University of Illinois Press, 1949, pp. 1–91.

Simmons, G. F. *Introduction to Topology and Modern Analysis*. New York: McGraw-Hill Book Company, 1963.

Simon, H. A. *Models of Man*. New York: John Wiley & Sons, Inc., 1957.

Simon, H. A. and A. Ando. "Aggregation of Variables in Dynamic Systems," *Econometrica*, **XXIX**, 2 (April 1961), pp. 111–38.

Smith, Adam. *An Inquiry into the Nature and Causes of the Wealth of Nations*. New York: Modern Library, Inc., 1937. Originally published in 1776.

Smolinski, L. "What Next in Soviet Planning?," *Foreign Affairs*, **XLII**, 4 (July 1964), pp. 602–13.

Sombart, W. *Der moderne Kapitalismus*. 6th ed. München and Leipzig: Duncker und Humbolt, 1928.

Sorter, G. H. "The Boundaries of the Accounting Universe: The Accounting Rules of Selection." Unpublished Ph.D. dissertation, University of Chicago, 1963.

Sprouse, R. T. (reporter). *The Measurement of Property, Plant, and Equipment in Financial Statements*. Boston: Harvard University Graduate School of Business Administration, 1964.

Sprouse, R. T. and M. Moonitz. *A Tentative Set of Broad Accounting Principles for Business Enterprises*. New York: American Institute of Certified Public Accountants, 1962.

Stedry, A. C. *Budget Control and Cost Behavior*. Englewood Cliffs, New Jersey: Prentice-Hall, Inc., 1960.

Stevens, S. S. "Measurement, Psychophysics, and Utility," in C. W. Churchman and P. Ratoosh, *Measurement: Definitions and Theories*. New York: John Wiley & Sons, Inc., 1959, pp. 18–63.

Stevin, Simon. *Principal Works*. Ernest Crone *et al.* (editors). Translated by C. Dikshoorn. Amsterdam: Swets & Zeitlinger, 1955.

Stigler, G. J. "The development of Utility Theory," *Journal of Political Economy*, **LVIII**, 4 and 5 (August and October 1950), pp. 307–27, 373–96, respectively.

Stuart, H. W. "Valuation as a Logical Process." Unpublished Ph.D. dissertation, University of Chicago, 1918.

Suppes, P. *Introduction to Logic*. Princeton, New Jersey: D. Van Nostrand Co., Inc., 1957.

———. *Axiomatic Set Theory*. Princeton, New Jersey: D. Van Nostrand Co., Inc., 1960.

Suppes, P. and R. C. Atkinson. *Markov Learning Models for Multiperson Interactions*. Stanford, California: Stanford University Press, 1960.

Suppes, P. and J. L. Zinnes. "Basic Measurement Theory," in R. D. Luce, R. R. Bush, and E. Galanter (editors), *Handbook of Mathematical Psychology*, Volume 1. New York: John Wiley & Sons, Inc., 1963, pp. 1–76.

Theil, H. *Linear Aggregation of Economic Relations*. Amsterdam: North-Holland Publishing Co., 1954.

———. "Linear Aggregation in Input-Output Analysis," *Econometrica*, **XXV**, 1 (January 1957), pp. 111–22.

———. "The Aggregation Implications of Identifiable Structural Macrorelations," *Econometrica*, **XXVII**, 1 (January 1959), pp. 14–29.

———. "Alternative Approaches to the Aggregation Problem," in E. Nagel, P. Suppes, and A. Tarski (editors), *Logic, Methodology and Philosophy of Science—Proceedings of the 1960 International Congress*. Stanford, California: Stanford University Press, 1962, pp. 507–27.

Torgerson, W. S. *Theory and Methods of Scaling*. New York: John Wiley & Sons, Inc., 1958.

Tritschler, C. A. "The Use of Specific Price Indexes in Accounting Valuation," a mimeographed paper. Stanford, California: Stanford University Graduate School of Business, December 1966.

Urban, W. M. *Valuation: Its Nature and Laws*. London: Swan Sonnenschein & Co., Ltd., 1909.

Vatter, W. J. *The Fund Theory of Accounting and Its Implications for Financial Reports*. Chicago: University of Chicago Press, 1947.

von Neumann, J. and O. Morgenstern. *Theory of Games and Economic Behavior*. 3rd ed. Princeton, New Jersey: Princeton University Press, 1953.

Walras, Léon. *Elements of Pure Economics*. Translated by William Jaffé. Homewood, Illinois: Richard D. Irwin, Inc., 1954. Originally published in 1926.

Walsh, C. M. *The Four Kinds of Economic Value*. Cambridge, Massachusetts: Harvard University Press, 1926.

Whinston, A. "Price Guides in Decentralized Organizations," in W. W. Cooper, H. J. Leavitt, and M. W. Shelly II (editors), *New Perspectives in Organization Research*. New York: John Wiley & Sons, Inc., 1964, pp. 405–48.

Whitaker, A. C. *History and Criticism of the Labor Theory of Value in English Political Economy*. New York: The Columbia University Press, 1904.

Whitrow, G. J. *The Natural Philosophy of Time*. New York: Harper & Row, Publishers, Inc., 1963. Originally published in 1961.

Whorf, B. L. *Language, Thought, and Reality*. J. B. Carroll (editor). New York: John Wiley & Sons, Inc. and The Technology Press of Massachusetts Institute of Technology, 1956.

Wiener, N. *Cybernetics: Or Control and Communication in the Animal and the Machine*. 2nd ed. Cambridge, Massachusetts: The Massachusetts Institute of Technology Press, 1961.

Yamey, B. S. "Introduction," in A. C. Littleton and B. S. Yamey (editors), *Studies in the History of Accounting*. Homewood, Illinois: Richard D. Irwin, Inc., 1956, pp. 1–13.

————. "Accounting and the Rise of Capitalism: Further Notes on a Theme by Sombart," *Journal of Accounting Research*, **II**, 2 (Autumn 1964), pp. 117–36.

Index

A

Abstraction, process of, 82

Account, *see also* entries
activity, 110, 113
asset, 110, 112
flow, 110
profit and loss, 108
stock, 110

Accountants, *see also* accounting, accounting measurement, accounting valuation
challenge to and response by, ix, x
and decision makers, 31, 145–46, 149–65
reaccounted, 164–65

Accounting, *see also* accounting measurement, accounting valuation
behavioral effects upon decisions, 149–50, 157–65
conventional, as objects of the study, x, 33, 88
and decision making, 31, 149–65
definition, 3, 33
equity, 67
foundations of, ix–xi
and noneconomic events, 33
operational, 67
outputs are always surrogates, 6
purpose of, 69
responsibility, 70, 113–14

Accounting measurement, *see also* accounting, accounting valuation
behavioral effects upon decisions, 149–50, 157–65
cost concept as the methodological characteristic of, 84
and decision making, 31, 145–46, 149–65
and linear aggregations of quantities, 117–20
malfunctioning of, 159–60

methodological foundation of, 33
and noneconomic phenomena, 33
objectivity of, *see* objectivity
reliability of, *see* reliability
role of, in setting up standard operating procedures, 158
substantive foundation of, 33

Accounting process
change in, 160–64
and decision process, 155–65

Accounting sociology, x

Accounting valuation, 64–67, *see also* valuation, accounting measurement
axioms of, 69–85
choice of, 65, 120, 150–51
effects of, upon behavior, 120
as a linear aggregation of quantities, 117–20
numerous uses of, 122
objectivity of, *see* objectivity
reliability of, *see* reliability
and theory of value, 64n

Accuracy, 142n

Active aggregation function, 191, 194

Activity
dual aspect of, 40
evaluation of, 97
profit making, 46

Activity account, 110, 113

Activity gain and loss, 119

Adams, E. W., 35n

Adaptation, 163–64

Addison, J. W., 28n

Additivity
of indifference, 77n
of monetary values, 59–61
of quantities, 75–76, 77
of values, 60–61, 62n, 119n

Advance payment, 96

Advance receipt, 96